COMMUNITY COLLEGE MOVEMENT IN INDIA AND ABROAD

COMMUNITY COLLEGE MOVEMENT IN INDIA AND ABROAD

Access and Success

XAVIER ALPHONSE, S.J.

GYAN

ISBN: 978-81-212-1186-4

Price: ₹ 1095

First Published 2013

Published by

Gyan Publishing House
23, Main Ansari Road, Daryaganj,
New Delhi - 110002
Phones : 23282060, 23261060
Fax : (011) 23285914
E-mail: books@gyanbooks.com
website: gyanbooks.com

Laser Typesetting : Rajender Vashist, Delhi
Printed at : G. Print Process, Delhi

Cataloging in Publication Data--DK
Courtesy: D.K. Agencies (P) Ltd. <docinfo@dkagencies.com>

Alphonse, S. Xavier.
Community college movement in India and abroad : access and success / Xavier Alphonse.
p. cm.
Includes bibliographical references (p.) and index.
ISBN 9788121211864

1. Community colleges--India--History. 2. Community colleges--History. I. Title.

DDC 378.15430954 23

Contents

PART II

COMMUN ITY COLLEGES OTHER PARTS OF THE WORLD

PART-III

BIBLIOGRPHY AND RESOURCE MATERIALS AVAILABLE AT ICRDCE

The Dire Need

The Right to Skills

It's been raining "rights" in Indian policy for the last few years — education, work, food, service, healthcare, and much else. This "Diet Coke" approach to poverty reduction — the sweetness without the calories — was always dangerous because of unknown side effects. Commenting in 1790 on the consequences of the French Revolution, Edmund Burke said: "They have found their punishment in their success. Laws overturned, tribunals subverted, industry without vigour, commerce expiring, the revenue unpaid, yet the people impoverished and a state not relieved." Not very differently, early results of this "policy revolution by fatwa" — NREGA, Right to Education, Right to Food, Right to Service, etc. — suggests that it has led to 15 interest rate hikes in 12 months, is destroying government finances, fuelling inflation and encouraging civil society to subvert democracy. It also reminds us that policy entrepreneurship, like all entrepreneurship, is not exempt from the rule that big ideas without execution and resources are ineffective. Outlays don't lead to outcomes because poetry is useless without plumbing.

But there is an alternative for reducing poverty to this impatient state-driven idealism—skills and jobs. Poverty reduction comes from an individual's ability to access opportunities. Unfortunately, unemployability is a bigger problem than unemployment; 58 per cent of India's youth suffer from some skill deprivation. India's skill crisis is a child of a fragmented regulatory regime (State vs Centre, 19 ministries vs 2 human capital ministries), the dead-end view of vocational training (the lack of vertical mobility between certificates, diplomas and degrees), a broken apprenticeship regime (we only have 2.5 lakh apprentices relative to 6 and 10 million in Germany and Japan), a weak job framework (the national occupation codes don't create a shared thought world for employers and educators), no linking of financing to outcomes (we pay for training, not jobs), no separation of financing from delivery (creating competition to government delivery by using government money for private delivery) and dysfunctional employment exchanges (1,200 of them gave 3 lakh jobs to the 4 crore people registered last year).

The policy agenda around skills is not impossible or unknown. Employment exchanges need to become public-private partnership career centres that offer counselling, assessment, training, apprenticeships and job matching. The Apprenticeship Act of 1961 must be amended to view an apprenticeship as a classroom rather than a job and shift the regulatory thought world from push (employers under the threat of jail) to pull (make them volunteers). The National Vocational Educational Qualification Framework must be accepted by the states and the ministries of labour and HRD as the unifying open architecture tool for recognition of prior learning and vertical mobility between school-leaving certificates, diplomas and degrees. Delivery systems are in the hands of states and every state must create a skill mission or vocational training corporation tasked with building capacity and quality. States should also create asset banks to make existing government real estate available for skill delivery. All schools must teach English because English is like Windows, an operating system that creates geographic mobility and improves employment outcomes by 300 per cent . Schools and colleges must selectively embed vocational subjects — particularly soft skills — into their curriculum. The regulatory cholesterol around national distance education (mail order, e-learning and satellite) must be reviewed to offer flexible options for workers already in the workforce and the geographically disadvantaged. We must create a national network of community colleges offering two-year associate degrees; these colleges, rooted in the local ecosystem, will serve the informal sector (92 per cent of employment). This missing mezzanine layer — their two-year programmes are not normal degrees on a diet but vocational training on steroids — would bridge the gap between vocational education and training but make the system more inclusive. Finally, we must create skill vouchers that will allow financially disadvantaged students to get trained wherever they want at government expense. Such vouchers would shift the system to funding students rather than institutions. They could be funded by money carved out of the NREGA budget.

Unlike the skill agenda, the job creation agenda is more complex and controversial. But few disagree about the shame in four employment statistics being exactly where they were in 1991; 92 per cent informal employment, 12 per cent manufacturing employment, 50 per cent self-employment and 58 per cent agricultural employment. Economists do not understand how jobs are created or why they cluster where they do. But the broad contours of fertile soil for job creation are obvious: a flexible labour market, skilled employees, robust infrastructure and predictable legislation. A flexible labour market is important; most economists agree that our labour law regime is poisonous. India's labour laws — our employment contracts are marriage without divorce

— have created a labour aristocracy (only 8 per cent of our labour force works in the organised sector) that perpetuates labour laws which cripple India's ability to compete with China in organised manufacturing. The labour law issue is closely related to the skill issue because expanding formal employment is the key to third-party financing of skill development and expanding manufacturing employment is key to getting people off farms (58 per cent of our people produce 18 per cent of our GDP).

It's late but not too late to change the tragic reality that the two most important decisions children in India make is choosing their parents and pin code wisely. Mughal emperor Jahangir told his gardener in Kashmir that if a tree takes 100 years to mature, that's all the more reason to plant it as soon as possible. In other words, the best time to start changing our skill system and reforming labour laws was 20 years ago. The second best time is now. India's new tryst with destiny — putting poverty in the museum where it belongs — doesn't need more "rights" but more jobs and more skills. And creating jobs and skills doesn't need new ideas but courage. Not more strategy but more execution. Any takers?

The Writer is Chairman,
Teamlease Service, express@expressindia.com
Manish Sabharwal
The New Indian Express, 1/8/2011

Preface

Introduction

India is a country with a population of 1.3 billion. Higher Education in India has expanded twenty five times since Independence. India has got 671 Universities and 32,294 Colleges. Inspite of this momentous growth, it is estimated that only 12 to 15 million students are going for Higher Education. Hence those who are left out of Higher Education is almost 85 to 90 per cent. They definitely need an alternative system to come into the main stream especially the rural poor, urban poor, tribal poor, women and all other disadvantaged sections of the society.

This alternative system should have a twin purpose. It should provide education for livelihood promoting skills development leading to gainful employment. This would give the much needed Horizontal Mobility to these disadvantaged sections. It is obvious one cannot deprive them of the opportunity to go forward in Higher Education through the process of credit transfer - Vertical Mobility.

In India this Community College movement began in 1995 leading to the establishment of 312 Community Colleges in twenty states of India under the banner of ICRDCE. These colleges serve the target group and provide them with Horizontal Mobility in terms of Job Placement fulfilling the needs and requirements of the Job Market.

Ways and means have been devised to bring these students to the main stream by providing them Vertical Mobility. This book explains the history of the Indian Community College system and touches upon briefly the similar system available in other parts of the world and also gives the list of resource material available on the system by way of publications and articles.

Part I : Indian Community College System

1. The Concept and Evolution of Indian Comunity College System (1991-95)

Appendix: Directions of Community College in India.

The Chapters offer a glimpse of nature, philosophy, mission, evolution, content, curriculum, assessment and Evaluation of skills, Job Placement, the beneficiaries, the role of Industrial Partners, the success stories of the target group and also the process of recognition right from the Central Government to the State Government to Open Universities including Indira Gandhi National Open University (IGNOU).

Chapter II of the book provide the various systems of skills development available in USA, UK, Europe and South Eastern and Far Eastern Countries of Asia. Though these countries may provide different models of skills development, they agree in one common aim of providing models of livelihood by serving as door openers to provide the needed opportunities for the target group and also the means towards Vertical Mobility. One can look at the Indian model in contrast to the other models from abroad which can lead to an understanding of the common features as well as local specificities responding to the call of the territory of the country.

Chapter - IV Directory of the Community Colleges - State-wise

The book also suggests ways and means of the quality management of Indian Community Colleges so that it should not be considered inferior to formal and professional Educational Institutions to the country. It is a serious effort made by the author as well as ICRDCE team to record and narrate 15 years of experience of the Indian Community College system. My sincere wish is that everyone reading this book will be inspired to understand, appreciate this system and also to start initiatives especially in the rural, urban areas to realize the dream of inclusive social development to bridge the gap between the rich and the poor, the educated and illiterate and men and women.

The ICRDCE team appreciates all those who have taken up this innovative system of Community Colleges in India and wishes them well in this devoted and dedicated service to the marginalized sections of the society.

Dr. Xavier Alphonse, S.J.,
Director, ICRDCE
Member, University Grants Commission (2006-2012)
Member, Distance Education Council
Member, working group on Higher Education for the XII Plan
MHRD and Planning Commission
Chennai, July 2011

PART I
INDIAN COMMUNITY COLLEGE SYSTEM

1

The Concept and Evolution of Indian Community College System (1991-95)

1991 October to December

Feasibility of Community Colleges Experiment and Experiences

"This brief description of the Community College, I believe, would give an idea about the versatility and resiliency of the Community College as a unique educational institution. It has acquired these qualities because of its underlying philosophy of finding out the educational needs of the community and meeting them with suitable educational programmes. Its present structure has been evolved out of the traditional college in the process of meeting the needs of the community. Therefore if we are considering the adoption of the Community College pattern in our higher education system, the first thing that we have to do is to pay heed to the philosophy of the Community College, couched in the expression *"Find the need and meet it"*.

The problematic aspects of our higher education have been discussed threadbare in the reports of the different Educational Commissions. The needed structural changes have also been spelt out. I can do no better than summarise the suggestions made by J.P. Naik in his book entitled Policy and Performance in Indian Education, 1947–74, which hold good even now. They include (a) the replacement of the single point entry system by a multiple point entry (b) altering the sequential character of the system so that it would be possible for older persons to join a prescribed programme at any time and complete it in a shorter period (c) supplementation of the fulltime institutional instruction which is almost exclusively adopted in the present system with a large programme of part time education (d) the utilization of part-time teachers to the present exclusive dependence on full-time teachers so as to take advantage of the special expertise and talents available in the community and (e) in general, the blending of the formal system with the programmes of non-formal education, in order to meet the needs of the developing and changing society and to provide the basis of a new system of life-long education for all.

It is important to realize that all these suggestions made by J.P. Naik refer to the mode of organizing and imparting education. The American Community College has succeeded in implementing all these measures and many more, in the process of meeting the educational needs of the community and the economy. But interestingly in our country whenever there is a new educational need, we have tried to meet it by introducing a new category of institutions which have eventually started functioning like the traditional institutions."

> *Prof. Victor S.D' Souza presented the above paper at the UGC sponsored seminar on The Feasibility of Community Colleges in India. March 14-15, 1994 at the India International Centre.*[1]

1993

The revised version of NPE 1986 was placed before the Parliament in monsoon session 1992. The action strategies for implementation are highlighted in Program of Action of 1993. The items concerning the present seminar reads as follows:

"To encourage establishment of Community Colleges dealing with Vocationalisation of subjects related to service sector on line with community polytechnics". The establishment has been viewed as a saviour in redressing the problem of college sector:

Justice Punnya Committee Recommendations (1992-93)

The following recommendations made by Justice Punnaya Committee (92-93) promote greater degree of self reliance and quality assurance in higher education. These recommendations that are visualized for the Central Universities could be made applicable to the Community College. They are:

- Additional resources generated by an institution should be kept in a separate fund to be utilized for furtherance of objectives of the institution;
- UGC may provide matching grant as an incentive for generating additional resources;
- There should be 100 per cent income tax concession on all endowments and contributions made and also additional concessions to be given to donors;
- State or Government funding must continue to support higher education;

- Quality, efficiency and innovativeness must be consciously rewarded and institutions failing to improve financial and academic discipline should face disincentives;
- Unit-cost system of calculation of eligibility for grants should be followed;
- Part of the development grant may be provided for organisation of new academic programs and development of existing programmes.
- If these were the committee's recommendations, different five year plans had different targets.[2]

1993 Canara Community College, Mangalore

The Canara Community College (CCC) is a non-profit making, autonomous institution. It was established in 1993 and has been registered as a Society under the Karnataka Societies Registration Act, 1960.

It owes its origin to the Centre for Technology Development (CTD), Bangalore. The idea of starting a Community College was first suggested by Mr. John Hubbard, former US Ambassador in India.

Community Colleges – US and Canada–Features

The Community College movement started in the US at the beginning of the century in response to the changing needs of the society and the growing demand for higher education. Later it spread to Canada, Great Britain, France and Japan and other countries. Some of the distinguishing features of Community Colleges in the US and Canada, where such colleges have been in existence for a long time, are:

- They are community focused and locally governed, administered and advised.
- They are students centered-decisions are made with the students in mind.
- They promote an open admission policy that allows the enrolment of any person who is a high school graduate and / or at least 18 years of age.
- There is no discrimination in the admission of students of recruitment of staff on the basis of age, race, colour, sex, religion, handicap or national origin.
- They exhibit flexibility in a variety of ways in meeting the needs of the students and the community.
- They are responsive, quick to recognize and address emerging changing needs of the students and the community.

- They provide vocational/technical courses and programmes that incorporate relevancy with useful technology transferable to the work-place.
- They exhibit low student costs with consideration of the "ability to pay Concept".

CTD, recognizing the role that a Community College could play in providing relevant education to meet societal and developmental needs, decided to promote one.

Mangalore City in Dakshina Kannada (South Canara) District of the Karnataka State was chosen for the experiment because of several of its merits: The Dakshina Kannada region is a small homogeneous region: it is a veritable beehive of successful service industries in the tertiary sector: Mangalore is emerging as a major sea port on the western coast: a petroleum refinery and several major industrial and business establishments are coming up in the area and these will give rise to employment opportunities to vocationally trained people; it has a century old tradition of active private sector involvement in education, banking and business; and the people of the Dakshina Kannada District have an unabated yearning for learning. Moreover, the Canara High School Association, which runs the over-a-century-old educational institutions like the Canara High School and the Canara Girls High School came forward and offered accommodation on the campus of their institutions in Mangalore for the College.

Thus, came to be established in Mangalore the first Community College of India - the Canara Community College.

Objectives

The main objects of CCC are:

- To conduct courses (which are generally employment oriented), providing theoretical knowledge and practical training in various fields.
- To establish and run educational institutions/centres.
- To collaborate with universities and other educational institutions in order to establish centres of vocational education and training.
- To produce skilled workers to meet the trained manpower requirements of the Community, industry and business in the region.
- To retrain the already employed in order to upgrade their skills.
- To help small entrepreneurs in starting new business enterprises by training them in the areas of their interest.

Features

CCC provides opportunities to people of all ages and from diverse backgrounds to further their education and training in a multitude of ways. The courses are generally career-related and employment oriented. Women-in-development is a major thrust area of the College and many of the courses are especially designed for the career development of women. There is a place for almost everyone at CCC. The courses cater basically to:

- Young students and other persons to prepare for a career.
- Employed persons to improve their knowledge and career prospects.
- Housewives to acquire useful skills.
- Men and Women to be helped to start their own business.

In keeping with the times, CCC also provides opportunities to school students to learn the fundamentals of computers. For adults, the courses are in a variety of career fields: Computers, business, food science, health science, engineering and trades.

Special courses are conducted to prepare students for professional examinations. Often courses are offered which combine in-college sessions with work sessions in business or other sponsoring organisations.

The duration of the courses varies from a few days to a year. The daily time schedules of the courses also vary. Some of the courses are full-time ones and some part-time ones. Some courses are available only on Sundays.

CCC starts new programmes whenever there is a demand by industry or business. It discontinues an existing programme if there is no longer a demand for it. In particular areas where there is a demand for instructors, the College trains trainers rather than trainees.[3]

1994 October

Community Colleges: Administration and Accreditation Systems

As a follow-up of the conference held in March, 1994 on "**The Feasibility of Community Colleges in India**" sponsored by the UGC, a team was sent to U.S.A. to study a few Community Colleges in U.S.A. The late Dr. Ram Reddy, Former Chairman of the UGC evinced a lot of interest in the concept and implementation of Community Colleges in India. The present UGC administrative team is seriously considering the scheme.

The Team Nominated by UGC

Professor Dr. Malla Mamidi Reddy, Vice-Chancellor, Osmania University, Hyderabad; Professor Dr. Bhoomittra Dev, Vice-Chancellor, Rohilkhand University, Bareilly; Dr. Vijaya Chouhan, Principal, Government Science College, Jabalpur; and Dr. Sr. Annamma Philip, F.M.M., Principal, Stella Maris College, Madras were nominated by the University Grants Commission to study a few selected Community Colleges in the U.S.A. The group was escorted by Mr. Frank Bourne, an eminent scholar and formerly in the U.S. Foreign Service.

The programme was sponsored by the United States Information Agency (USIA). The programme began in Washington, D.C., followed by stops in Dayton, Ohio; Cocoa/Melbourne, Florida; Orange Country, California; Davenport, Iowa; and ending in New York.

At each place the members had the opportunity of visiting several Community Colleges situated in the area. This report is based on the study of Community Colleges with reference to their objectives, academic, administrative, and financial structure of each institution with a view to making suitable recommendations to the University Grants Commission, Government of India, New Delhi. The exact report is given below.

Recommendations

The broad philosophy on which the Community College is founded is not new to the Indian educational system. Many departures have already been made in the Indian educational system based on the recommendations of major education commissions, such as Kothari Commission (1966) and the National Policy on Education (1986). The restructuring of courses with greater thrusts on frontline areas, such as Science and Technology, emphasis on rural and agricultural education, extension dimension of higher education, open door admission policy and reservation policy based on positive discrimination, speaks volumes about the vision and perspective of the authors of these reports and their concern for the goal of equality of educational opportunities and pursuit of excellence. However, in spite of such vital policies of the Indian educational system and several measures adopted to reach the goal of equality of opportunity, one notices the growing crisis in higher education in the country.

The committee, on the basis of its study on Community Colleges of the U.S.A. suggests a few recommendations for the consideration of the University Grants Commission and the Ministry of Education, Government of India.

It is not out of place to mention here while we are committed to an open door admission policy, that the percentage of students in the respective age group who enroll into the college is very small and insignificant. The mode of distance education though serving the cause of educational needs of large number of people, unfortunately is not able to offer the programme in vital areas such as Science and Technology and job-oriented courses. The higher education system has not yet established linkages with industry. There are large number of jobs for which the students must go through the middle level technical courses. We have not been able to design courses, such as job-oriented courses, which alone probably can solve the growing unemployment problem in the country. Thus, the system is lagging behind to meet the needs of changing economy and technological advancement.

The Committee also carefully studied the "Project Report on Community Colleges" (U.G.C. workshop at New Delhi: March 1994) and found that the report reflects the philosophy of Community Colleges and the recommendations of the Committee are very timely and appropriate. The Committee therefore recommends the adoption of the concept of Community Colleges in the Indian higher education with suitable modifications. The following are some of the recommendations:

1. The committee recommends incorporating this concept of Community Colleges in the existing degree programme by increasing its duration by another year. This may be done on experimental basis in a few selected colleges. The programmes in the first two years must be restructured with an emphasis on vocational and job-oriented courses. In the subsequent programme of two years the student is given an opportunity for specialization. In order to maintain some distinction between the three-and four-year degree programmes it is necessary that students are awarded the Honour's degree. In the case of four-year degree course, a student with Honour's degree should be eligible for Master's degree programme of one year duration.

2. Taking into consideration the present constraints in Indian higher education the committee is of the opinion that the vocationalization of education at the undergraduate level may be strengthened as an alternative. However, to broaden its objectives and to organize the programmes on the model of Community Colleges it is necessary to introduce divergent vocational and technical courses catering to our changing economy. The vocationalization of U.G. level has been conceived by offering the vocational courses in three years. This may be evaluated after five years and restructured if need be.

3. It is also proposed that we should use the existing infrastructure in colleges for offering job-oriented programmes in the morning, evening, and on week-ends allowing flexibility in terms of time and duration of the programme and permitting the students to move at their own pace to complete the course. A credit system needs to be introduced for this purpose.

4. Starting Community Colleges as independent institutions mobilizing community resources could be yet another alternative. A definite policy has to be evolved for this purpose.

5. The present polytechnic college may be modified and founded on a broader philosophy to serve the community needs. The model of the Community College in the U.S.A. may be kept in view while modifying these institutions.

The admission policy can be as in the Open University system. The student should be given the freedom of registering at a particular college and be able to take courses in different institutions. Transfer of credits between institutions should be allowed.

Establishing of Community Colleges in terms of models suggested above, designing and offering job-oriented programme involves many challenges. It is, therefore, crucial to evolve certain detailed strategies for implementation of the programme and to meet the challenges. In order to evolve these strategies and work out various details for establishing institutions, it is necessary to organize a series of national and regional workshops involving persons from different walks of life - education, industry, business, government, etc. After arriving at a certain consensus, with respect to administrative structure, funding, industry-institutional relationship etc., a few institutions may be selected to initiate the programme.[4]

1995 May

UGC Report on the Feasibility of Community Colleges in India

A feasibility report prepared by a committee under the chairmanship of Prof. A. Gnanam, Vice-Chancellor of Pondicherry University is under consideration of the UGC. A news item that appeared in *The Times of India*, New Delhi, 14, April 1995 *"UGC to promote Community Colleges"* gives the summary of the feasibility report.

"In seeking to effectively address the constraints on higher education, the University Grants commission (UGC) is actively considering promotion of the Community College concept by modifying polytechnic institutions, bringing them in line with a broader philosophy to serve collective social needs.

This concept is expected to take up from where the present system is widely seen as having ended up short of expectations. Foremost amongst the shortcomings that it is intended to tackle is the unsatisfactory level of reach and access, with higher education so far being the prerogative of a few. What has also made the system appear beleaguered is the expected move towards privatisation, which will inevitably increase costs and thus make it economically discriminatory, defeating the Government's avowed policy of equal opportunity.

An alternative had also been necessitated in view of the fact that conventional distance education, though serving the scholastic needs of a large number of people, has unfortunately not been able to offer programmes in such vital areas as science and technology as well as job-oriented courses. Not many curricular packages had been designed to solve the growing unemployment problem in the country.

Educational opportunities would be provided not only to students who lag behind educationally and economically, but also to those who wish to resume scholastic involvement at one of the several stages either for retraining or to pick up on an interrupted academic programme. Training and education would be, therefore, uniquely student-centered, extremely flexible and community-focused. The feasibility study takes into account the average age of students as 30 years, with most of them employed.

The profile of a community college would be reflective of societal needs of the community living around it. A high level of community involvement in the decision making process in such areas as course delivery, range of services, determination fee and budget and recruitment of administrative personnel has been thought of. In essence, the entire community would learn from and have a stake in the college.

Since the major goal of such institutions would be to identify and fulfil the needs of the community, especially the weaker sections, the fee structure has been kept very low in the proposals.

Unlike the approach in traditional colleges, teaching would be given the primary priority and research almost given the go-by. Consequently, the teachers in Community Colleges will have to work a minimum of 15 contact hours per week. A greater proportion of part-time faculty has been favoured here than in any other sector of higher education. This may substantially reduce the cost of education and may even improve the quality of the faculty by drawing upon a variety of experienced resource-persons or professionals from the community.

Also, in contrast to traditional educational institutions, the emphasis is not so much on degrees as on knowledge and skills. Equal importance has been conceived for "non-credit courses" to attract a large section of the community into the process of higher learning. Divergent courses catering to the needs of working people and housewives for training and upgrading their functional knowledge and skills would be offered.

An important objective is retraining industrial workers to adapt to the changing technologies.

The criteria for admission would be flexible and similar to the procedures adopted in open universities in the country. However, in the case of students seeking admission with inadequate preparation, there would be a provision for remedial or preparatory education.

With a view to maintain standards of excellence, a strict evaluation system, which would make exit requirements highly demanding, has been provided for. Thus, while not much of a fuss will be made over entry requirements, the exit criteria are to be exacting.

Paradoxically, this concept of a community-centric educational institution originated in that bastion of capitalism and free enterprise, the USA. At present, there are around 1,400 Community Colleges in that country, with 43 per cent of the total student strength of 12 million on their rolls.

A UGC-nominated delegation was conducted around these institutions by the United States Information Agency (USIA) last year to examine the possibility of the concept being replicated in India. This team has recommended just this, incorporating certain modifications for the Indian context." The recommendations have been enumerated above.[5]

1995 October

Pondicherry University Community College

The Pondicherry University Community College was inaugurated by Dr. (Miss) A.S. Desai, Chairperson, UGC on 16th October 1995 during the Decennial celebration of Pondicherry University. It is located at Lawspet, Pondicherry.

The motto of Pondicherry University Community College is "Education for Employment" through skill formation. This goal is sought to be achieved by four fold functions, namely, teaching, training, research and extension. More specifically, the objectives of this Community College are:

- To promote the general educational well being of the community
- To ensure wider opportunities for higher education to those who are denied access to other forms of education
- To provide job oriented courses based on the perceived community demand for manpower
- To offer facilities for training and retraining of Government servants and the other workers in the organised sectors
- To initiate socially relevant and community based research projects
- To undertake extension activities on behalf of the University.[6]

Salient features of the Community College are

- The Community College has been able to draw expert faculty from various institutions like Hospitals, Government, Banks, Industries and college and University Departments.
- For each programme of study, an advisory committee constituted of senior resource persons well known for their contribution in the field, identifies the competent course staff from various other institutions and various areas of specialisation. This enables the Community College students to get the best expertise available.

- The Community College has been able to establish a rapport and collaboration with other institutions like General Hospital, Pondicherry Engineering College, Government Press, Law College, Leather and Tanning Industries and Institute of Hospitality Crafts. Such a linkage helps the Community College to provide hands on experience in the state of the art technology to the students in the labs and libraries of these collaborating institutions.
- Classes are scheduled according to the convenience of the learners. There are part-time courses to suit the timing of the employed people and full time courses to the unemployed.
- Practical training, visits to industrial sites and other areas of interest form integral aspects of every programme.
- The College provides counseling and guidance service to the students with a view to provide information on the prospects of their employment.
- Efforts are being made to ensure placements to the students in various organisations after the completion of their programmes.
- Considerable amount of infrastructure has been created to facilitate effective training and teaching. The establishment of a sophisticated computer lab, a library and a typewriting centre deserve a mention in this regard.[7]

References

1. Dr. Xavier Alphonse, S.J., *Changing Track – Community Colleges in India*, AIACHE Publications, New Delhi, First Edition - December 1996 and Second Edition – June 2001, pp. 27-30.
2. K. Sudha Rao, *Community Colleges in India: Need and Relevance*, *New Frontiers in Education*, New Delhi, Vol. 24, No. 23, 1994, p. 376.
3. Dr. Xavier Alphonse, S.J., "*Changing Track – Community Colleges in India*", AIACHE Publications, New Delhi, First Edition - December 1996 and Second Edition – June 2001, pp. 143-147.
4. *Ibid*, pp. 131-135.
5. *Ibid*, pp. 135-137.
6. *Ibid*, pp.. 155-156
7. *Ibid*, pp. 157-158.

2

Experiment and Expansion of Community College System (1996-2000)

Madras Community College

1996 August : The idea to start a Community College in Madras emerged gradually during the last academic year 1995-96 in a series of meetings and discussions with the principles of various colleges in the city, educational administrators, committed leaders of the Community, through interaction with professors from Community Colleges in USA who visited the Centre for Vocational Education, on the basis of the research done by the Centre and also the influence of the Indian delegations that have visited Community Colleges in USA. It is also the result of a fruitful exchange with the representatives of business, industry and service sectors.

The Madras Community College is established by the Archdiocese of Madras-Mylapore in response to the educational and employment needs of the people of Madras and its neighbourhood. Talking to newsmen on the 1st of July, the Archbishop of Madras-Mylapore, His Grace Aruldoss James expressed lucidly the need for such an institution.

"The Catholic church has been a pioneer in education. It owns and operates a large number of primary, secondary and tertiary educational institutions in and around the city of Madras. Extensive resources have been put into these institutions over the last hundred years and more. I am inclined to believe when these institutions were created, they had a relevance and fulfilled the needs of those times. But times have changed and I am afraid our educational institutions have been left behind.

I am concerned with the large number of students coming out of our secondary schools and University colleges being unable to find suitable employment and not being fully equipped to face life and its challenges. It is necessary to ask the question, for whose good are these educational institutions, if they do not prepare young men and women for life in the real world. It is said that only 18 per cent of those who finish school go on to higher education. About 82 per cent enter the world of work with no skills, open to exploitation with low wages under poor working conditions. I believe that our institutions should change track and pay a little more attention by providing relevant and quality work skills for this large group.

The time has come for the community to be involved in the shaping of the life of young people whether as educators, religious leaders or potential employers.

I take this opportunity to promote the Madras Community College which will offer skills and work oriented education to meet the needs of the students who have finished the higher secondary school. This institution will open for all sections of our society".

Madras Community College as an educational alternative to provide skill oriented, work related, value based and employment oriented education with employability guarantees. It is aimed at everybody in the community who is interested in acquiring work-oriented skills.[1]

Origin, Evolution and Motto

The Madras Community College was established in 1996 by the Archdiocese of Madras – Mylapore in response to the educational and employment needs of the people of Madras and its neighbourhood. The idea to start a community college in Madras emerged gradually during the academic year 1995-96 in a series of meetings and discussions with the Principals of various colleges in the city, Educational Administrators and Committed Leaders of the Community. Interactions with Professors and Community Colleges in USA and the influence of the Indian delegations that have visited the Community Colleges in USA also contributed in the formation of the concept. It is also the result of a fruitful exchange with the representatives of business, industry and service sectors.

Objectives

- To provide an opportunity for higher education to the economically underprivileged.
- To equip individuals with work skills in order to meet the demands of the prospective employers.
- To secure good placements for the successful students.
- To bring about an overall development in the students through value-based education and through a holistic approach.

Characteristics

- It is a unique and pioneering venture in providing an alternative system in the field of higher education where academic skills, life skills work skills training and job placements are done under one roof.
- It is an answer to the students who are unable to register in other colleges due to their poor economic background and poor academic performance.
- It is called a Community College because:
  - The whole is involved in the formation of the students in Madras Community College. To be precise, experts from the fields of business, industry, counseling, psychology and people from other sectors teach and train the students. Hence this college depends more on the community for the training of the students than formal classroom teaching.
  - To also cater to the needs of the people of the locality. In other words, it meets the needs of both the students and the employers of their respective area/place.
- The Madras Community College is a pioneer in the Life Skills Programme which helps the students to realize themselves and develop a self-identity. It brings in an overall growth in their personalities through boosting their self-esteem. This programme helps the students to appreciate labour in any form.
- Career counseling is a feature of the college where the families of the students are involved to help the students choose the right area of work skill in accordance to their interest and aptitude.
- The 'hands-on' experience or apprenticeship training after the completion of their three years of study in MCC is another characteristic which helps the students to put into practice the theory they have learnt. This serves as an entry point, for the students, into the work force.
- Job placement is also an important feature where the community goes hand in hand with the college to provide the right jobs, as soon as the students graduate out of the college.

Courses Conducted by the Community College

- Sales and Marketing
- Cargo Management
- Office Administration and Secretaryship
- Computer Software

- Computer Hardware
- Small Business Management

Challenges particular to the College

The most important challenge faced by the College is the recognition. Even though the Industrial sector accommodates the students, the recognition of the courses would help them to get better opportunities. Apart from that, the students will also be able to avail themselves of the benefits (like bus passes) meted out to other regular college students. In keeping with the objective of the college, the fees collected from the students is deliberately kept at a minimum. This limits the availability of funds. Hence, the staff remuneration is not in keeping with their qualification. Even though most of the fulltime staff have completed M.Phil, the college is unable to give them a pay scale and at present only a consolidated pay is given. This leads to greater staff turnover hindering the progress of the college.

Inspite of all these challenges, Madras Community College is a pioneer and one of its kind providing life skills, academics, work skills and all the above mentioned under one roof.[2]

1996 December

AIACHE General Body meeting and Triennial Conference of Principals – Statements and recommendations – Community College – AIACHE News Letters

The book *Changing Track: Community Colleges in India* written by Fr. Xavier Alphonse S.J., was released at the conference of principals, held in Bangalore. The extract from the Statement of the Conference is given below.

Community Colleges : We welcome the concept of Community Colleges as adapted to the Indian conditions, as an alternative mode of education and training. The vocational, lifelong and self-reliant character of the Community College is a refreshing change from the traditional, age-specific and Government dependent mode of education prevalent. We urge the Churches, College Managements and other interested groups to study the feasibility of Community Colleges as a timely response to the challenges of unemployment and the irrelevance of the present education system. AIACHE should facilitate the feasibility study, job-market survey setting up of Community Colleges in all possible ways.[3]

1997 August

Plea for an Educational Alternative: Emerging occupational patterns and social relevance of higher education have significant bearing on the shape of post-secondary education. While educational goals are generally discussed in terms of instruction methodology, establishment costs and social aspirations, the format of institutions of higher education has more or less remained untouched. The present system of education has lost its competitive efficiency. It also does not fully provide for freedom, flexibility, innovation, equity and excellence in its approach while it is always described as a pathway of development with a human face. The book under review attempts a new definition of higher education through its new delivery system with a new format. The present educational scenario is full of well-intentioned schemes, yet its output is not quite satisfactory.

Changing Track: Community Colleges in India offers an articulate survey and study of the author to bring out the concept of community colleges for adoption in the context. It contains a statement of his first hand experience of the working of community colleges in United State of America gathered from December 1995 to April 1996. As a sponsored study the book is prefaced with an introduction containing valuable perceptions about the success story of the implementation of the schemes in America. Such eminent persons as Dr. Maxwell C. King. Dr. Bill F. Stewart, Dr. Kollar, Dr. Ponitz, Dr. Blong, Dr. Fanelli, Dr. Anandakrishan, Prof. D'Souza, Dr. Sudha Rao, Dr. Sawakar and Dr. Almeida, have painstakingly brought out the linkage of community colleges with local needs, diversity of technical and occupational programmes, citizen's ability, community environment etc. Through assiduous accounts of their success in America in offering opportunities and access to non-traditional students, independent of parental financial support, their curriculum has been referred to be as diverse as the students body while taking into account their abilities. These colleges have been called low cost alternative with a mission for work preparation and life long learning opportunities. They constitute a process compensatory education for existing and emerging business needs while also educating people for meaningful role in society. Among their noteworthy features is flexibility of studies. Autonomy of the institutions in their functioning is another features responsible for their success. Their governance and mechanism are related to such public functionaries as have the desire, dynamism and orientation for making the system a success. The finances come from the beneficiaries and the particular private industries of the area where these are located. Referring to the Indian context, community colleges are proposed to be either new institutions or within the existing colleges and polytechnics or industrial locations, they could offer restructured courses in consonance with UGC Policy on vocationalisation with due innovation, change and integration of new concepts and ideas. Referring to the many dimensions involved in industries – university linkages for which a community college could be an answer, it is suggested that the industries and the government should contribute finances in the form of sufficient grants to the colleges thus bridging the gap between higher education and needs of the market place.

Part – II of the book – *The inspiration: Community Colleges in USA* contains laudatory references to the role of community colleges as 20th century phenomenon generated in America to extent the reach of education and terms them as valuable community resource, Generally this part repeats what has been said by numerous protagonists of the concept in the earlier part of the book. Infact, this is an account of a few successful American community colleges. In all, it recounts their philosophy, outreach, governance, educational service or students support services, industrial linkage, community service, etc. In short the perspective of community colleges has been with alternative learning programmes. There is no doubt that community colleges in America enjoy an overwhelming social support and have their district role in accommodating enrolment growth and addressing professional growth opportunities through sharing of information and through technical education assistance. Against this background this writer's vital interest in replicating this paradigm to the India set up is understandable. However, it entails translating a concept in the context of the needs of our community.

Part-III of the book focuses on the need of Community Colleges in India. This part gives some statistical scan about the level of employment vis-à-vis outreach of our higher education system and its alternatives while establishing vocationalisation as the felt need of our students vis-à-vis UGC initiative through its scheme. The focus is on building vocational competence through courses not fully known to the industrial sector. The author has made the need for the establishment of community colleges a social imperative on account of the need to remove the mismatch between academic inputs and job requirements and also briefly to add value and utility to undergraduate courses.

In Part IV 'the Feasibility of Community Colleges in India', the author shares his views that educationists, industrialists and others have to establish close linkages between community and modifications, training needs and public requirements. This part also refers to the UGC Report of Feasibility of the Community Colleges in India (May 1995). This report attempts to suggest some modifications of polytechnic institutions so as to bring them in line with a broader philosophy to conceptualise social needs with this it linked the important objective of retraining industrial workers to suit changing technologies.

The author of the book after having visited 14 Community Colleges in America and after having interacted with them has offered a series of modifications in terms of constitution of advisory boards, placement procedures, teaching and learning processes, flexibility in courses etc, to plant them in the Indian soil. He has also outlined areas of American role collaboration in curriculum development, faculty exchange, operational management etc. Against this background he has called this a viable and practical, timely and relevant reform in Indian Higher Education set up.

Part-V – deals with the 'Existing Experiments of Community Colleges in India'. The author focuses on the three available initiatives at Bangalore, Pondicherry and Madras and finds them community focused, students centered, flexible, vocational and cost effective. He finds them useful for preparing students for career prospects. Giving an overview of the useful courses introduced in these three institutions, the author is at pains to point out that a Community college is an institution which attempts to match students educational needs and is poised to be a social success.

The book features the author's experience of the role of community colleges in America through a sponsored study tour. While establishment of community colleges is a social-education phenomenon there on account of the rich support of the community to sustain IIT, its survival in Indian context in spite of the suggested modifications cannot be vouched. The poverty of Indian social support and its reluctance to share collective experiences would always be deterrent to this otherwise useful alternative. Despite the fast changing pattern of collegiate education with an ever-increasing focus on vocational education, establishment of community colleges, as social phenomenon with all its relaxed entry rules, flexibility of course choice would not have many promoters except in a few cosmopolitan cities. The book does not offer a competent look at the financial aspect of the schemes in the India context. It also overlooks the largely rural and intensively poor social strata of our society. In a country of little academic inputs and with features of growing indifference in our universities and affiliated college, the system cannot be offered as a sound and viable alternative. So, "Changing Track" despite containing positive suggestions will not find a very encouraging response in the Indian set up with limited availability of funds and lopsided social priorities.

Written in a lucid style, the book makes an interesting reading and offers a valuable contribution to the literature on Community Colleges, the success of which is a function or a range of variables several of which may not be with us.[4]

1997: Changing Track: Community Colleges in India – Book Review: The inspiration for writing this book came to the author from the example of community colleges functioning successfully in the United States for the past few decades. These institutions impart vocational education of a high standard relevant to the community around them and also manage to give a dose of liberal arts and science as well. They award associate degrees in the two-year period the students spend in their campuses; the credits secured here can be transferred to the four year Baccalaureate degree. The learners are enabled to practise some profession with the skills acquired.

What is significant is the fact that wide range of courses are offered by the community colleges within the reach of all. Easy accessibility, open admission, low tuition fees, opportunity for part-time education and life – long learning may be considered the hallmarks of the community colleges. Therefore, the concept of community colleges can fit in very well in a country like India. The author who had the benefit of visiting several community colleges in the U.S. makes out a good case for starting such institutions in this country. The initiatives taken here already are: Canara Community College, Mangalore (1993), Pondicherry University Community College, Pondicherry (1995) and Madras Community College, Madras (1996).

There are a number of programmes like computer applications, information technology, food processing, early childhood care, nutrition and dietetics and tourism and ticketing that are already being offered in these institutions. With the virtue of flexibility and adaptability to the needs of the neighbouring communities, these institutions have the potential to transform the education scene. There is, however, one serious impediment; the preference for while collar work and prejudice against blue collar work that is still prevalent in the public mind. People pay only lip service to the "dignity of labour" but think highly of deskwork. This attitude must change and if a number of community colleges spring up in different parts of the country, the better the country will be. [5]

1997 November

The Madurai Community College: An educational alternative

The Origin: The Madurai Jesuit Province has been involved in the field of primary, secondary, technical and higher education in South India for the past 150 years. The Jesuit order has been running four primary schools, eleven secondary schools, one technical institute, one institute of management and five university colleges. In the past ten years, it has been concentrating with preferential concern on students belonging to rural areas and disadvantaged sections of society. More than 33,000 students are currently being educated in these institutions.

For the past 150 years, Jesuits have been pioneers in the field of education. They have taken innovative steps within their limited resources to improve the quality of education given in the institutions run by them. One more step in the same direction is the Madurai Community College, a job–oriented, skill-based, work–related institution situated in the Loyola Technical Institute Campus from July 1997. This new educational alternative has been the result and fruit of much study, research and wide consultation with leaders engaged in education, industry and administration.

The Environmental Scan

The Level of Education: Each year around 20, 000 students pass out from 63 higher secondary and matriculation schools. Only 50 per cent of these students are enrolled in 23 arts and science colleges and other professional institutions of higher education. One third of the students drop out or are unable to complete higher education due to economic and social constraints.

All these individuals form a large part of the unskilled labour force in India and need opportunities for training in some type of skills either in the traditional occupation of their families or in other areas to enable them to become gainfully employed. There is also a backlog of school dropouts such as individuals who are beyond the usual school age of sixteen and are working as unskilled and semi-skilled workers.

The Level of Employment: Most graduates from arts and science colleges and early school leave-outs are unable to find employment because they lack competence and skills required for jobs that are available in business, industry and service sectors. Very often, the employers have to retrain them in order to enhance their employability in terms of work-skills, life adjustment skills. It is obvious that the turning out of the graduates in general arts, science and commerce colleges in a routine fashion has not only contributed to the problem of unemployment but also the unemployables. There is a serious mismatch in India between the jobs that are available and the graduates with inadequate skills.

The Need: It is in this context, the community college system-job-oriented and skill-based education is gaining currency in India and in particular Tamil Nadu during the last two years. The Madras Community College was born in August 1996, started by the Archdiocese of Madras – Mylapore to fulfil the need of bridging the gap between employment opportunities and required skills in the city of Madras. These type of Colleges, skill-based and competency–based institutions are becoming educational alternatives to the traditional arts and science colleges in the country.

In the explosive and depressive environment of the educated unemployment, semi-skilled and unskilled labour force and the increasing demands of the commerce, business, industry and service sectors (influenced by globalization and economic liberalization of the country) for competent individuals with the necessary skills, the community college system becomes a feasible and viable educational alternative.

Keeping this perspective, the Madurai Jesuit Province decided in January 1997 to establish the Madurai Community College by upgrading its only technical institute during the course of the academic year. Serious and well thought out preparation began towards the establishment of the Community College from February, 1997.

The Preparation: A research study to explore the employment opportunities and possibilities available in and around Madurai was carried out for six weeks during February – March 1997. The findings of the study were the following:

Employment Opportunities and Possibilities Around Madras

Names of the Programmes	*Jobs Available by 2000 A.D*
Textile Technology (35 Units)	1,000
Printing Technology (105 Units)	1,500
Hospital and Allied Health Service (Multi – Specialty Hospitals and other Health Centres 86 Units)	1,200
Sales and Marketing Management (33 Marketing and Advertising Consultants)	3,000
Automobiles Service and Maintenance (67 Sales and Service Units)	4,500
Cargo Management (25 Units)	1,250.
Small Business Development (500 Units-188 Projects are available)	
Soft Beverages Manufacturing (11 Units)	750
Office Technology	2,500
Small Home Appliances Service and Repair	800 to 1,000
Construction Management and Interior Decoration (22 Construction Companies)	500
Computer Hardware and Software (52 Small and Medium Sized Training Units)	Innumerable
Air conditioning and Refrigeration	750
Transport Fleet Management (67 Units)	1,000
Plantations Management	500

Extreme care was taken to make sure that the Madurai Community College will offer only need-based courses to meet the demands of the community. The research study was carried out by Fr. Xavier Alphonse, S.J., Director of Curriculum Development and Project Planning of the Madras Community College with Mr. T.A. John Nelson, Manager, Human Resources Development, Radha Park Inn International, Chennai.

The findings of the study were presented to a group of educationists, Jesuits, Non-Jesuits, representatives of business, industry and commerce on the 14th of April, 1997 in order to elicit their views and suggestions on the feasibility of a Community College in Madurai. The theme of this First Consultations was 'Re-engineering Education to Employment and Life'. The entire group endorsed the idea of the establishment of a community college in Madurai at the earliest opportunity. The consultation was presided over by the Jesuit Provincial Fr. D. Jeyaraj, S.J., and he explained the purpose of the institution.

- Madurai Community College will serve the people of Southern Tamil Nadu by catering to the employment needs of the economically and socially disadvantaged groups in particular by providing job-oriented, skill-based and work-related quality education at an affordable price to all who desire it, encouraging open access and equal opportunity with cost effectiveness, life-long and continuing education.
- It has a great potential and promise leading to the unfolding of the creative potentialities of the people who have been denied access so long and thus empowering them to lead a life of dignity leading to human resource development.
- It will fill the gap--matching education with employment, skills with jobs, competencies with opportunities.
- It will have both urban and rural campuses taking care of the community education and service programmes in the rural areas.
- The Jesuit Province of Madurai will provide the platform but the entire community will participate in the establishment and administration of the college. Member belonging to various religions and sections of the society will be in the Governing Board of the College. All the people irrespective of their caste and creed will have access to the college.
- The Madurai Community College stresses and emphasizes the option of the Madurai Province i.e. preferential option for the poor especially the rural poor. This option will be realized by conducting courses for the early school leavers and community service programmes.

The Second Consultation was held on the 4th of July, 1997 with representatives of industries in Madurai. Their presence in large numbers encouraged the whole venture. The theme of the consultation was 'Towards Relevance, Challenge, Access in life and Work skill Education'. The industrialists were given a clear understanding of the concept and implementation of the community college system. Mr. A. Selvaraj, the president of Madurai District Tiny and Small Scale Industries Association (MDITISSIA) and Vice-president of TANSTIA presided over the deliberations and all the industrialists, representatives from commercial, service sectors supported the establishment of the community college unanimously. They expressed their willingness to sign a memorandum of understanding with the college to help the college to design the curriculum, to send part-time faculty to teach the students, to train the students on site and to prepare them for placement. The Managing Directors of Hi-Tech-Arai Ltd, Susee Autos, Sahay

Tools Ltd, representatives of NABARD, representatives from NGO group were also present.

Mr. Selvaraj expressed his great dream to make Madurai an Industrial city and emphasized the urgent need to have the right man for the right job. He said that the industries have to be proactive to bring about the necessary change.

The College without Walls: The Madurai Community College will be making use pf the existing infrastructural facilities of LTI campus, St. Mary's Higher Secondary School with its new computer centre, Dr. Ambedkar Cultural Academy (DACA) and the Ideas Centre of Madurai. The effort to provide meaningful and relevant education is truly communitarian and collaborative.

The Objectives

1. It aims at matching education with employment.
2. Its emphasis is on application and employment orientation and skill promotion.
3. It seeks to develop socially responsible, community oriented and industrially skilled quality individuals.
4. It aims to provide skill-oriented education with professionalism and cost effectiveness.
5. It will promote active participation and collaboration and provide vital linkage between industries and the community college.

The Beneficiaries

The college offers One Year Diploma Programmes (middle level skills) to the following categories:

- Graduates who have completed their undergraduate degree in arts and science colleges.
- Higher secondary school completed and those who are doing their undergraduate programmes in the existing arts and science colleges.

The college also offers *Certificate* programmes for school drop outs in various trades.

- People already in the work-force by upgrading their skills especially computer literacy through weekend programmes.
- People in the rural areas—Basic skills of reading and writing, Literacy and other community service programmes that will improve the quality of life of the rural poor.
- The college is open to both men and women.

Programmes Offered

1. Air-conditioning and Refrigeration
2. Automobile Service and Maintenance Technology
3. Cargo Management
4. Construction Management and Interior decoration
5. Computer Maintenance Technology
6. Office Technology
7. Plantations Management
8. Crop Plant Management Technology
9. Printing and Allied service
10. Small Business Development
11. Small Home Appliances Service and Repair
12. Soft Beverages Manufacturing
13. Sales and Marketing Management.
14. Two Wheeler Maintenance Technology.
15. Allied Health Courses.

Programmes on offer during 1997-98

1. Automobile Service and Maintenance Technology
2. Two Wheeler Maintenance Technology
3. Office Technology
4. Computer Maintenance Technology
5. Crop Plant Management Technology

Curriculum

The curriculum has three distinct components. It is taught in two semesters.

FIRST SEMESTER

1. Life Skills Programme

(a) Understanding and coping with Life challenges
(b) Interpersonal Relations and Communication Skills
(c) Computer usage and applications
(d) Developmental course in spoken and written English

SECOND SEMESTER

2. Work Skills Programme

This is divided into three parts:

First Part : Intensive input sessions on the field of specialization chosen for 40 sessions (Each session is for three hours)

Second Part : Field placement, Library work and assignments for 50 sessions.

Third Part : Hands on Experience: Third component will be the internship and on campus training for finding a job and keeping it for 50 sessions.

All students have to go through the life-skills programme before they start the work skills programme. Career guidance and counseling will be conducted for all the students at the end of the life-skills programme to choose the right work-skill programme. The curriculum is learner-centred, need-based and has a large component of hands on experience.

Faculty for the programmes is composed of experts, professional consultants, managers and scientists working currently in their field of specialization.[6]

1997 December, 4-6

St. Joseph's College (Autonomous), Tiruchirapalli–620 002

National Seminar on "Framework of Education for the Indian Context" (A New Perspective) – Recommendations of the Seminar

Drawn from different regions in India, 2000 delegates discussed several issues for making the education system relevant to the present Indian context. Realizing the urgency to take a fresh look at our educational endeavours at this historical moment in Indian History the 50th year of our Independence, the delegates of this conference made the following recommendations.[7]

We recommend to the State and Central governments to promote the community college system as an educational alternative promoting skill-based, work-related and job oriented education.[8]

1998 February

Changing Track: Community Colleges in India – Book Review

The book is an informative and resourceful introduction to the concept of Community College and its realization in India and abroad.

In the present situation of countless young men and women especially from the lower strata of society struggling to get gainful employment, the promising concept of community college and its gradual emergency in India are very significant in the educational field. Community Colleges developed very well in the USA. Their expertise and resources have provided a model from experimentation with such colleges in India. It is encouraging to note that the UGC and other educational research organisations have taken note of this new model and began to promote it.

The book's title *Changing Track* suggests that community colleges are an emerging alternative in vocational and technical education for the great bulk of students who may not and cannot venture into higher professional schools. In a country of massive unemployment, the community college as presented in the book is commonly practical, truly integrative and very promising for the young students. Its concept, programme content, management of resources, especially local resources its emphasis, nature, creatively developing the potential of the students, its value education and the personality growth and human relatedness it fosters are Laudable. Dr. Xavier Alphonse has put together the points of view of experts from the US and India on the community college, presented the arguments for the need for such colleges very cogently and convincingly, demonstrated their feasibility for the country and given a good picture of the existing community colleges in India. Besides the notes and references there is a very useful bibliography at the end for those who would like to be informed about this novel concept. The book is a "must" for any one interested in community colleges, especially in India. AIACHE a prime supporter of community colleges has done a great service in publishing author; Programme Director of the Madras Community College deserves credit for a well-written resource book.[9]

1998 June

Melrosapuran Rural Community College – An Educational Alternative

During this Golden Jubilee year, the Diocese of Madras of the Church of South India has launched a novel project of Melrosapuram Rural Community College both Rural Campus and Urban Campus to offer job-oriented, skill-based, work related quality education at an affordable price to all those who desire it, to meet the local needs of various industries, commerce and community. The very purpose of the Melrosapuram Rural Community College is to find gainful employment for all those who are socially and economically depressed.

The Problem

One of the basic problems faced by India is unemployment. This complex problem assumes new dimensions, when we consider the unemployed youth. The number of youngsters entering schools and colleges is on the increase. A vast majority of them drop out either at the tenth std. level or at the 12std. level. Very few of them enter college. They belong to the age group of 14 to 16 years.

These students seek employment with no particular skills. Many of them are under employed or unemployed. The worst part of the problem is that they are not employable. This is because of the curriculum, they were taught at schools. Hence, it becomes essential that the students are taught job oriented, skill-based and work-oriented courses.

The Church of South India shares this deep human concern. The Diocese of Madras has initiated the project of Rural Community College as memorial of the Golden Jubilee of the Church of South India. Bishop M. Azariah has clearly expressed the need for such a project.

"The Church of South India, Diocese of Madras with one of its focus on service to the educated unemployed people has been offering skills training opportunities over the last seven years, so far covering 1400 young men and women mainly drawn from the rural areas. And yet, there are several thousands of more young men and women with qualifications of SSLC and +2 education both drawn from our rural churches and Dalit communities from among the deprived sections of our society within the limits of our Diocese of Madras".

"It is this felt need that has led the Executive Committee of our Diocese to think of an alternative avenue for skills development training opportunities. One such project that emerged is the Tool Room Training Centre under the umbrella of the Rural Community College that is being developed on the ten acres of the land available with Rural Church at Melrosapuram, 40Km South of Madras".

"This Tool Room is going to be situated at the edge of the expanding city of Madras where many industrial factories and production Centres are coming up such as Ford Mahindra Automobile Engg. Project. It is this climate that can be expected to offer the specific kind of job opportunities for our young trainees through Tool Room Training Centre by establishing close linkages with industries in this region.

The Need Analysis

It is in this context, the church of south India, Madras Diocese, strives to impart the required skills to the job seekers through need based training. To design this need based training, the Madras Diocese of the Church of South India has undertaken the study to identify the middle level jobs that are available in various fields and the expectations of the employees, the skills to be acquired by the potential job-seekers. The Need Analysis was done for five months interviewing 320 employers, covering 32 areas of employment opportunities both rural and urban.

Employment Potential: (Need Analysis at a Glance)

Areas of Employment Potential	*Units*	*No. of Jobs Available*
1. Advertisement	78	2,000
2. Air Conditioning and Refrigeration	45	4,000
3. Aqua Culture	19	1,000
4. Automobile Service and Manufacturing	17	2,600
5. Bakery and Confectionery	24	1,300
6. Beautician and Health Care	27	570
7. Book Publishing and Selling	120	5,500
8. Cargo Management	103	11,800
9. Commercial Photography	36	750
10. Community Workers		1,400
11. Computer Hardware	100	1,000
12. Computer Software	348	78,750
13. Construction Management	98	16,500
14. Courier Services	108	18,000
15. Dairy Farming	13	850
16. Export Garments Manufacturing	152	20,000
17. Fashion Designing	13	350
18. Horticulture .	12	850
19. Hospital and Allied services	86	18,000
20. Hotel Management and Hospitality Services	120	19,000
21. Interior Decoration	163	12,600
22. Journalism	21	1,500
23. Office Management and Secretaryship	80	5,000
24. Plantations Management	14	400
25. Printing Technology	224	8,500
26. Road Transport Management	207	12,100
27. Sales and Marketing management	55	11,000
28. Small Home Appliances Repairs and Service	135	8,500
29. Soft and Hard Beverages Manufacturing	16	1,500
30. Travel and Tourism Operations	254	14,000
31. Two Wheeler Mechanism	30	4,200
32. Visual and Graphics Mixing	22	350

Community College System

Community College System is emerging as an alternative response to the problem of finding gainful employment and better livelihood. It provides access and equal opportunity. It is cost effective. It seeks to serve the economically and socially disadvantaged groups. It works in collaboration with Industry, Commerce and Service Sectors. It provides skills and enhances human resources development of the area and aims at alleviation of poverty, through economic regeneration by creating individuals to fulfil the needs of the industry and community. The Melrosapuram Rural Community College with its rural and urban campuses implements the above Philosophy of the Community College System in its totality and the entire functioning of the college is based on the scientific analysis that has been made of the job opportunities available in the Madras City and its neighbourhood.

Rural Campus

The Rural Campus with its Tool Room and the Technical Training Centre will train Multimechanics with the variety of skills. It will also be a production centre to provide Industrial accessories as it is situated ideally 1km away from the Ford Mahindra Factory and the industrial town of Maraimalai Nagar with more than hundred units just six km away from the college. Even as the campus is under construction, five industries have approached the college to produce precision instruments for them. The college will conduct Two Year Diploma courses for 10th and 12th passed students and certificate programme for school dropouts.

The courses will be offered in the following trades: Cylindrical Grinder, Miller, Turner, Surface Grinder, Radial Driller, Pointer Press, Sheet Metal, Tool Die Maker, Mechanical Grinder, Fitter, General Fitter, Mason, Carpenter, Electrician, TV and Radio Mechanic, Air Conditioning and Refrigeration, Small Home Appliances Services and Maintenance.

Each year the college will train a batch of hundred students mostly from the economically and socially backwards sections from the rural areas.

Community Oriented Courses

It will also provide community oriented courses like Community Health workers, Community Counsellor, and Agro product manufacturing, dairy Farming, Family and Child Welfare, Literacy Mission Worker, Environment Management, Soil Analysis, Seed Technology. The college will also design courses for rural women for self employment leading to self reliance.

These courses become inevitable because Melrosapuram is surrounded by 80 villages.

Since the college is also a production centre it is hoped that it will make 20 per cent of profit over the accessories sold to the industries. This money will be used to support the economically poor students. The college also contemplates hostel facilities for the rural students.

Urban Campus

This is situated in the city of Chennai, using the existing infrastructural facilities of St. Ebba's Girls Higher Secondary School, Mylapore, Chennai. The Classrooms and a well-equipped computer centre are used for the college. The following programmes are presently offered as One Year Diploma courses at this campus in the evenings for graduates and those who have completed Plus Two.

1. Computer Hardware Maintenance and Software
2. Office Technology
3. Hotel Management
4. Sales and Marketing Management
5. Travel and Tourism
6. Printing Technology

The following courses may also be offered in future: 1. Cargo Management; 2. Road Transport Management; 3. Garments Export; 4. Beautician and Health Care; 5. Advertising and Visual Communication; 6. Allied Health Courses: (a) Medical Lab Assistant, (b) Radiology Technician, (c) Nursing Assistant, (d) Physiotherapy Assistant, (e) Operation Theatre Assistant, (f) Data Record Technician, 7. Journalism and T.V. Production.

These Programmes have three distinct components:

A. Life skills and Developmental English for 3 months – 10 weeks,
B. Work skills in the area chosen for 7 months – 28 weeks;
C. Internship and hands on experience for three months – 10 weeks

Total Number of credits = 48 = 48 weeks = 720 hours

1 Credit = 15 hours a week = 3 hours a day.[10]

1999 January

Community College Movement

The Community College Movement is taking deep roots in Tamil Nadu and Pondicherry. It is emerging as an alternative system to provide the need based, job–oriented, work–related and skill based training to young men and women of all categories, thus brightening their lives with hope, through skills development.

Objectives

- *To include the excluded* - To suggest an alternative to the present system of education that promotes exclusion and elimination right from kindergarten to higher education.

- *Giving the best to the least* – In providing access and equal opportunity and ensuring cost effectiveness in skills development training to the economically, socially and educationally backward segments of society.
- *Matching education with employment* – To increase and enhance the employability of our young men and women so that they could take advantage of the innumerable employment opportunities that are available in the locality, determined by the indicative surveys and need analysis of the area.
- *Close linkage with industries* – Commercial houses and service sectors so that the curriculum and the training are relevant, purposeful and fulfil the needs of the community
- *The participation of the community* – Membership in the advisory boards of the Community College is ensured by the leaders of the industry and community becoming , and some of the Community Colleges have signed Memorandum of Understanding with the industries.
- *The development of skills and competencies* – As a necessary stage in the growth of social reengineering and economic regeneration, after all our efforts at conscientization, organisation of people to fight for their rights, basic literacy and health and so on.
- *Enhancing the employability* – It would lead to the acquiring of jobs that are available thus resulting in the alleviation of poverty and furtherance of human resource development.

Community Colleges in South India

The Pondicherry University started the Pondicherry University Community College in October 1995. This was followed by the Madras Community College, started by the Archdiocese of Madras – Mylapore as the pioneering effort in Tamil Nadu. It is encouraging to note the phenomenal growth of Community Colleges in Tamil Nadu which numbers fifteen.

The Madras Centre for Research and Development of Community Education proposes to start Community Colleges at Periyakulam, Nanguneri, Kuthenkuly, Salem, Thanjavur, St. Thomas Mount, Sriperumbudur, Chennai, Dindigul Chennai Corporation Community College. Tenali and Guntur in Andhra Pradesh.

All these Colleges follow these five stages towards their establishment as institutions: (a) the Conceptual Clarification of the Community College system (b) Need analysis of the employment potential of the area (c) The feasibility study (d) Industrial Collaborators meet and (e) Determination of the programmes to be given and the starting of the college.

Many of the colleges are functioning without recognition or approval by any recognized educational body. The Manonmaniam Sundaranar University has approved five colleges under its jurisdiction. The University is making a serious attempt to formulate guidelines and norms towards the establishment and governance of these colleges. The University is keen to encourage this movement with all the necessary checks and balances in order to maintain the quality and standard of the training given and also to prevent educational agencies from commercializing the system which would obstruct the fulfillment of the objectives of the Community College.

All the colleges follow the curriculum with four distinct components: (i) Life Skills, (ii) Work skills, (iii) Internship and hands on experience (iv) Preparation for employment.

Madras Centre for Research and Development of Community Education

As the Community Colleges are emerging, it becomes imperative to monitor the process of the development in order to give a distinctive direction and focus and the need analysis of the local community backed by scientific research, publication of books and articles, curriculum development, training programmes and preparation of resource materials in collaboration with industries, commercial houses, service sectors and experts in community education and rural development.

All these could be done effectively through the establishment and promotion of Madras Centre for Research and Development of Community Education.

The objectives and activities of the Research Centre include:

- To promote and popularize the concept of the Community College system in India as an educational alternative through seminars and workshops.
- To help the community colleges to form and develop relevant, meaningful, need based, skill oriented and life coping curriculum and prepare the necessary resource material based on the need analysis of the employment opportunities of the local area.
- To establish links with industrial partners for curriculum development and training.
- To publish books and articles in the leading journals of higher education in the country in order to give a clear focus and direction to the Community College Movement.
- To evolve short term and certificate courses for school dropouts, rural youth and rural women in order that they can find employment and also create self-employment. One-year diploma courses at a higher

level with advisory boards from industries and trades for those who have completed their secondary school education.

- To train the teachers of Community Colleges in Life Skills and Work Skills.
- To create a learning resource centre for the development of various job-oriented programmes.
- To document the process and evolution of the community college movement in south India.
- To enter with the international networking of Community College in USA, U.K. Germany, Australia, South Africa and Canada through Internet and E-mail.
- To influence the State and Central Governments, Universities and UGC (University Grant Commission) to recognise and accept Community College System as an educational alternative and to work for the recognition of the diploma and certificate programmes.
- To serve as the coordinating agency and clearing house for Community College in South India in order to share the experience and expertise by all.

The Madras Centre for Research and Development of Community Education was inaugurated on the 10th of January 1999 by the secretary of the University Grants Commission, Dr. G.D. Sharma.

The Centre aims at serving the following target groups: School dropouts below 10th grade – Certificate courses; +2 (Higher Secondary Grade) Completed – One year Diploma Courses: Existing Arts and Science students – one year Diploma Courses; Those who have completed their Under Graduate Degree – One year Diploma Courses: Life long continuing education and updating skills for the workers of the respective areas; Self employment for rural youth and women.

The Centre would be happy to assist in the preparation towards the establishment of the Community College, in providing the curriculum for life skills and work skills in conducting training programmes for the Community College teachers, in being accessible through the learning resource centre which will have important books and relevant material for the various job-oriented programmes and the documentation on the Community College movement in India and abroad.

The centre aims at application oriented, need based, job and skill oriented research to fulfil the needs of the local community in serving the economically, socially and academically disadvantaged groups in order to equip them with the skills required for the job market which would help them to earn their livelihood. This will be a tangible source of alleviation of poverty and human resource development.

All educational agencies that are interested to look into the Community College system as an educational alternative could contact Dr. Xavier Alphonse, S.J., Director, Madras Centre for Research and Development of Community Education (MCRDCE), 13, Madha Church Road, Mandavelipakkam, Madras – 600 028.[11]

1999 September

Community College: Meeting Society's Needs

Preamble – Need for Community Colleges

The formal system of education in India is unable to deliver the goods because of these two important reasons – exclusions elimination and mismatch between education and employment. The exclusion rate is 96%.

The mismatch between education and employment results in producing people who are not only unemployed but also made ineligible for employment.

The school drop out rate in Tamil Nadu at the level of 10th standard is 61.6% (1997-1998) and the 12th standard is 79.86% (1997-98). The statistics that are available with the employment exchange as on 31.12.97 tells us about the dismal and alarming picture of people waiting for jobs in Tamil Nadu.

Perspective and Philosophy of the Community College System

The vision of the Community College is to include the excluded – the academically, economically and socially disadvantaged groups and to give the best to the least. The Community College is a job-oriented, work-related, skill-based institution, which provides access and cost effective skill based and life coping education. It is promoted as an educational alternative to 12th standard students, 10th standard passed students, school dropouts, rural youth and rural women, and there is no age limit for admission. It is considered as supplementary education to graduates or would-be-grades in order to make them employable. It encourages life long and continuing education, updating the skills of the existing workforce. It is a learner-centered, student-centered institution.

The Community College aims at making the above target groups eligible for employment and prepare them for jobs that are really existing. It makes every possible effort to find employment opportunities for them. Need Analysis of the employment opportunities of the local area is done prior to the starting of the institution. The Need Analysis has to embrace not merely the industrial and the commercial needs but also the rural, agro based and social needs of the area. After all efforts at conscientization, organisation of people to fight for their rights, basic literacy and health programme, the Community College is aiming at the development of skills and competencies as a necessary stage in the process of social re-engineering and economic regeneration.

The close and active linkage between industries and Community College is a must for the success of the Community College system. The industries, commercial houses, NGOs and Social Voluntary organisations help the college in designing curriculum, in sending help to the college in designing curriculum, in sending part time instructors from the various field advisory boards of the Community College, in taking the students for on-site training and finally helping the college for job placements and the follow-up of the students. Consultation with the industries of the local area prior to the start of the Community College is essential and necessary. The Community College follows flexibility in curriculum, teaching methodology and evaluation because of its continuous response given to the growing demands, needs and development of the Industrial / Commercial / Agricultural and Service sectors and social issues.

The Community College trains people not only for jobs available but also for self-employment and small business development.

The local Community college is a College without walls. The emphasis on using the unused and underutilized infrastructural facilities available in the community. The governing body of the college is composed of representatives from different religions, community leaders, educationists, administrators, industrialists, rural entrepreneurs and Government officials. Scholarships are mobilized for the needy and the deserving students from the members of the Community.

The creation of Community College is in accordance with programme of action of NPE that recommends the establishment of Community Colleges in India: "To encourage establishment of Community Colleges dealing with vocationalization of subjects related to service sector on line with Community Polytechnics."

Community College are clear about their mission – "Including the Excluded, Giving the Best to the Least."

The vision of the Community College is – Empowerment of the Disadvantaged.

"The Community Colleges aim at the liberation and employment of the exploited and deprived groups of society by releasing and developing the sources within, through middle level skills development and facilitating self-actualisation. This would lead to restoring the human right to education denied to them."

Colleges have fixed the Target groups from the socially, economically and academically poorer sections of society and ensured access, equal opportunity and cost effectiveness in training. The different organizations that have taken up the Community College experiment are NGOs, Religious Congregations, Christian Dioceses, Civic Bodies like the Chennai Corporation and Private Agencies. [12]

2000 August

Community College Movement – An Overview

The Essence of the Community College System

The Community College is an alternative system of education, which is aimed at the empowerment of the disadvantaged and the underprivileged (Urban Poor, Rural Poor and Women) through appropriate skills development leading to gainful employment in collaboration with local industry and community.

- The Community College promotes job oriented, work related, skills – based and life coping education.
- The Community College initiative is in conformity with the Indian political will with priorities in education, primary education, information technology education and vocational education.
- The key words of the Community College system are access, flexibility in curriculum and teaching methodology, cost effectiveness and equal opportunity in collaboration with industrial, commercial and service sectors of the local area and responding to the social needs and issues of the local community, internship and job placement within the local area, promotion of self employment and small business development, declaration of competence and eligibility from employment.

Milestones and Achievements in the History of the Community College Movement

- The Community College has come to stay as an alternative system of education. The Movement began in 1995 with the Pondicherry University Community College followed by Madras Community College 1996. The total number of Community Colleges functioning in India right now are 37 (34 in Tamil Nadu, 2 in Andhra Pradesh, 1 in Goa). The Community Colleges under preparation are 13 in Uttar Pradesh, Maharashtra, Gujarat, New Delhi and Tamil Nadu.
- When we observe the Community College Movement the following salient features emerge:
    1. There is a certain clarity about the concept of the Community College System and its implementation has been undertaken by

religious congregations, diocese, NGOs, Philanthropists and civic bodies like the Corporation of Chennai.

2. The Colleges have developed a system which needs to be consolidated and standardized without sacrificing autonomy and flexibility.
3. The Madras Centre for Research and Development of Community Education, Chennai (MCRDCE) has been established in January 1999 and it has been performing the role of facilitation and co-ordination.
4. The colleges have reached a consensus in preparing the document for recognition and approval. We have made the following efforts:

- The first Consultation on the 4th of July 1995 at Madurai Community College with 13 participants representing 7 Community Colleges in which the articulation of the concept and the implementation took place. The document was submitted to the feasibility committee of the Manonmaniam Sundaranar University, Tirunelveli.
- First South Indian Conference on the 8th and 9th of January, 1999 in which 150 delegates from 14 existing Community Colleges and 11 Upcoming Colleges, Vice Chancellors, educationists, industrial partners and community leaders expressed clearly the need for an alternative system of education not merely for developing skills for employment but also responding to the social needs of the community. A mandate was given a MCRDCE to explore the possibilities for recognition and approval with the central and state governments.
- Second Consultation of Community Colleges took place at Madurai on the 26th and 27th of March 1999 to draft the document for recognition and approval guided by Dr. Louis Xavier, S.J., Director, LIBA, with 71 participants from 12 existing and 9 upcoming community colleges. the document has been submitted to the Government of Tamil Nadu.
- Since Manonmaniam Sundaranar University has the maximum number of affiliated Community Colleges numbering 21, a day's Workshop was held at Tirunelveli on the 21st of August 1999 where certain constraints and difficulties were expressed by these colleges in affiliating themselves with the University. 70 participants from 17 Community Colleges of the University area participated.
- Third Consultation on the 9th of October, 1999 at the request of Mr. P. Selvam, IAS, Education Secretary of the Government of Tamil Nadu to finalise the document for recognition and approval was submitted to the Government of Tamil Nadu on the 20th of October

1999. It is under scrutiny at the highest administrative level of the Government of Tamil Nadu.

- The National Workshop on Community Colleges was organised by MCRDCE in collaboration with the HRD Ministry, New Delhi at Chennai on the 18th and 19th of February, 2000 in which 46 NGOs from all over the country and representatives from 13 Community Colleges, HRD Minsitry Officials, Tamil Nadu State Government Officials participated. The entire group affirmed the urgent need for Community Colleges as an alternative system of education. The time has come for the movement to become national. MCRDCE was recognised as a nodal agency to facilitate the growth of Community Colleges in India.

5. The State Government of Tamil Nadu and Andhra Pradesh have taken note of the movement. The Ministry of Human Resource Development, New Delhi is looking at the model seriously for the whole country. The Director of MCRDCE gave two presentations to the officials of the HRD Ministry in New Delhi in August and September 1999.

6. The Community Colleges have kept the target group in focus in spite of their financial constraints – the socially, economically, educationally, disadvantaged groups especially the school dropouts, those who cannot go in for further education. Recently an evaluation of 13 Community Colleges in Tamil Nadu and Andhra Pradesh was undertaken and the cases of 1934 students were studied by the Madras Centre for Research and Development of Community Education (MCRDCE) and the following findings reflect the philosophy of the Community College System.

   - 80 per cent of the target group are below Rs. 3000 / monthly family income.
   - 70 per cent of the target group of the community colleges takers are women.
   - 113 married women are studying in these Community Colleges
   - The age group of the Community Colleges takers is between 16 and 35 years.
   - All qualifications are taking the Community College System: 101 (below 10th), 362 (10th passed), 1322 (12 passed) and 149 (degree holders).
   - The caste-wise distribution has been 405 (Scheduled Caste), 4 (Scheduled Tribe), 427 (Most Backward Caste), 766 (Backward Caste), 322 (Other Castes).

7. The success of the Community Colleges in the Job Placement has been 60 to 70%
8. The Community College Movement is becoming an All India Phenomena. The MCRDCE team went to Roorkee in U.P., Jalgaon in Maharashtra and Vapi in Gujarat for the preparation of the Community Colleges in the respective places. There is a great desire and commitment to replicate the model.
9. The Community College is a non-governmental initiative taken by non-commercial, non-profit making, community based organisations.
10. The Community Colleges are trying to establish a vital link and active collaboration with industrial partners.
11. We have four types of Community Colleges
   - University Community Colleges
   - Affiliated Community Colleges under the umbrella of Manonmaniam Sundaranar University
   - The Voluntary Agency Community Colleges recognized and accepted by the society and industries and have not obtained any official recognition from the state and central governments.
   - The Community College run by a civic body like the Chennai Corporation.

Community College Benefits

The Community College System touches the most needed and deserving sections of society. It offers the following benefits to the society.

- Includes the Excluded
- Gives the best to the least
- Enhances the Human Resource Development
- Alleviates poverty
- Empowers the disadvantaged groups, particularly women
- Competency and capacity building system.
- Creates self-employment opportunities
- Constructive channeling of the energies of vast proportions of the education unemployed.
- Movement of the people
- Democratic response to the current processes of privatization, globalization and liberalization.

- Catalyst to rural development.
- Instrument to promote communal harmony and national integration.[13]

2000 July – September

Community College system towards Vertical Mobility

The Concept of the Community College

The Community College is expected to be an alternative system education, which is aimed at the empowerment of the disadvantaged and the underprivileged (Urban poor, Rural poor and Women) through appropriate skill development leading to gainful employment in collaboration with the local industry and the community and achieve skills for employment and self employment of the above sections of people in the society.

The Community College is an innovative education alternative that is rooted in the community providing holistic education and eligibility for employment to the disadvantaged.[14]

2001 April to June

Community College Movement

The Community College Movement started in India in 1995. However, its activities are largely concentrated in Southern part of India, mostly in Tamil Nădu. The Movement draws its inspiration from community colleges of USA. Proponents of the movement are of the view that Community Colleges are still in the infancy in India and are trying to carve out a local and indigenous identity. These colleges aim at providing job oriented, work related and skill based education to empower the disadvantaged and the underprivileged. This is to be done through appropriate skill development leading to gainful employment in collaboration with local industry and the community. The target group of the community college includes school dropouts, secondary and higher secondary pass-outs, rural youth, rural women, existing workforce that wants to update its skills, and all other interested in skill based and need based education.

The community colleges are supposed to work in close collaboration with industrial, agricultural, commercial and service organisations. The collaborative arrangement includes helping in designing the curriculum, serving on advisory board, providing part-time instructor, on-the-job training, job placement etc.

Four models of community colleges are in vogue. These are NGOs model, University model, Local body model, and affiliated model. As per latest information available there are 63 community colleges (56 in Tamil Nadu and 7 in other part of India) run by Christian Dioceses, religious congregations, NGOs, philanthropic trusts and Chennai Corporation. In order to coordinate the working of the community colleges the Madras Centre for Research and Development of Community Education (MCRDCE) was started in January 1999. The Department for International Development (DFID) UK is supporting the project under its development programme – 'Colleges without Walls'. Community Colleges generally are located in separate wing or rooms of the existing buildings in the premises of institutions like schools or Industrial Training Institutes (ITIs) sharing the existing facilities.[15]

References

1. Dr. Xavier Alphonse, S.J., *Changing Track – Community Colleges in India*, AIACHE Publications, New Delhi, First Edition - December 1996 and Second Edition – June 2001, pp. 165-167.
2. Dr. Xavier Alphonse, S.J., *Best to the Least – Profile of Community Colleges in India*, MCRDCE Publication, Chennai, November 2004, p. 46-54.
3. Dr. Xavier Alphonse, S.J., *Including the Excluded – History of the Community Colleges in India*, MCRDCE Publication, Chennai, January 1999, p.178-179.
4. *Ibid*, pp. 215-221.
5. *Ibid*, pp. 231-232.
6. Xavier Alphonse, S.J., and Pushparaj, S.J., "The Madurai Community College – An Educational Alternative", *University News,* Vol: 35 (41), October 13, 1997, pp. 8-11.
7. Dr. Xavier Alphonse, S.J., *Including the Excluded – History of the Community Colleges in India*, MCRDCE Publication, Chennai, January 1999, p.266.
8. *Ibid*, p. 269.
9. *Ibid*, pp. 283-284.
10. Xavier Alphonse, S.J., and S.M. Joe Rajan, "Melrosapuram Rural Community College – An Educational Alternative", *University News,* Vol: 36 (23), June 8, 1998, pp. 11-12.
11. "Community College Movement", *Campus News*, *University News*, New Delhi, Vol. 37 (1), January 4, 1999, pp. 17-18.
12. Xavier Alphonse, "Community College: Meeting Society's Needs", *University News*, New Delhi, Vol. 37(36), September 6, 1999, pp. 13-15.
13. Xavier Alphonse, S.J., "Community College Movement", *University News,* Vol: 38(35), August 28, 2000, pp. 8-11.
14. Xavier Alphonse, S.J., "Community College System towards Vertical Mobility", *Extracts from New Frontiers in Education,* New Delhi, Vol: 30(3) July-September 2000, p. 278.
15. Prof. Sen Gupta, "Community College Movement", *Extracts from Vocational Education*, Vol. 8, Issue-1, April to June 2001, p. 10.

3

Recognition of the System (2001-2010)

2001 June - July

Community Colleges: A National Phenomenon

The Community College system is promoted as an alternative system of education aiming at the empowerment of the underprivileged through appropriate skill development leading to gainful employment. It is an open system where there is no age limit and minimum qualification. It provides job-oriented, work-related, skill-based and life-coping education.

The target group of the Community Colleges is the rural poor, the urban poor, the tribal poor and women i.e. the socially, economically, educationally backward groups in the society. The whole system is characterized by access, flexibility, cost effectiveness, equal opportunity and quality. It promotes an ongoing and vibrant industrial partnership with potential employers and other organisations. The industrial partners design the curriculum, serve as members of the Advisory Boards and Government Boards and take the students for internship and hands-on-experience and help in job placement. The difference between Community Colleges and other systems of vocational education in the country are:

- The teaching of life skills
- The evaluation and assessment of skills
- The active industrial partnership
- Hands-on experience or internship
- Declaration of eligibility for employment by the Community Colleges and the industrial partner.

The Community Colleges use the existing infrastructural facilities in order to reduce the cost of training and to make it available to the poor and those who cannot afford it otherwise.[1]

2002 April – June

Best to the Least: Community College Movement in India – An Update

The Concept of Community College

- The Community College is an alternative system of education, which is aimed at the empowerment of the disadvantaged and the underprivileged (Urban poor, Rural poor, Tribal poor and Women) through appropriate skills development leading to gainful employment in collaboration with the local industry and the community and achievement of skills for employment and self employability of the above sections of people in the society.
- The community college is an innovative educational alternative that is rooted in the community providing holistic education and eligibility for employment to the disadvantaged.
- The vision of the Community College is to be of the community, for the community and by the community and to produce responsible citizens.
- The community college promotes job oriented, work related, skill-based and life coping education.
- The community college initiative is in conformity with the Indian political will that prioritizes in education, primary education, information technology education and vocational education.
- The key words of the community college system are access, flexibility in curriculum and teaching methodology, cost effectiveness and equal opportunity in collaboration with industrial, commercial and service sectors of the local area and responding to the social needs and issues of the local community, internship and job placement within the local area, promotion of self employment and small business development, declaration of competence and eligibility for employment.[2]

2003 Book Review – Mismatch - Developing Community Colleges

The traditional system of education has not been able to develop character among the youth nor has it succeeded in providing job opportunities. The Community College movement aims at empowering the disadvantaged, the defenseless, the marginalised and the weak through appropriate skill development. The author of this book, Dr. Xavier Alphonse S.J., is a pioneer in the community college movement in India. This book is the product of six years of experiment with the concept of community college and its implementation.

The Community Colleges are established by non-profit making organisations. There is no age limit for admission into a community college. There should be close linkage between industries partners to help the college in several ways – designing the curriculum, providing part-time instructions, helping students to find job placement etc.

In a community college, importance is given to a number of job-oriented courses like nursing, health and hygiene and hotel management. The college itself assesses the skills of the incumbents of course with the help of technical and field experts. The knowledge and skill component is given equal weightage (p. 92).

The main aim of a community college is to help students secure suitable jobs. Hence, industrial/community partnership is sought. While the courses offered in community colleges are need-based and demand-driven, more and more emerging areas are required to be introduced harnessing local resources (p.180).

The MCRDCE should be congratulated for bringing out this volume which throws useful light on the importance, functioning and challenges of community colleges.[3]

2004 April

Best to the Least: Education for Livelihood – Community Colleges in India

Inception and Growth

With the this vision and philosophy the Community College Movement began in India in 1995, after a Community Colleges from the US whose project was approved through the University Development Linkage project made the pertinent observation that while India does a great job in producing PHDs, it has not infrastructure to produce skilled technicians. The First consultation of Community College was help the Manonmaniam Sundaranar University, Tirunelveli to understand the nature, philosophy and functioning of the Community College system. It was the first effort towards articulation of the system. The First South Indian Conference of Community College coincided with the establishment of the Madras Centre for Research and Development of Community College in 1999. The conference provided an awareness among Educationists, Teachers and Administrators of Community College, Community Leaders and potential employers. It also provided a comparative study of the Indian systems vis-à-vis that of the British, American, Australian and German systems of the Community College. The second consultation of the Community College was held in March 1999 which evolved the self Regulatory Guidelines to be submitted to the Government of Tamil Nadu. The Third Consultation was at the direction of the Secretary, Higher Education, Tamil Nadu for submission of the Document for Recognition. In February 2000, a National Workshop on Community College system was held at Chennai with a number of NGOs and the Community college in collaboration with the Ministry of HRD, Union of India, participated by a dozen of MHRD officials.

It was followed by a national consultation on Community College System that was held on New Delhi in collaboration with the MHRD Ministry, New Delhi. The Fourth Consultation on Community College system was graced by Dr. K.S. Venkatasubramaniam, Member Union Planning Commission. The Fifth Consultation was on recognition and accreditation particularly to the National Institute of Open Schooling and the Indira Gandhi National Open University.

The Community College Movement began with that of Pondicherry University in 1995 followed by the Canara Community College in the same year, the Madras Community College in 1996 and the Madurai Community College in 1997.

Soon the Movement spread among the NGOs and universities in Tamil Nadu and Andhra Pradesh like the Manomaniam Sundaranar University and Avinashilingam Deemad University. The establishment of MCRDCE provided the Community College system with great impetus and today 82 out of 111 of the Community College work with MCRDCE. Already there had been five Consultations, 29 Regional workshops and two National Consultations. Teachers were provided with 12 training programmes so far. Dr. M. Sengupta, Head Humanities, Science and Education Division, Central Institute of Vocational Education, Bhopal and two nominated members of NCRET, New Delhi visited eight Community Colleges to do an evaluation, and submitted their report to the Government of India. By 2004, 18 of the Community College have been accredited to the National Institute of Open Schooling. It is significant to note that a mention has been made of the Community College in the Draft document of the Tenth Five Year Plan (2002-07) as "There should be focus on convergence of schemes like the Sarva Shiksha Abhiyan, Adult Education, Vocational Education at Schools, Polytechnics, Community College etc." (Chapt. 2.4. Vocational Education p.51).[4]

2004 June

"A Community College is an alternative system of education; an education meant to make people for fit for life and a job". [5]

2005

Integration of Community College System with TNOU

Summary of the Proceedings

The Consultation started with the registration of the participants from

9.30 a.m. Dr. Xavier Alphonse, S.J., welcomed the delegates and introduced the theme of the Consultation and also shared his experience with Yashwantrao Chavan Maharashtra Open University, Nashik and the offer of the Vice Chancellor, Dr. Rajan M.Welukar, to recognise Community Colleges in the states of Maharashtra, Goa, Gujarat and Karnataka. The Consultation started with the prayer dance performed by one of the students of Nano Nagle Community College. Rev. Sr. Sophie Joseph, Director, Nano Nagle Community College welcomed all the delegates.

Dr. Xavier Alphonse, S.J., Director, MCRDCE made a PowerPoint presentation on this theme covering the following aspects.

Background

- Development of Concept and implementation of Community College System
- Running effectively and efficiently without formal Recognition
- Collective effort and decision making through Consultations
- Led to the formulation of the Indian Community College system (University of Madras)
- NIOS and HRD Ministry – only limited Colleges went for this option
- Manonmaniam Sundaranar University affiliated Community Colleges and difficulties experienced
- Consultation with TNOU, Vice Chancellor and Team
- First Phase of Nine Courses accepted and recognised
- TNOU accepting all the Community Colleges recommended by MCRDCE as Vocational Programme Centres. Dr. Xavier Alphonse, S.J., appointed to be the member of Academic Council of TNOU
- Integration of TNOU Diploma courses with the Community College System Workshop.

Aims and Objectives of the Community College System

- Fit for Life and Fit for Job
- Along with Education providing job opportunity
- Principles governing the Community College System
- Merit is an Opportunity, Education = Skills + Information + Attitude, Excellence is tapping the untapped potential in the individual
- Life Coping Skills, Communication Skills, Computing Skills and Developmental English, Work skills, Internship, job placement
- Industrial and Community Partnership promoted vigorously

Advantages in going for the TNOU

- Formal Recognition
- Demand of the target group and the parents and the public
- Closer to the Community College System in philosophy, practice and implementation
- Diploma is valid all over India
- Possible for registering in the employment exchanges of the country
- Possibility of taking care of the School dropouts since minimum qualification not prescribed except for Pre-Primary Teaching and Health Assistant Programmes
- Vocational Programme Centres
- Ensures status in the society
- Possibility of Vertical mobility through credit transfer since credits have been prescribed by the TNOU
- Scholarships (SC/ST and Common Wealth Scholarship) can be obtained through TNOU.
- Integration is useful to the Beneficiaries
- Final Products have to be eligible for employment and should be able to meet with the demands of the required skills by the employers.
- Broad spectrum of skills.

Skills Required for an Office Assistant

Social Skills : Acceptability, Listening, patience, Ability to solve interpersonal conflicts, Overcoming inhibitions, Hospitality, Overcoming shyness, Accepting one's faults, Handling hardships and failures and Approachability.

Personal Skills: Punctuality, Pleasing Personality, Sincerity, Loyalty, Responsibility, Reliability, Spontaneity, Ethical, Industrious, Self Esteem, Good Perception, presentability, Stress Management, Problem Solving, Presence of Mind, Hard Working.

Communication skills: Dialogue, Group Communication, Clarity, Public Speaking, Good Expression, Ability to understand, Interpretation: Oral and Written, Formal and Informal, Presentation Skills, Presentation of a good Curriculum Vitae.

Language Skills: Multilingual

Work Skills: Computing Skills, Handling of Office Automation Products: Xerox, Fax, Record Maintenance, EPBX, Business Correspondence, Drafting, Typing and Shorthand, Handling stationery, Utilisation of Resources Electricity.

Cost Consciousness, Office Assistance, Computer Assistance, Accounting Skills, Banking Skills and Awareness of Competitors.

Creative Skills: Updating of Knowledge and Skills, Innovative, Risk Taking, More Imaginative.

Leadership: Empathy, Impartiality, Co-ordination, Animation, Facilitator, Team Building, Approachability, Dynamic, Crisis Management, Resourcefulness, Focused, Participatory Leadership, Decision Making, Counselling, Service Minded, Initiative, Delegations, Self Motivations, Appreciative, Organisation Skills.

Skills required for Health Assistant

Leadership Skills: Resourcefulness, Dynamic, Impartiality, Empathy, Co-ordination Facilitator, Team Building, Approachability, Crisis Management, Focused, Decision Making, Counseling, Service Mindedness, Initiative, Delegation, Self Motivation, Appreciative, Organisation Skills.

Personal Skills: Punctuality, Pleasing personality, Sincerity, Loyalty, Responsibility, Reliability, Problem solving, Presence of Mind, Hard Working, Good Perception, Commitment.

Communication Skills: Dialogue-Oral and Written, Presentation Skills, Group Communication, Clarity, Public Speaking, Good Expression, Ability to understand, Interpretation.

Language Skills: Multi lingual and well versed in the regional language.

Social Skills: Hospitality, Patience, Listening, Acceptability, Overcoming Inhibitions, Accepting one's own faults, approachability, Overcoming Shyness, Handling hardships and failures, Solving interpersonal conflicts.

Creative Skills: Updating of Knowledge and Skills, Innovative, Risk Taking.

Work Skills: Hygiene, Basic Nursing Skills, Observing and reporting, Utilization of resources and equipments, assisting the nurse, developing interpersonal relations, awareness towards environmental sanitation, Knowledge about legal aspects, maternity and delivery, identifying and treating of emergency cases.

Skills required for Pre Primary Teacher Training

Job Description Task and Responsibilities: Impartiality, Kindness, Loving, Motherly, Child Psychologist, Understanding, Model Teacher.

Advisory Board: Child Psychologist, parents, faculty, Head Master of the School, Child Specialist, Director of the Community College, Professional Social Worker, Child Specialist.

Social Skills: Facing hardship, Listening, patience, Acceptance, and Approachability.

Personal Skills: Lovable, hardworking, Problem Solving, Responsibility, Presence of Mind, Practice Ethics, Hard Working, Listening, Creativity, Approachability.

Communication Skills: Effective Order, Pronunciation, Good Expression, Intonation.

Work Skills: Maintaining play toys, Chart making, Maintaining records, clay modeling, resource utilization, cleanliness, social awareness, sense of humour, presence of mind.

Courses to be Given: Teaching of the Alphabets, Identifying the given picture, Clay Modeling, Child development, story telling.

Leadership: Impartial, Appreciation, Acceptance, Crisis Management, Service Mindedness Facilitator.

Creative Skills: Innovation, Singing, Story telling, Body Language, Drawing, Imagination colouring.

These skills have to be provided for employment from our experience.

Points to be remembered

- We are not producing Diploma holders for TNOU, but we are producing people fit for job, with eligibility for employment and with skills mentioned above, as required by our industrial partners.
- We cannot be satisfied, merely with the study material provided by TNOU. The material may be insufficient. It is common to all the Vocational Programme Centres.
- We need to divide our time in the following manner to take care of all aspects:
    - Teaching of Life Coping Skills
    - Theoretical knowledge combined with practice in the Community College System
    - Good knowledge of English (written and spoken)
    - Flexibility in curriculum
    - Basic Computing skills
    - Skills required by the Industrial Partners : Knowledge of English, Communication Skills
    - Additional work skills (Theory) enhanced with reference books
    - Guided and monitored internship with due follow-up
    - Job placement

- Only when we will fulfil the above points then only we can call our institution a Community College.
- At no point of time, we will compromise with the target group which is indicated in the Indian Community College System developed in the last ten years.
- We are going to make the TNOU Diploma successful by the implementation of Community College System rather than merely following the TNOU System.
- Every student of the Community college will be given the over all performance certificate by the Community College and the TNOU Diploma for work skills for recognition and upward and vertical mobility.
- Our final aim is job placement not distribution of Diplomas. Diploma is only the value addition in terms of vertical mobility and horizontal mobility.

Requests made to TNOU

1. 42.5% of the total money collected for each course 6,500 / 3,500 to be paid to the University with the filled-in application form.
2. Recognition sought for Community Colleges in states other than Tamil Nadu
3. Life coping Skills and Interpersonal Relationship and Communication Skills to be added to pre-primary teachers and Health Assistant courses. All communication from the University and received by the colleges. a copy to be sent to MCRDCE for immediate reference.
4. The curriculum for Pre-Primary Teachers and Health Assistant to be worked out by the teachers of Community Colleges where the courses are already conducted for many years.
5. Any representation or request for special needs to be routed through Fr. Xavier Alphonse, since he has been nominated as the member of the Academic Council by the Tamil Nadu Open University.

Mr. Anto Vincent complemented Fr. Xavier Alphonse and made the following deliberations:

Growth means change. Integration of the TNOU with the Community College is a challenge and a threat. He raised the question how do we sustain and preserve the uniqueness of the Community College System while going for the TNOU certification.

1. It is our choice to have the tie-up or not to have the tie up. We have functioned without the external certification.

2. Integration with TNOU is an additional feather in our cap but the feather cannot become a bird.
3. Our Community College System has been a programme of success in reality because of the following aspects
   (a) Need Analysis – Responding to the call of the territory
   (a) Syllabus has been unique to us. It was customer and consumer oriented because of which we got 70% employment.
   (c) We have established a strong industrial and social partnership. We should not over emphasize the TNOU diploma at the cost of the Community College System.
   (d) The teaching of the Life Coping Skills has given us the desired results 41% of our time we have spent in teaching Life Coping Skills in Community College System. When we come into TNOU it comes to 14%. We need to take care of this aspect.

He referred to the ISO certificate for quality control.

1. Tell me what you do
2. Do what you have said
3. Quality comes with authenticity and effort

He concluded saying that the Diploma of TNOU is a value addition to the Community College Programme.

Questions for Group Discussion

1. What is your response to the presentation?
2. What are the difficulties we foresee in integrating the TNOU System with the Community College System? (5 difficulties)
3. Five ways and means of integrating the two systems.
4. Three concrete suggestions for the networking of Community Colleges at the Zonal level for monitoring the integration.
5. What are the three special helps that we can offer to the Tsunami affected young men and women whom we have admitted in our colleges.
6. The way to administer the bridge course offered by the University to the failed candidates to make them eligible for diploma courses.
7. How do we deal with off campus students who will be attached to our institutions by TNOU for contact classes and evaluation?

Participants were divided into Madras Zone 1 and 2, Trichy Zone, Madurai Zone, Tirunelveli and Nagercoil Zone. The discussion took place for 1½ hours.

Group Discussion Deliberations

1. What is your response to the presentation?

- The subjects taught under Life Skills Programme be continued to all the students irrespective of the course they opt for without compromising the teaching of life skills programme.

2. What are the difficulties we foresee in integrating the TNOU System with the Community College System? (5 difficulties)

   - Provisioning of syllabus and guidelines for each trade.
   - Conducting and evaluating the Life Skill Programme / training should be entrusted to the respective Community Colleges.
   - Teaching Developmental English and Basic Computer should be integrated in the TNOU Diploma Course Programme.
   - Medium of instructions of TNOU Diploma Courses may be bilingual for teaching certain trades such as Fashion Designing and Garment Making.
   - Students to be allowed to write the TNOU Exam both in English and Tamil.

3. Five ways and means of integrating the two systems.

   - TNOU Course fees may be allowed to be remitted in two instalments rather than at one single go.
   - Uniqueness of Community College System should be protected and maintained.
   - Credit System of Life Skills subjects included in the TNOU Examination pattern be redistributed to suit the Community College System.
   - TNOU officials should have periodic discussions with directors of the Community Colleges in order to update the latest developments.
   - Community Colleges should be distinctly differentiated from VPE / PSC (Ref: Page No: 20 of TNOU Prospectus).

4. Three concrete suggestions for the networking of Community Colleges at the Zonal level for monitoring the integration.

   - Arrangements may be made to share the expertise at Zonal / State / national levels.
   - Interaction with other colleges at the Students level may be organised.
   - List of Courses, course contents and methodology be shared among the colleges of the zones concerned.

5. What are the three special helps that we can offer to the Tsunami affected young men and women whom we have admitted in our colleges.
    - One to one counseling
    - Bus and Train Pass
    - Lunch
6. The way to administer the bridge course offered by the University to the failed candidates to make them eligible for diploma courses.

   Community Colleges should get autonomy to conduct the bridge course by themselves
7. How do we deal with off campus students who will be attached to our institutions by TNOU for contact classes and evaluation?
   - Minimum Attendance be enforced
   - Certain degree of life coping skills be taught to the off campus students.

General Discussion

After the Lunch break, there was a General Session chaired by Dr. Xavier Alphonse, S.J., and the Zonal reports were read out and passed.

The functions of the zonal level clusters of community colleges

1. Once in three months, colleges will meet, review and share their experiences.
2. The Minutes of the meeting will be sent to MCRDCE
3. The Zonal Committee takes responsibility for organizing the Refresher Courses by way of workshop for two days each for the following courses:
   (a) Life coping skills
   (b) Communication skills
   (c) Spoken English
   (d) DTP
   (e) Work skills
4. Creation of Job Placement Cell at the Zonal level.
5. Creating Website of the Zonal Colleges

Input from TNOU

Dr. Thiyagarajan, Reader and Head, School of Continuing Education, Tamil Nadu Open University, gave a clear PowerPoint presentation of the expectations of TNOU from Community Colleges. Some of the important clarifications were:

1. We do not entertain other students who have applied from Study Centres of TNOU in our Community Colleges.
2. Last date of admission of students could be extended to 15th of September.
3. Only those students who have passed +2 and should be 17 years of age can be admitted to DPPTT.
4. 10th failed students can be admitted to Diploma in Health Assistant. They should complete the bridge course prescribed by the University. Except DPPTT and DHA in all other courses below 10th can be admitted. They have to be 18 years of age.
5. Resource Sharing

The Community Colleges are expected to pay 42.5% to TNOU for DHA and DPPTT Rs. 2, 762.50. For all the other courses Rs. 1,487.50. For bridge course Rs. 212.50.

Particulars	*Rs. 6500 for DHA & DPPTT*	*Rs. 3500 for other 7 Courses*	*BPP Rs. 500*
Admission Fee 15%	975	525	75
SSS i.e. C.C's 42.5%	2762.50	1487.50	212.50
TNOU University 42.5%	2762.50	1487.50	212.50

6. Community Colleges can make a representation that students 15 years of age completed can take the bridge course excluding DPPTT by taking the bridge course of TNOU.
7. Old students of Community Colleges can be enrolled for the TNOU diploma and they could be charged with the following fees:

For DHA and DPPTT	Rs. 2, 762.50
Application Form	Rs. 100.00
Examination Fee	To be charged separately

8. Students can write their examination in Tamil
9. Prof. Thiyagarajan, Reader and Head, School of Continuing Education, TNOU can be contacted at this no. 044-22352898.
10. Any communication sent to the University a copy of it has to be marked to MCRDCE as a follow-up.
11. The TNOU is asked to send the checklist of things and facilities to be kept ready when the inspection team comes to the Community Colleges.

12. Community Colleges will also issue a comprehensive certificate and also a diploma as we have been doing in the past. In order to give a clear picture of the attainment level of skills by our students.

4

Seminar on Indian Community College System

A seminar and a workshop was conducted on the 8th and 9th of February 2005 at the University of Madras in collaboration with The US Consulate, Chennai. The theme of the seminar and workshop is the formulation of the Indian Community College System. Both were organised as a sequel to the working committee for the formulation of the policy document on Community Education constituted by the University of Madras in September 2004. The committee has eight members with Prof. Thiyagarajan, Vice Chancellor, University of Madras as the Chairman.

The Seminar was inaugurated by Prof. V.N. Rajasekharan Pillai, Vice Chairman, University Grants Commission (UGC), New Delhi. In his keynote address he remarked. "Community Colleges should be integrated into higher education if the percentage of citizens with higher education has to expand from 6.7 per cent to 10 per cent by the end of the Tenth plan. He endorsed the idea of an Indian Community College System put forth by the University of Madras, in consultation with the United States Consulate General for South India. Access to Higher Education was a key parameter of development. "We have the largest youth force in the world," he observed "including 40 million registered unemployed youth – not because there is a lack of work but because there is a mismatch between education and employment". In Community Colleges, academic and occupational education took place simultaneously".

Dr. Robert G. Templin, President, Northern Virginia Community College, Virginia, USA who was the Chief Resource Person of the Seminar remarked "Community Colleges must first be considered a legitimate part of Higher Education. Universities must recognise Community Colleges and allow students to cross over. India cannot afford to compete on the basis of cheap labour forever. India must create entrepreneurs and workers who can innovate and create new products and services." Prof. Thiyagarajan said that "Unless there was a paradigm shift, it would be impossible to ensure that 20 per cent of the population received higher education (the projected target) within a decade. The existing 365 Universities and 16,000 colleges could not cater to all. We still aren't helping rural youngsters between 14 and 20 years get into higher education. Drawing from several models, he said the Indian Community College System could well be the 'missing link' between secondary school education and higher education. Vocational Training Centres, Polytechnics, Indian Technical Institutes (ITIs), SHG Training and value-added courses could be brought under this system.

Mr. Ravi S. Candadai, Consul for Public Affairs, US Consulate General, Chennai referring to the wide variations in value assigned to different kinds of education in the country (for example, B.Tech degrees and ITI courses) and the lack of opportunity for students to upgrade from one 'education currency to another remarked', "The time has to come to stop dealing in different currencies".

The Seminar was attended by Academicians, Educationists and Vice Chancellors of Universities of Bharathidasan, Trichy, Thiruvalluvar, Vellore and Dr. Ambedkar Law University. It was largely attended by 70 representatives from 43 Community Colleges and from the Madras Centre for Research and Development of Community Education (MCRDCE), Chennai a Co-ordinating agency for Community Colleges in India.

Dr. Xavier Alphonse, S.J., Director, MCRDCE presented the Community College: A Contemporary Experience and Mr. Ravi S. Candadai, Consul for Public Affairs presented Community College: A Comparative Experience between USA and India. A workshop was conducted on the occasion in which the participants were divided in five groups in which the Indian Community College System was discussed under five aspects – Framework, Credit Transfer, Accreditation, Programmes and Areas of Study, Entrepreneurship and Employment Opportunities. All the suggestions were presented in the Plenary Session presided over by Prof. Thiyagarajan.

The policy document committee deliberated over the format of the document ably assisted by Dr. Robert G. Templin, President, Northern Virginia Community College, Virginia, USA. The Committee has decided to finalise the document and submit the same to UGC and the Hon'ble Chief Minister of Tamil Nadu by the 2nd week of March 2005. All the participants lauded the Role of MCRDCE in creating so many Community Colleges in the country. Right now there are 118 Community Colleges in 14 States of India.

5

Committee on Role of Community Colleges in Education System

Recognition from Ministry of Human Resource Development, New Delhi

MINUTES OF THE FIRST MEETING OF THE COMMITTEE

1. The first meeting of the Committee was held under the Chairpersonship of Addition Secretary (Education) on February 28, 2005 in Room No. 115 'C', Shastri Bhawan, New Delhi.
2. The following were present:
   - (i) Shri Sudeep Banerjee, Additional Secretary - Chairperson
     Ministry of HRD, Department of (S and HE)
   - (ii) Prof. H.P. Dixit, Vice-Chancellor
     Indira Gandhi National Open University and Chairperson
     All India Council of Technical Education
   - (iii) Shri Sunil Kumar, Joint Secretary (Higher Education)
     Ministry of HRD, Department of (S and HE)
   - (iv) Prof.Ved Prakash, Secretary
     University Grants Commission
   - (v) Dr. Xavier Alphonse, Director
     Madras Center for Research and Development in Community Education
   - (vi) Dr. D.K. Paliwal, Deputy Education Adviser
     Ministry of HRD, Department of (S and HE)
3. As (Education), after introducing the members gave a brief welcome address thereafter, Dr. Xavier Alphonse presented a brief over view of the community colleges in the country. The highlights of the presentation were as under:

1. The approach of the community colleges is 'by community and for community'
2. There is no eligibility bar or minimum prescribed qualification for education in community colleges.
3. Community colleges impart education in the courses relevant to the local needs by using existing infrastructure.
4. The courses are designed after the analysis of the need and in partnership with the industry / employer as far as possible.
5. Community colleges follow credit based system and one credit is offered for thirty hours of work.
6. The student of Community colleges is receiving good response from the employer and in some case the employers are ready to offer them employment when they are approached with the request of internship for the students.
7. The finding is that employers give considerable weightage to the attitude of the candidates in addition to the skills they have and information they possess.
8. Community colleges consider this in designing of their programme.
9. Community colleges focus on the education of weaker and educationally deprived sections of the society.
10. The community college system offers bridge courses to the educationally deprived before offering them education in life skills.
11. The difference between community colleges is designed to tackle unemployability and not the unemployment.
12. Community colleges do not have concepts of pass or fail and they give due weightage to the self assessment by the students. After successfully completing the programme, diploma and certificate are awarded by the community colleges under the signatures of the Principal of the College and Sponsoring industry.

4. Dr. Xavier Alphonse also gave a brief presentation on Madras Centre for Research and Development in Community Education (MCRDCE), stating that this Centre was inaugurated by Dr. G.D. Sharma. Former Secretary, UGC and acting as a coordinating agency for community colleges, organizing national as well as regional workshop, conducting refresh courses, bringing out publication on community college education.
5. After the presentation, Dr. Alphonse said that as per his experience the starting of the community colleges by NGOs is not feasible because of certain reasons including sustainability. He added that there could be five kind of community colleges, on the basis of their focus, as under:

(i) Urban Community Colleges
(ii) Rural Community Colleges
(iii) Integrated rural community colleges
(iv) Community colleges for women
(v) Tribal Community colleges

6. Dr. Alphonse has suggested the following:
   (i) The Government and its agencies such as UGC, AICTE, universities etc. may recognize the community colleges and their programmes for the purpose of employment as well as academic advancement of their graduates.
   (ii) There could be an apex coordinating body for community college education at national level with Regional offices.
   (iii) There could be a four tier system as follow:
      (a) First Tier - Short duration certificate courses without credit
      (b) Second Tier-Diploma level courses of 36 credits
      (c) Third Tier - Associate Degree level courses of another 36 additional credits
      (d) Fourth Tier - Distance Education courses of another 36 credits equivalent to university degree
7. Vice-Chancellor, IGNOU raised the issue of recognition and accreditation of the programme of Community Colleges in nursing area and also of the cost effectiveness of its certificate / diploma programme.
8. JS (HE) commented on the point of attitude as one of the component of Community College Education, bridge courses recognition of courses and their cost effectiveness. He also desired to know who would implement the Community College's programme.
9. Additional Secretary, in his concluding remarks, appreciated the presentation and concept of Community Colleges. He said that various departments and ministries of Government of India are implementing the programme for education empowerment of masses, especially deprived one. These programme have similar objectives to that of community colleges, therefore, there may not be the need for a new scheme. It should be explored, if the concept of community colleges could be embedded in any of these schemes.

   Additional Secretary also said that an incremental expansion of programme, as run by Dr. Alphonse should continue, even as we explore the possibility of a larger programme. All support to such an expansion would be given by the HRD Ministry.

10. Dr. Alphonse thanked AS (Education) for his offer and said he would come back with request for assistance after consultation with his colleagues.
11. Following decisions were taken:
    - (i) The material on all the schemes of Ministry of Human Resource Development and other Ministries with similar objectives be collected.
    - (ii) The report on Community College, prepared by different agencies be obtained.
    - (iii) On the basis of material (mentioned in (i) and (ii) above), UGC and IGNOU would develop a concept of an integrated approach to achieve objectives of community colleges Education through community colleges in India.
    - (iv) National Council for Rural Institute may act as coordinating body for Rural Community College.
    - (v) Members of the Committee may visit community colleges in Tamil Nadu to have a feel of them.
    - (vi) Officers of Ministry of Human Resource Development and Directorate of Adult Education dealing with programmes having objectives common to community colleges may be co-opted in the Committee.
    - (vii) The Committee may meet after one month.

The meeting concluded with thanks:

The Second meeting of the National Committee was held on the 10th of May 2005 in which all the Government agencies that are offering Vocational Programme were invited to work out the equivalence of credits that could be integrated into the mainstream of Higher Education.

6

Community College: Consultations and Spread to Africa

Fourth National Consultation of Community Colleges in India

The Fourth National Consultation of Community Colleges in India was organised by Madras Centre for Research and Development of Community Education (MCRDCE), Chennai recently. The Consultation was attended by 186 representatives from 14 states of India. The agenda of the meeting was to review the Community College Movement in India and the Association with Tamil Nadu Open University (TNOU) since TNOU has given recognition to 18 Job Oriented Courses conducted by the Community Colleges.

The resource persons of the Consultation were Dr. Mani Jacob, General Secretary, AIACHE, New Delhi, Dr. Muthukumaran, Member Secretary, Tamil Nadu State Council for Higher Education, Prof. K.S. Raghavan, Member Secretary, Committee on Policy Document on Indian Community College System, Mr. Ravi Candadai, Consul for Public Affairs, US Consulate, Chennai, Mr. Peter Merkx, Mr. Hans Wennink, both of them from Stichting Porticus, Netherlands and Prof. Planichamy, Vice-Chancellor, Tamil Nadu Open University (TNOU). The valedictory session was presided over by Fr. B. Jeyaraj, Rector, Loyola College. A Seven Member team from South Africa headed by Mr. Hans Wennink, Stichting Porticus, Amsterdam also attended the Consultation.

On the occasion of the consultation the books edited by Dr. Xavier Alphonse, S.J., Director, MCRDCE. Viz. Miracles of Hope; Walking the Extra Mile; Computer Made Easy; Neglected Majority; co-authored by Dr. Peter Xavier, S.J., Loyola College, Chennai were released. The statement of the Fourth National Consultation of Community Colleges in India is as follows:

- Community College System has evolved in the Indian education scenario at the right time to put education in the right track.

- Community College provides educational opportunity to the underprivileged and
- Community College provides educational opportunity to the underprivileged and the marginalised paving a path to universal education.
- It is an alternative system of education which has all the elements necessary to make a person fit for life and fit for job.
- Community College System is an answer to the problem of unemployed youth.
- The formal education is right now taking only 7 per cent of students in the higher education whereas the Community College is capable of catering to the educational needs to a greater extent due to its flexibility.
- Community College System emphasizes on Communication Skills and Life Coping Skills which has been proved as an important element in the Human Resource Development.

Hence the members of the Fourth National Consultation of Community Colleges in India suggest the following recommendations.

- The Ministry of HRD may formally announce that the Community College education will be part of the Indian Education System.
- The State Government may be advised to accept the Community College as a desirable and feasible unit of the State Level education system.
- Adequate provision may be made separately in the Central and State Government budgets for the promotion of the Community College System.
- The students who have passed out from the Community Colleges need more opportunities to get integrated into the higher education system.
- The infrastructure facilities of Community Colleges should be improved.
- Adequate funds may be made available in the form of scholarships and other subsidies to the students of Community Colleges.
- National Council for Community Colleges may be set up on the pattern of AICTE, NCTE etc.
- Government should sponsor teacher training programmes of Community College education.
- Government should not interfere with the flexibility of Community College System.

- Tamil Nadu Open University (TNOU) has recognised the Community College System and we request the other Open Universities to recognise the Community College Education.
- EDUSAT should be linked with Community Colleges and necessary hardware should be provided to the Community Colleges.
- An agency should be set up at Delhi to spread the Community College Movement in Northern India.
- All the Colleges and Schools with good infrastructure facilities should start community colleges.

*National Consultation of Community Colleges in India, Campus News, *University News*, Vol: 43 No. 16, April 18-24, 2005, p. 21-22.

Yashwantrao Chavan Maharashtra Open University, Nashik, Maharashtra: MCRDCE conducted one day's Consultation in Collaboration with Yashwantrao Chavan Maharashtra Open University at Nashik on 12th of August in Which sixty-six participants took part from Maharashtra, Gujarat, Madhya Pradesh and Goa. Vice Chancellor Dr. Rajan M. Welukar wanted by all means the Community College System to be recognised by the Open University. Ten Centres promised to submit their project proposal to the University by the end of September 2005 for recognition.

Community College Movement spreads to the African Continent: A brief report of visit to South Africa, Lesotho and Kenya 27th August to 4th September 2005. Lesotho is a small independent kingdom situated within the Republic of South Africa.

Consultation of Community College System: 72 participants from the entire Lesotho Kingdom attended including Rt. Rev. Bernard, Archbishop of Maseru and Rt. Rev. Everests, Venue: Assumption High School, Berea Date: 29th August 2005:

Highlights

(i) Enthusiasm, dedication and commitment of the entire Church of Lesotho for the skills development of the unemployed poor youth.

(ii) The entire proceedings was documented by Mr. Mark Potterton, CIE will bring out the documentation as a booklet.

(iii) The detailed discussion was made with Mr. George Mohlapiso, Secretary, Education Commission, Bishop's Conference of Lesotho.

(iv) The following Centres have been suggested for experimentation of the Community College System in Lesotho about the follow up action:

(a) Assumption School

(b) St. Elizabeth School

(c) Good Shepard Centre (Centre for unwed mothers)

(d) Catholic Technical School of Leribe

(v) A master trainer to be sent to Chennai, India from the 7th to 12th of November 2005 and also to have the experience of functioning of Community Colleges in India from the 14th to 18th of November 2005.

(vi) Meeting with the officials of Department of Education Government of Lesotho on the 30th August from 9.00 a.m to 10.00 a.m. A detailed presentation on the Community College system was made by Dr. Xavier Alphonse, S.J., and cooperation of the Government was sought for recognition and scholarships for skills training. The Director of Technical Education has promised to follow up the matter with Mr. George Mohlapiso.

(vii) We had the visit to Good Shepard Centre for unwed mothers. This Centre could be easily converted into a Community College / Skills Development Centre. Young women of the entire area could benefit. Providing them with residential and other basic facilities by way of hostel building and other equipments.

(viii) Mr. Charles, Principal of Assumption School could be thought of as a pioneer in starting the Community College system in Assumption School for the school dropouts.

Visit to South Africa

(i) 28th August Meeting with Bro. Douglas, Pax Vegetable Farm, Petersburg. He has done the initial work of situational analysis and need analysis. He has chosen 26 young farming students for whom he would like to give Life Skills and Work Skills. He is also trying to obtain the certification for the courses from primary agriculture SETAs. Mr. Mark Potterton of CIE was also present for the meeting.

(ii) Visit to Citrus Valley, Port Elizabeth. A good interaction with Bro. Christopher and visit to Farm Schools and also a meeting with Mr. Steven Lloyd and Peter Crawford, owners of the Dun Brody Estates (orange farm). Mr. Steven Lloyd and Mr. Peter Crawford are the enthusiastic community partners who have clear expectations of the required skills for work in the farm. Dr. Xavier Alphonse, S.J., suggested the following steps

Step I: Identification of trainers within the farm

Step II: Developing the course curriculum

Step III: Identifying the benefacries (target group)

Step IV: Training – Life skills, Work skills, Internship

Step V: Job placement in the farm itself

Step VI: Approaching the Government for recognition after making it a success

This venture would result in successful experimentation of courses on farming including Life Skills and Community participation of experienced workers for skills training.

(iii) Visit to St. Antony's Skills Training Centre, Johannesburg on 1st September. It is a laudable effort on the part of Mr. Alan Kichenbrand who has introduced Entrepreneurial Skills in eleven weeks skills based programme. They have the state of art equipments. They have also produced two training manuals on Life Skills and Small Business Development. The introduction of Life Skills has made a big difference in the whole training process and also in the job-placement. This is to be continued.

Nairobi, Kenya

Two days Conference on the Community College System. There were 35 participants from Kenya, Uganda and Tanzania. 12 presentations were made about the Indian Community College System by Dr. Xavier Alphonse, S.J. It was received enthusiastically by the participants. They also had detailed group discussions on the following seven questions:

1. What is your response to the presentation to the Indian model and How you can implement with necessary modifications in your local context?
2. What do you think are your community's needs – Situational Analysis and five needs in the order of priority?
3. Identify FIVE different target groups that you would like to serve through the Community College System?
4. Name five trades you would like to suggest that would give employment (Need Analysis)
5. What are the benefits this system of skills development will bring to your community (Vision)
6. Name five possible centres that could start Community Colleges in the three Countries?
7. What kind of structure would you like to have as a follow up of this Conference to help in starting Community Colleges?

Then the action plan emerged in the final session which had the following features:

A Coordination Committee to set up Community Colleges in the three countries was elected.

1. Bro. Nicholas Banda, Coordinator of the Committee, Administrator, Marist International Centre.
2. Ms. Elemina Musundi, Secretary of the Committee, GRAIL International Centre, Kisumu, Kenya.
3. Fr. Joseph Buzabaryaho, Apostles of Jesus, Youth Technical Institute, Karen, Nairobi, Kenya.
4. Mr. Amos Wambugo, Mjwa Furaha. Sisters of Precious Blood, Tanzania
5. Mr. Aden Raj, Jesuit Refugee Service, Uganda.

The following five centres were identified as Community Colleges in three countries:

1. Grail Centre, Kisumu, Kenya.
2. Ongata Rougai, Evangelizing Sisters of Mary, Kenya.
3. Apostle of Jesus, Langata, Kenya.
4. Inter Displacement People (IDP), Centre, JRS, Kitku, Uganda.
5. Mjwa Furaha, Zanzibar, Tanzania.

Three Master Trainers to be sent to Chennai, India for the Teachers Training Programme to be held on the 7th to 12th of November 2005 and also have experience of functioning of Community Colleges from the 14th to 18th November.

The Coordination Committee met with Dr. Xavier Alphonse, S.J., and Johnson of MCRDCE and finalised the action plan. Bro. Nicholas will document the entire proceedings of the Conference.

Evaluation of the last ten days was done by a group consisting of Mr. Hans, Mr. Michael, Bro. Jude Pieterse, Bro. Nicholas Banda, Dr. Xavier Alphonse, S.J., and Mr. Johnson on the 4th September. The entire group expressed their satisfaction in inspiring and increasing the commitment and involvement of South African, Lesotho, Kenyan, Ugandan and Tanzanian participants who had come for looking for an answer for the problem of unemployment. They went back with the conviction of introducing the Life Skills in their programmes which will build better human beings and better employees.

As a fruit of the visit we hope to have three Community Colleges well established centres by 2006 in South Africa and also five Centres as Community Colleges in Kenya, Uganda and Tanzania and three centres in Lesotho. The visit has given concrete direction and focus to the centres. All the participants in Nairobi were given a set of the important books written by Dr. Xavier Alphonse, S.J., on the Community College system and also the manual on the South African Conference held last year at Johannesburg in August 2004.

The visit of the Indian team served the twin purposes of follow up in South Africa of the Conference in August 2004 and introduction and inspiration to the Kingdom of Lesotho, Kenya, Uganda and Tanzania about the Community College System.

MCRDCE has been continuously publishing promotional literature and text books on Community College System from 1995. The following is the useful list for the handy immediate reference:

Promotional Literature

1. Alphonse, Xavier, *Changing Track – Community Colleges in India*, AIACHE Publications, New Delhi – December 1996.
2. Alphonse, Xavier, *Including the Excluded: History of the Community Colleges in India*, MCRDCE Publications, Chennai – January 1999.
3. Alphonse, Xavier, Editor, *People Building Business: Proceedings of the National Workshop on Community College System*, February 2000, MCRDCE Publications, Chennai – September 2000.
4. Alphonse, Xavier, *Reaching Out: Community College Movement in India – An Update*, MCRDCE Publications, Chennai, July 2001.
5. Alphonse, Xavier, *Mismatch: Establishing and Developing Community Colleges in India*, MCRDCE Publication, Chennai, June 2002.
6. Alphonse, Xavier, *Best to the Least – Profile of Community Colleges in India*, MCRDCE Publication, Chennai, November 2004.
7. Alphonse, Xavier, *Miracles of Hope – Success Stories of the Community College Students*, MCRDCE Publication, Chennai, March 2005.
8. Neglected Majority - *The Problem of School Dropouts and Possible Alternatives*, Co-authored by Dr. Peter Xavier, March 2005.

Text Books

9. Alphonse, Xavier, *We shall overcome: A textbook on Life Coping Skills*, MCRDCE Publication, Chennai, March 2004.
10. Alphonse, Xavier, *Walking the Extra Mile: A Textbook on Interpersonal Relationship and Communication Skills*, MCRDCE Publication, Chennai, March 2005. *(Pages. 284)*
11. Alphonse, Xavier, *Computer Made Easy: A Textbook on Basic Computing Skills*, MCRDCE Publication, Chennai, March 2005.

All these books are available at MCRDCE

7

Community Colleges: Role, Concept and Focus

Community Colleges – Playing Vital Role

Dr. S.P. Thiyagarajan, Vice Chancellor, University of Madras, distributed diploma certificates to 52 students who passed out from Dr. Chandran Devanesen Rural Community College in Karanai Village of Thiruporur Panchayat recently. The Vice-Chancellor acknowledged the role of the rural college in imparting "life-coping skills" that helped nearly 98 per cent of its students get employment.

Dr. Xavier Alphonse, Director, Madras Centre for Research and Development of Community Education, highlighted the concept of community colleges to help the less privileged sections of society. Dr. Alphonse, a former principal of Loyola College, paid glowing tributes to Dr. Chandran Devanesen, an educationist and the founder of Roofs for the Roofless, which established the community college.

Prabhu, a 22-year-old youth from Pallikaranai, who studied computer software application and multimedia, recalled with pride his one-year stint in the college after which he became a "team leader" with a private bank. Ammu, daughter of a casual labourer, in Chitlapakkam, was keen to take up nursing as a career but lacked the funds to be trained in a regular institution. She found an answer in the community college. She was employed in a private hospital in Pallikaranai, as a health assistant. (Courtesy: Community Colleges play vital role, *The Hindu*, *Education Plus*, 12.09.2005)[6]

Empowerment of Socio-Economic Weaker Sections through the Community College System and the support of the Universities in India.

The Community College Movement has been growing in India during the last ten years. It was aimed primarily at the socio economic weaker and disadvantaged sections of the society leading to empowerment through skills development thus providing education for livelihood. This article traces the role of many universities in India in support of this alternative system of education.

The Concept of Community College and its Salient Features

- The Community College is an alternative system of education, which is aimed at the empowerment of the disadvantaged and the underprivileged (urban poor, rural poor, tribal poor and women) through appropriate skills development leading to gainful employment in collaboration with the local industry and the community and achieve skills for employment and self employability of the above sections of people in the society.
- The Community College is an innovative educational alternative that is rooted in the Community providing holistic education and eligibility for employment to the disadvantaged.
- The vision of the Community College is to be of the community, for the community and by the community and to produce responsible citizens.
- The Community College promotes job oriented, work related, skill - based and life coping education.
- The Community College initiative is in conformity with the Indian political will that prioritises in education, primary education, information technology education and vocational education.
- The key words of the Community College system are access, flexibility in curriculum and teaching methodology, cost effectiveness and equal opportunity in collaboration with industrial, commercial and service sectors of the local area and responding to the social needs and issues of the local community, internship and job placement within the local area, promotion of self employment and small business development, declaration of competence and eligibility for employment.

The Curriculum of a Community College

Category	*Programme*	*Weeks*	*Hours*	*Credits*
Part I	Life Skills	21 Weeks	630 Hours	21 Credits
Part II	Work Skills	21 Weeks	630 Hours	21 Credits
Part III	Internship and Hands on Experience	8 Weeks	390 Hours	13 Credits
Part IV	Preparation for Employment and Evaluation	2 Weeks	60 Hours	2 Credits
	Total	**52 Weeks**	**1710 Hours**	**57 Credits**

One Credit = 30 Hours of work.

Focus on Socio-Economic Weaker Sections (Target Group)

The unique achievement of the Community College has been the empowerment of the socially economically and educationally backward sections of society in the last ten years. The Madras Centre has been able to gather the data regarding 23,609 from 99 Community Colleges. The breakup gives a complete picture of the Target Group served.

Women- 74%

Married - 7%

Age- 16-48

Qualification

Below 10th - 16%; 10th Passed - 22%; 12th Passed -55%; Degree- 07%

Caste

SC - 25%; ST- 06%; MBC - 15%; BC - 44%; OC - 10%

Monthly Family Income

Below 1000 - 39%; Below 2000 - 34%; Below 3000 - 17%; Above 3000 - 10%

Religion

Hindus - 55%; Christians - 42%; Muslims - 03%

Job Placement – 75%

Focus on Rural Development through Community Colleges

There is the urgent need to link agriculture and Rural Development with education for Livelihood and skills development. Due to the new emerging trends in agricultural farming and Rural Developmental Approaches to reach up to International standards, there is the need for the enhancement of Human Resourses and the developmental of newer and updating of skills. There is also the urgent necessity of harnessing the human resources and manpower of the Rural Community. This fits in well with the search of the Community College Movement.

What is a Rural Community College?

- Rural Community College has arisen as an urgent requirement for empowering the rural people through skills education for self-employment as well as group employment in rural areas.

Features of Rural Community College

- Meets the needs of the local community
- People participating and people benefiting

- Aims at capacity building of rural people
- Improves talents of youth
- Taps resources and potentialities in rural areas.
- Provides skills for self-employment
- Creates job opportunities for eradicating poverty
- More field oriented with practical inputs
- Trains rural youth in traditional sectors.
- Enhances collaboration between government and service sector.
- Facilitates self-reliant initiatives in rural areas.
- Makes interested youth to upscale their education and skills
- Transforms the qualitative aspects of life of the rural poor
- Initiates sustainable livelihood options for poverty alleviation
- Empowers rural people through integrated development.

Rationale for the Promotion of a Rural Community College

There is a great need for people, especially the young to discover great meaning and dignity in their lives and find positive, healthy, productive alternatives to unemployment, isolation, boredom, alienation, addiction and violence. Over 72% of the population in rural areas are not able to make a decent living mainly because of regular employment and income generation. Hence, creating gainful employment opportunities is the biggest challenge today.

The opportunities for regular employment and income generation in rural areas can be grouped into on-farm and off-farm activities. Initially, the agro-based activities cannot provide adequate opportunities for the landless laborers. But, subsequently, with the optimum use of resources and enhanced productivity, demand for labour will rise and even the landless will have increased employment opportunities with improvement in agriculture productivity, job opportunities for ancillary services will also increase and hereto, the landless laborers can take advantage of the situation. Based on the above rural development focus, two community colleges have been started in Siruganur, Tamil Nadu and Lachragarh, Jharkhand

Lachragarh, Jharkhand

Montfort Community College is run by the Montfort Brothers of St. Gabriel, Ranchi Province. It is hoped that Montfort Community College would come up with a new educational system against the present system learning and give options to those who cannot progress in life due to poverty, weakness and injustice in the society. Therefore Community College aims at full development of those unemployed youth who cannot complete or cannot go to school. Community College will provide work efficiency to more youth every year which will give them much confidence to live prestigious life in the society and provide them the atmosphere for job opportunities. The institute will also provide them with a moral education and leadership programmes so as to form a good society.

Objectives

- To provide skills and knowledge needed to cope with life's problems and challenges.
- To develop a positive attitude
- To understand the meaning of life and its challenges
- To train to be successful and useful citizens through positive thinking.
- To cope with criticism, failure, anger, loneliness, physical and verbal abuse
- To manage time and stress.
- To develop one's personality to its full potential.

Aims

1. To prevent labour migration especially the migration of unskilled labours and migration of girls for working and maid servants.
2. Provide skill training, appropriate to make the youth get at least part time – employed.
3. Empower the powerless tribals and dalits.
4. Prevent the youth from becoming anti social elements and criminals and support them to become responsible citizens of the society.
5. Improve the economic status of tribals.

Courses Conducted by the Community College

1. Tailoring
2. Motor Mechanic
3. Carpentry
4. Welding
5. Masonry

Ertram Rural Community College

Ertram Rural Community College is situated at the Human Resource Development Training Centre of VOICE Trust at Siruganur village in Mannachanallur Block, Trichy District, State of Tamil Nadu, and South India.

Siruganur is 25 Kilometers north of Trichy in the Trichy-Chennai National Highways (NH 45). It is linked by bus transportation between Trichy and Perambalur, the District Head Quarters of the neighbouring district of Perambalur at a distance of 30 kilometers north of Siruganur.

Siruganur is a village Panchayat of Mannachanallr blocks which has 156 villages big and small. It is one of the 38 village Panchayats of Mannachanallur Block.

Voice Trust (Voice for the Oppressed through Integrated Community Emancipation) was registered in 1985 under Trust Act as a Non Profit and Voluntary Organisation. Being a NGO, VOICE Trust is involving in various social action initiatives for the disadvantaged groups of people especially, women, children, landless, small farmers, unemployed youth, the disabled, the destitute and the ageing.

Voice Trust obtained permission in 1986 from the Ministry of Home affairs, Government of India under the Foreign Contribution Regulation Act (FCRA).

Courses Conducted by the Community College

1. Diploma in Sustainable Farming Systems for Integrated Rural Development
2. Diploma in Pre- Primary Teacher Training
3. Diploma in House Electrician
4. Diploma in DTP Operator
5. Diploma in Plumbing Technology

   Diploma in Fashion Designing and Garment Making

Village Placement Programme

President (eastwhile) APJ Abdul Kalam has appreciated the Village Placement Programme of the Alagappa University and expressed the belief that such programmes would help the objectives of project achieved for Providing Urban Amenities to Rural Areas (PURA).

Kalam conveyed these views when Alagappa University Vice-Chancellor P. Kanniappan called on him at Rashtrapathi Bhavan to brief the President of the programme.

The Vice-Chancellor made mention of his meeting with the President at the feedback meeting on the university's innovative Village Placement Programme (VPP). He said that it was the first time that such a programme had been introduced by any university in the State. Over 400 students, both men and women, participated in the programme by staying in seven villages. Students, who participated in the programme, told at the feedback meeting about their work in the villages, which included desilting village tanks. (*The New Indian Express*, 13.10.2005).

Role of the Universities

Tamil Nadu Open University helped the Community Colleges to receive recognition as Vocational Programme Centres.

Association with Tamil Nadu Open University

- The announcement in "*The Hindu*" dated 15.08.2004 "Job Oriented Programmes – The Tamil Nadu Open University (TNOU)" has introduced six job-oriented vocational programmes at the certificate level through the distance mode. In a statement here, the Vice-Chancellor, M.S. Palanichamy, said an intensive practical training to provide hands-on experience would be the mainstay of the programmes for DTP operator, house electrician, refrigeration and air-conditioning technician, plumbing technician, four Wheeler mechanic and catering assistant. Community Colleges, Polytechnics, industrial training and other institutes with infrastructure would provide the practical inputs. Interested institutions may contact the Registrar, TNOU, Directorate of Technical Education Campus, Guindy, and Chennai for obtaining forms and details within 15 days.
- Having seen the advertisement Dr. Xavier Alphonse, S.J., and the MCRDCE team approached Prof. M.S. Palanichamy, Vice Chancellor, Tamil Nadu Open University met him on the 17th of August 2004 and had a long discussion for about two hours about the possibility of offering above six courses in the Community Colleges.
- Dr. P. Thiyagarajan, Head, Continuing Education, TNOU was sent as a representative of the University as a one-man commission to visit Colleges in the city of Chennai. He visited Tabitha Community College, Vadapalani and Dr. Chandran Devanesan Rural Community College, Karanai Village on 20.08.2004. He was very much impressed by the functioning of Community College System. He was also happy to visit MCRDCE to get all the necessary information to know about the system.
- On 24.08.2004 Dr. Xavier Alphonse, S.J., made a presentation about the Community College system and its working at the Tamil Nadu Open University. The Members present were Prof. Palanichamy, Vice-Chancellor, Registrar, Dr. Thiyagarajan, Head, Continuing Education, Prof. Shanmugam, Consultant TNOU, Prof. Murugan, Director, Student Support Services, Prof. Subramanian, Continuing Education, Mr. Emmanuel, Manager, Dr. Chandran Devanesen Rural Community College, Mrs. Mercy Joy Joshua, Director, Chennai Corporation

Community College, South Campus, Joseph Johnson, MCRDCE, Jothilingam, MCRDCE were present. We had a meeting of two hours at the end of which Vice-Chancellor requested Dr. Xavier Alphonse, S.J., to have a consultation with Community Colleges in the State and also to arrange for a meeting of the Directors of Community Colleges with the whole team of Tamil Nadu Open University (TNOU).

Seventh Consultation of Community Colleges in Tamil Nadu

- Accepting the invitation of the Vice-Chancellor, a consultation of Community Colleges in Tamil Nadu for recognition was organised and the dialogue with the TNOU Team on the 16th and 17th of September 2004 was conducted at Chennai.

The Purpose

(i) To familiarize with the working of the Tamil Nadu Open University especially with regard to the Six Vocational Courses.

(ii) To explore the feasibility of offering these six courses in our community colleges.

(iii) To request the university to accept the other popular courses that is run by the community colleges.

(iv) To have a dialogue with the TNOU about the modalities of offering the job-oriented courses.

(v) To review and evaluate the functioning of the Community Colleges in Tamil Nadu in terms of achievements, challenges and concerns.

Tamil Nadu Open University: Objectives

(i) To provide an alternative non-formal, cost effective channel for obtaining tertiary education to those who seek it.

(ii) To supplement the efforts of Conventional University System in providing tertiary education thereby reducing the pressure on those systems.

(iii) To provide a "second chance" to those who had to discontinue their formal education for reasons of their own.

(iv) To provide easy access to good quality Higher Education to "all" in general and "the disadvantaged" in particular, by delivering the same at their door steps.

(v) To provide an opportunity to those who are gainfully employed to upgrade their knowledge and skills tailored to meet specific vocational/ professional needs, whenever they wish to do so.

(vi) To design an innovative system of good quality University Education that is flexible not only with respect to entry criteria, but also with respect to what to learn, when to learn and how to learn?

(vii) To design and provide local specific employment oriented programmes.

Prominent Features

(i) State Jurisdiction

(ii) Flexible admission rules

(iii) Individualized study: flexibility, in terms of place, pace and duration of study

(iv) Use of latest information and communication technologies

(v) Student support services network

(vi) Cost-effective programmes

(vii) Modular programmes

(viii) Resource sharing, collaboration and networking with other Open Universities

(ix) Relevant programmes

Based on the above Consultation Tamil Nadu Open University (TNOU) has recognised 79 Community Colleges in Tamil Nadu as Vocational Programme Centres. The recognition has also been extended to other Community Colleges in other parts of India. The following nine courses have been recognised as Diploma Courses to be conducted by Community Colleges from this year including Life Coping Skills and Communication Skills.

(i) Pre School Teaching

(ii) Health Assistant

(iii) Fashion Design and Garment Making

(iv) DTP Operator

(v) Refrigeration and Air Conditioning Technician

(vi) House Electrician

(vii) Plumbing Technician

(viii) Catering Assistant

(ix) Four Wheeler Mechanism

Advantages in going for the TNOU

- Formal recognition.
- Demand of the target group and the parents and the public.

- Closer to the Community College System in philosophy, practice and implementation.
- Diploma is valid all over India.
- Possible for registering in the Employment Exchanges of the country.
- Possibility of taking care of the School dropouts since minimum qualification not prescribed except for Pre-Primary Teaching and Health Assistant Programmes.
- Vocational Programme Centres.
- Ensures status in the society.
- Possibility of Vertical mobility through credit transfer since credits have been prescribed by the TNOU.
- Scholarships (SC/ST and Common Wealth Scholarship) can be obtained through TNOU.
- Integration is useful to the beneficiaries.
- Final Products have to be eligible for employment and should be able to meet with the demands of the required skills by the employers.
- Broad spectrum of skills.

Yashwantrao Chavan Maharashtra Open University– Nashik

MCRDCE Conducted a day's Consultation in collaboration with Yashwantrao Chavan Maharashtra Open University at Nashik on 12th of August in which 66 participants took part from Maharashtra, Gujarat, Madhya Pradesh and Goa. The Vice Chancellor Dr. Rajan M. Welukar wanted by all means the Community College system to be recognised by the Open University. The proposals are being sent to the University for Consideration.

The Central University of Hyderabad

The MCRDCE Team was invited by the Central University of Hyderabad to speak to 60 participants of the Academic Staff College from all over India on the 2nd of November 2004. The Director of MCRDCE met the Vice–Chancellor, Dr. Kota Harinarayana who made a formal request to MCRDCE to help the rural youth in the neighbourhood. The University has started a Community College for the Rural Youth under the auspices of the Distance Education Centre with a course in Industrial Security.

- 1998 September – Establishment of Five Community Colleges by Manonmaniam Sundaranar University (M.S.University), Tirunelveli, Tamil Nadu. It was further strengthened by starting of 36 Community Colleges during the years 1998-2005.
- **Avinashilingam Deemed University** is running a Community College for women from 1998

Pondicherry Central University

This University started a Community College in October 1995 at the initiative of Dr. Gnanam, the then Vice –Chancellor of the Central University of Pondicherry. It is offering 5 Associate Degrees, 31 post graduate diplomas for those who have completed their degrees, One five year integrated course in M.A. Economics, 21 Diploma Courses for those who have completed +2, 18 certificate courses for those who have completed +2 and 10th standard with the duration of 2 months to 6 months. All these courses are conducted in close collaboration with the industries of the area. The college was inaugurated by the UGC Chairman Ms. Desai. As the prospectus of the college indicates, "Pondicherry University Community College endeavors to create an innovative alternative model of higher education in which academicians, administrators, industrialists, agriculturists, traders, students and other members of the community become partners in the development of human resource with adequate mutual collaboration and co-operation. In fact, the educational activities are designed in response to the needs of the local community, business, industries and Government. In other words, the community college is for the community and of the community and by the community.

Madras University - Indian Community College System (ICCS) Document

The Vice Chancellor, Dr. Thiyagarajan of the University of Madras at the direction of the Chief Minister of Tamil Nadu constituted a working group to formulate a policy document of Indian Community College System (ICCS) in which Dr. Xavier Alphonse, was nominated as one of the six members. The document has been prepared with a clear idea of vertical mobility to bring in the Community College Students into the mainstream of Higher Education non-credited courses, Diploma, Associate degree and degree.

University Grants Commission

The UGC proposed to introduce a scheme for institutionalising community colleges as a direct linkage to the conventional university/ collegiate educational system. A report from the University of Madras on community colleges in Tamil Nadu was received and a committee of experts would examine it and place it before the Union Human Recourse Development Ministry, Dr. Pillai said.

Under the scheme, the programmes conducted by the existing community colleges would be recognised by the higher education system. Madras University studied the community college – university linkage system in the United States.

The University Grants Commission studied the importance of community colleges run by non-governmental organisations. Governmental agencies in

India, as also the successful experience in the U.S. Canada and other countries. (*The Hindu*, March, 7, 2005).

Conclusion

It is very encouraging to note the involvement of the Universities in support of the Community College Movement in India. The Community College System is gaining gradual acceptance because of the Universities coming forward to recognise and accept the system. The following suggestions can bring in a sea change in the whole scenario of the Higher Education in India.

- The four tier system of Higher Education non-credited, diploma, associate degree and degrees.
- Helping the Community College Students to have credit transfer to do the associate degree and degrees programmes.
- There is a need to develop new programmes through Distance Education Centres of various Universities to suit the learning needs and enhancement and updating of skills of the Community College students.

It is very promising if all these suggestions could be implemented, the takers of Higher Education will increase from 7 per cent to 20 per cent in India and 13% would be definitely from the socio economic weaker sections of the society.[7]

8

Community College System and its Future in India

Introduction

The Community College movement has come a long way from 1996. With the beginning of just one College 'Madras Community College' at Chennai in 1996, we have to-day 187 Community Colleges in 21 States of India. It has served more than 40,000 students from the socially, economically, educationally, backward sections of society and has obtained for them 90% employment in middle level jobs all over the country. It is highly commendable and remarkable that the service minded organisations, Dioceses, religious congregations and NGOs have taken up this mission of empowerment and capacity building of the poor and the marginalised to match up to the challenges of globalization. In this article, This chapter records the new developments of the Community College movement during the last two years (2004 – 2006).

The Target group served

Profile of 33,853 Community College Students from 132 Community Colleges

Summary of the Finding:

Women	- 75%	**Caste**	
Married	- 8%	SC	- 26%
Age	- 16 – 52	ST	- 07%
Qualification		MBC	-15%
Below 10th	- 16%	BC	-42%
10th Passed	- 23%	OC	-10%
12th Passed	- 54%	**100%**	
Degree	- 07%		

Monthly Family Income		**Religion**	
Below 1000	- 37%	Hindu	-55%
Below 2000	- 35%	Christian	-43%
Below 3000	- 17%	Muslim	-03%
Above 3001	- 11%	Buddhism	-01%
	100%		**100%**

Job Placement - 75%

Job Placement – Generation of Employment

The Community Colleges have tried their best to place their students in respective fields of employment as it is shown below:

Research Study	*Students*	*Community Colleges*	*Actually in Jobs (%)*
Feb 2000	1934	13	70
March 2001	4226	26	71
May 2003	1002	29	83
June 2003	10107	54	75
Nov 2004	14929	69	75
July 2005	23609	99	75
March 2006	33853	132	75

Overall Percentage 75%

The Fifth National Consultation of Community Colleges in India (August 2006), at Chennai

The Fifth National Consultation of the Community Colleges in India with the theme "The Community College System and its Future" was a big success. It was held on the 30th and 31st of August 2006 M.O.P. Vaishnav College for Women. There were 198 delegates from 118 Community Colleges from 15 States of India.

The Consultation was inaugurated by Mr. David Hopper, the U.S. Consulate General, Chennai, Mr. Aludiapillai, I.A.S., the former Secretary of the Tamil Nadu State Council for Higher Education gave the keynote address. The Technical session that followed the inauguration was on the response from various quarters to the Community College movement in India.

The members of the panel were.

1. Dr. S. P. Thiyagarajan, Vice Chancellor, University of Madras
2. Dr. Palanichamy, Vice Chancellor, Tamil Nadu Open University
3. Dr. Sundari Krishnamurthy, Academic Dean, Stella Maris College

4. Dr. Nirmala Prasad, Principal, M.O.P. Vaishnav College for Women
5. Prof. Ponnu Ram, Special Officer, M.S. University Community College
6. Mr. Anto Vincent, Former Vice-President, HRD, FORD India Ltd and Master Trainer of Community College Teachers

The discussion was on the document "Indian Community College System" prepared by Dr. S.P. Thiyagarajan, Former Vice Chancellor, University of Madras and the Team in which I was a member. The panelists gave their criticism of the document and also the unique features of the Community College movement which could not be compromised with. This was an enlightening session.

The participants were divided into twelve groups and they spent nearly five hours deliberating on the document, suggesting their modifications especially with regard to the target group and the one year diploma programme that leads to a job and livelihood.

The second day began with a multi religious prayer service. The twelve groups read their reports. Dr. Xavier Alphonse, S.J., summarized the deliberations and the entire assembly agreed upon the core features of the Community College system which is to be included in the document.

(i) Target group should not be sacrificed at any cost.

(ii) Vertical mobility is not our chief concern. Diploma is to be given importance since it is education for livelihood.

(iii) ICRDCE to be a nodal and coordinating agency.

(iv) Funds from Ministry of Human Resource Development, New Delhi – Scholarships and stipends to be solicited.

(v) The Community College students to have the provision to be registered in the employment exchanges, job placement in Government agencies.

(vi) Train and Bus passes to be provided like the other recognised institutions.

(vii) National recognition is to be given as an alternative system of education.

(viii) The working out of Credits, uniform and clarity 1 Credit = 15 hrs of work to have uniformity and clarity.

(ix) Autonomy of the Community College should not be disturbed.

(x) Less control and interference from the Government.

(xi) Original spirit of the Community College movement adaptability, accessibility, flexibility, innovativeness relevant to the community response to the local needs should not be sacrificed.

(xii) Training programme for teachers and updating of the skills in curriculum development.

(xiii) Operational modalities

- Autonomous functioning of Community Colleges
- Tamil Nadu Open University (TNOU) model with open Universities.
- Separate independent body constituted by the Ministry of Human Resource Development recognised by University Grants Commission, e.g. Mahatma Gandhi University of Community Colleges for Diploma and lateral entry to associate Degree and Degree programmes.

The *agenda* of the consultation was clearly articulated and agreed upon:

1. To seek National recognition of the system from the Government of India.
2. To ask for scholarships and stipends from the Planning Commission as one third of the training cost for every student of the Community Colleges Rs. 5,000.
3. To enable the Community College student to go forward with vertical mobility and to make the lateral entry into the second year through distance education in the respective disciplines recognized by the Open Universities of India.

After the lunch break, the participants were divided into Subgroups State-wise. They discussed ten issues and challenges facing the Community College movement especially the bus pass and train pass to the Community College students and registering their names in the employment exchanges of India to get Government jobs.

In the evening, Dr. Xavier Alphonse, S.J., and also the Community Colleges were felicitated in the presence of the Member of Parliament Mr. Ponnusamy, M.P. of Lok Saba. The distinguished visitor was Prof. Moolchand Sharma, the Vice Chairman of the University Grants Commission (UGC) who promised to include the Community College system in the agenda of the UGC and to be a partner in all our efforts to get the recognition from the Government of India. The day ended with a cultural programme of Indian dances by the Community College students followed by the Conference dinner.

All the participants of the National Consultation gathered at the tomb of St. Thomas on 1st of September at 7.30 a.m. We offered a thanksgiving mass for all that the Lord has done through the Community College movement to thousands of young men and women.

At 10.00 a.m. Rt. Rev. Chinnappa, Archbishop of Madras-Mylapore felicitated the participants. The Tenth year celebrations of Madras Community College (1996-2006) was marked by Industrial Partners meet in which representatives from 10 trades spoke about the skills needed for employment. Rt. Rev. Lawrence Pious, the Auxiliary Bishop and the Chairman of Madras Community College concluded the meeting.

The Request to the Ministry of Human Resource Development and the Planning Commission

National Recognition for the Community College

National recognition for the community college system is requested from the Ministry of Human Resource Development.

Vertical Mobility through Credit Transfer

A concept document on the Indian Community College System will be submitted by 184 community colleges in 21 states of India to the MHRD and UGC for ensuring the vertical mobility of the community college students through the Open Universities and conventional Universities with the three tier system: Diploma, Associate degree and Degree.

Soliciting Government Funds, Stipends and Scholarships

Soliciting Government Funds, Stipends and Scholarships to the disadvantaged sections of society especially SC/ST/BC/MBC/Women/ Minorities – Rs 250 Crores for scholarships and stipends (each year 50 crores) scholarships per student Rs 5000 per annum -10000 students will benefit by the scheme each year and 50000 students during the XI Five year plan.

Central Placement Cell

Central Placement Cell in collaboration with Confederation of Indian Industries and Chambers of Commerce.

- Community Colleges to be established in educationally backward districts with emphasis of soft skills development.
- Setting up the Community colleges can go long a way for correcting the regional imbalance in the system of Higher Education.
- Institutions of repute can adopt neighboring villages and open Community Colleges in them to promote vocational/skills training and pre-college training/bridge courses.[8]

Best to the Least – An Eye Opener

Alphonse Xavier, Ed, (2004), *Best to the Least: Profile of Community Colleges in India*, Chennai, MCRDCE, 405 p. 125.

Education improves not only the character, conduct and behaviour of an individual but also enhances his professional knowledge and skill. In our country only about 6 to 8% of those in the appropriate age group of 18 to 25 are receiving tertiary education. In order to achieve a better level of quality of life in our country, higher education must be made accessible to a much larger number of persons in the age group of 18 to 25 and also to those in the middle age. Some 40 years ago, evening part time programmes, summer programmes and correspondence courses were started to make higher education accessible to the working youth. In the last ten years, apart from open universities, a new innovative type of educational institutions namely community colleges were established by service minded compassionate men who desired to empower the disadvantaged through skill development.

The editor of the book under review, Rev. Dr. Xavier Alphonse S.J. who is involved in higher education for over two decades joined with others to found in 1996 the Madras Community College. There are now about 120 such colleges spread all over the country. Of course, Tamil Nadu State leads with 83 community colleges.

As more than eight years have passed since the first of these colleges was established and as it is of public interest that the facilities available at these colleges are made known to one and all, Rev. Dr. Xavier Alphonse has taken this initiative to publish a profile of these colleges.

The book consists of two parts: Part I provides an overview of the community college movement in India. Part II provides a profile of the community colleges.

The editor has brought out how these colleges have strived during the last few years to take higher education to the deprived lot and developed their knowledge and skills so that they can find good job placements. He has also shown how each institution has evolved its own mission and vision. The general pattern of education however is to develop life skills, work skills, providing internship and field experience and a final evaluation and assessment of the capabilities of the students.

The editor has also classified these colleges into the following four distinct groups and presented their nature of work and their contributors to the society around them; Urban Colleges, Rural Colleges, Colleges for Women and Tribal Community Colleges.

Anyone who reads this book will be amazed by the wide variety of programmes being offered by these institutions. This book will be an eye opener especially to those who are under the illusion that there are only two options open to the youth today i.e. Engineering and Medical studies.

This book also brings out the contributions of the Madras Centre for Research and Development of Community Education (MCRDCE) which is a coordinating agency. It is organizing training programmes and publishing books in addition to various other activities for advancement and popularisation of the community college movement.

In the olden days when the society depended mostly on crafts, the formal education required to learn the skills associated with such crafts was elementary. But today as more and more vocations are based on secondary and tertiary level educational knowledge, there is a need to develop a system of education that does not demand the rigours of a formal educational system, but provides only the needed secondary and tertiary level educational inputs. This need is fulfilled by the Community College system.

The book establishes the following conclusion of Dr. Xavier Alphonse: The Community College Movement is marching on and it is emerging as a collective and community effort to serve the most deserving and disadvantaged sections of society pro-poor educational system and education for livelihood.

9

Community College and Empowerment

Empowering the Marginalized

Community colleges were mooted in order to provide education for livelihood to the socio-economically weaker and disadvantaged sections. This system is flexible, accessible and cost-effective. Community colleges provide vocational training to students and channelise their skills for the development of society.

The community college movement has been growing in India in the last 10 years. It was aimed primarily at the socio-economic weaker and disadvantaged sections of the society leading to empowerment through skills development thus providing education for livelihood.

The community college is an alternative system of education, that seeks empowerment of the disadvantaged and the underprivileged section such as urban, rural and tribal poor and women) by providing them appropriate skills development leading to gainful employment. The local industry and the community collaborate to provide these skills. In essence, the community college promotes job-oriented, work-related, skill - based and life-coping education.

The key words of the system are access, flexibility in curriculum and teaching methodology, cost-effectiveness and equal opportunity in collaboration with industrial, commercial and service sectors of the local area and responding to the social needs and issues of the local community. The Madras Centre has been able to gather the data regarding 23,609 from 99 Community Colleges. The break-up gives a complete picture of the Target Group Served.

Women: (74 per cent, Married - 7 per cent, Age - 16 - 48),

Qualification: (Below 10th - 16 per cent; 10th Passed - 22 per cent; 12th Passed - 55 per cent; Degree - 7 per cent).

Caste: (SC - 25 per cent; ST- 6 per cent; MBC - 15 per cent; BC - 44 per cent; OC - 10 per cent),

Monthly Family Income: (Below 1000 - 39 per cent; Below 2000 - 34 per cent; Below 3000 - 17 per cent; Above 3000 - 10 per cent).

Religion: (Hindus - 55 per cent; Christians - 42 per cent; Muslims - 3 per cent), Job Placement: (75 per cent).

Thus the concept is totally a secular one breaking all barriers of religion, caste, region, language and educational qualification.

Education for a Livelihood

The alternative system of community colleges aims at helping the disadvantaged find employment in collaboration with the local community and industry.

The Community College Movement has been growing in India during the last ten years. It was aimed primarily at the socio economic weaker and disadvantaged sections of the society leading to empowerment through skills development, thus providing education for livelihood.

The Community College is an alternative system of education aimed at helping the urban poor, rural, tribal poor, and women find gainful employment in collaboration with the local industry and the community.

The system is of the community for the community, and by the community to produce, skill-based, and life-coping education. The key attributes are access, flexibility in curriculum and teaching methodology, cost effectiveness and equal opportunity. All this is in collaboration with industrial, commercial and service sectors of the local area and responding to the social needs and issues of the local community.

The results are internship and job placement within the local area, promotion of self employment and small business development, declaration of competence and eligibility for employment. There is also an attempt to evolve a profile exclusively for the rural community college.

The Community College is the need of the hour. It responds to the Challenges of Exclusion and Elimination from the formal system, Mismatch between Education and Employment, Capability Poverty, Problems of Unemployment, Under Employment and Unemployability and School Dropouts.

The Community College Movement began in 1995 with the Pondicherry University Community College. The first Non-governmental organisation to start the Madras Community College in 1996 was the Archdiocese of Madras-

Mylapore. Today we have 153 Community Colleges in 17 States of India. It has helped 35,000 students from the socially, economically and educationally backward groups. Thus, it has become a National phenomenon.

The Madras Centre for Research and Development of Community Education (MCRDCE), Chennai is the agency for promoting and implementing the concept in India. The MCRDCE has helped in the establishment and monitoring of 135 Community Colleges. It has conducted 15 Teacher Training programmes involving 1000 teachers from the Community Colleges in India. It has conducted more than 100 workshops all over the country and four National Consultations to propagate the concept.

It has also been working to get the National recognition and Accreditation from the State and Central Governments.

MCRDCE is also helping to establish Community Colleges in South Africa, Kenya, Lesotho, Tanzania and Uganda. The development of the system has been accepted internationally by Association of American Community Colleges (AACC) and Community Colleges for International Development (CCID).

The unique achievement of the Community Colleges has been the empowerment of the socially, economically and educationally backward sections of society in the last ten years. The Madras Centre has been able to gather the data regarding 23,609 from 99 Community Colleges.

The community college prepares its students and makes them fit for life and for jobs through its curriculum.

Part –I is Life Skills (21 weeks, 630 hours, 21 credits);

Part – II is Work Skills (21 weeks, 630 hours, 21 credits);

Part – III is Internship and Hands-on Experience (eight weeks, 390 hours, 13 credits);

Part – IV is Preparation for Employment and Evaluation (two weeks, 60 hours, two credits).

One credit is 30 hours of work.

The Community College System has been working successfully with 75 per cent Job Placement without getting recognition from any approved educational bodies of the country. However, most of the Community Colleges felt there is the need for recognition from the State and Central Governments to facilitate the horizontal mobility and the vertical mobility of the students. MCRDCE has succeeded in influencing the State and Central Governments for recognition and accreditation of the system and for student Centred funding. The issue of accreditation was examined closely by the National Institute of Open Schooling (NIOS), New Delhi at the direction of the Ministry of Human Resource Development (MHRD), Government of India,

New Delhi. The NIOS has given accreditation so far to 18 Community Colleges in the country. Tamil Nadu Open University has recognized 80 Community Colleges as approved Vocational Programme centres with nine recognized job-oriented courses. The Madras University has submitted a comprehensive document on "Indian Community College System" to MHRD and UGC ensuring the vertical mobility of the Community College students.

The National Committee set by MHRD prepared its recommendations to be submitted to the then Union Minister Dr. Arjun Singh. The system has found a mention in "Tenth Five-Year Plan (2002 - 2007), Chapter 2.4 Vocational Education p. 51. "There should be focus on convergence of schemes like the Sarva Shiksha Abhiyan, Adult Education and Vocational Education Programme at Schools, ITIs, Polytechnics, Community Colleges etc."

It is very promising if the Community College system achieves national acceptance. The takers of Higher Education will increase from 7 to 20 per cent in India and 13 per cent would be definitely from the socio economic weaker sections of the society.

Marching with the Marginalized [Alphonse Xavier, Ed. (2005) Marching with the Marginalized – The Contribution of MCRDCE to the Community College Movement in India [(1995 – 2005) MCRDCE, 248 p., Rs. 150].

There are a few credible agencies in the country totally committed to the growth and development of the weaker and disadvantaged sections of the society by imparting training in life skills and work skills. Enhancing the employability of youth through appropriate assessment of the opportunities in the area for employment and self employment and provision of professional training in life-coping skills relevant to their needs have been felt for several decades in our country.

Promoting the concept of community colleges in 1995, the founders have been able to convince the society of its usefulness as a unique idea in empowering the marginalized groups through well planned exercises. The concept, on acceptance by various sections of the society throughout the length and breadth of the country, has flowered into a movement. This is evidenced by the fact towards the end of the year 2005, 153 community colleges spread across 17 states in India functioning.

The Madras Centre for Research and Development of Community Education (MCRDCE), Chennai is known all over the country today as the champion and facilitator of the Community College Movement in India. In its own right, it has emerged as an umbrella organization by consensus for coordinating the activities of Community Colleges. It has assisted the colleges in standardizing the curriculum, training of teachers, publishing textbooks and promotional literature, evolving an evaluation system and above all, in getting societal recognition and acceptance.

Through National Consultations, regional workshops and presentations the concept has been propagated. With the cooperation of the National Institute of Open Schooling (NIOS), New Delhi and Tamil Nadu Open University (TNOU) some of the colleges have been recognised for the vocational programmes run by them.

The publication under review provides a cogent and comprehensive documentation of the evolution and functioning of the Community College Movement and the MCRDCE as a facilitating, research and supporting agency.

The systematic manner in which the consultations took place, workshops were conducted and authorities such as governments and Universities were approached, have been brought out in an authentic manner. This publication will serve as a ready reckoner and guide for all those interested in the study of the Community College Concept, the steps taken to gain the acceptance of the society and the authorities.[12]

Community College Empowerment Endorsed, Alphonse, Xavier, (2005) Community College – Empowerment Endorsed: The History of Recognition and Accreditation of Community Colleges in India. MCRDCE Publication, Chennai.

The above book by Xavier Alphonse S.J., Director Madras Centre for Research and Development of Community Education, Chennai is highly informative venture about Community College Movement in India. All through the book Alphonse put his scholarly efforts to highlight the efforts initiated by Madras Centre for Research and Development of Community Education (MCRDCE), Chennai for recognition and accreditation of community colleges in India.

The editor of the book who is also the father of Community College movement of India has a definite and purposeful vision for accomplishment of a mission that is primarily aimed at empowerment of the socio-economically weaker and disadvantaged sections of society through their skills development, thus providing education for a livelihood.

The book has been exclusively covering the efforts and initiatives undertaken by Alphonse and MCRDCE, Chennai to focus the concept of community college as an alternate system of education. The book has ten chapters starting from history of the process of recognition to efforts with Ministry of Human Resource Development, Government of India towards a part of national system of education.

Chapter I of the book deals with various efforts in process of recognition starting from April 1997, when Madras Community College started its efforts for recognition with the Government of Tamil Nadu to October 2005, when the recognition is extended to community colleges in other parts of India by Tamil Nadu Open University.

Chapter–II of the book is about consultations and workshops of community colleges and its major recommendations are:

- To create autonomous accreditation agencies which will device norms, guidance and prescribe standards for all community colleges of the country.
- The nature of the community college movements is to be kept autonomous in all aspects: Academic, Administrative and Functional.
- Recognition of MHRD as an alternative system of education and to include in the 10th Five year plan.

Chapter – III of the book deals with how the MHRD Government of India and State Government get involved in the process of affiliation of community colleges. Chapter – IV is about evaluative study of the working of community college movement in Tamil Nadu which recommended that the community colleges should be de-linked from the University affiliation system. The next three chapters are about Accreditation of National Institute of Open Schooling and IGNOU; Diplomas and Certificates of Community Colleges and accreditation by Tamil Nadu Open University to different courses of Community colleges respectively. Chapter – VIII deals with Indian Community College system and next chapter is about fourth national consultation of community colleges in India and last part deals with efforts with MHRD, Government of India.

The Community College Movement started in India in 1995 with the inspiration and model of the system from U.S.A. The Madras Centre for Research and Development of Community Education (MCRDCE), Chennai is co-ordinating to promote the concept and its implementation in India. Within a decade it has helped in the establishment of 153 community colleges: has published 11 books as promotional literature and four textbooks of life coping skills, conducted over 100 workshops to propagate the concept.

The Community College is an alternative system of education, that seeks empowerment of the disadvantaged and the underprivileged sections of the society by providing them appropriate skills development leading to gainful employment. In essence the community college promotes job-oriented, work-related, skill based and life-coping education.

Throughout the book efforts have been made by the editor to cover all the events / aspects of recognition and accreditation of community colleges of India. It will be beneficial for all the stakeholders of alternative education to enrich their knowledge about movement for process of recognition and accreditation.

Overall it is a well planned book. Dr. Alphonse has put his efforts in organizing the events in details pertaining to all the aspects discussed in ten chapters of the book. Though within a decade, community college could find a mention in tenth five year plan but it is yet to receive national acceptance. Out of the 17 States / UT where the community college has been established, only four states have more than five colleges of this type. It is yet to receive autonomous status with regard to affiliation. The success story of Tamil Nadu should set an example for others as a successful alternate education.[13]

Inauguration of ICRDCE

Article 1 : Dropping the dropout rate

'Knowledge and skill-based human resource is the need of the hour. With just 10 per cent of students reaching the higher education-level, we need to reduce the ratio of school dropouts', said Sukadeo Thorat, Chairman, University Grants Commission (UGC).

Inaugurating the Indian Centre for Research and Development of Community Education (ICRDCE), an upgraded centre of Madras Centre for Research and Development of Community Education (MCRDCE) in Chennai Thorat said, "Around 41 per cent of students dropout of high school for reasons such as poverty, family compulsions and others. It is this section that ICRDCE would be concentrating in by offering skill and demand based courses to improve employability among them", he added.

Thorat also said, 'at an increased demographic profile we should have a large educated workforce. For this, we need to channelise our human capability by implementing education to the rural and ordinary people.'

Speaking on the occasion, Dr. Palanichamy, Vice-Chancellor, Tamil Nadu Open University (TNOU), said, 'Community college acts as a catalyst to the rural people and education.'

TNOU alone has affiliated 79-89 colleges which offer nine diploma programmes like desktop publishing (DTP), four - wheel mechanism and catering services.

Xavier Alphonse S.J., director of ICRDCE, and Ramamurthy Naidu, member, University Grants Commission, were also present on the occasion.[14]

Article 2 : ICRDCE launched in Chennai

The Indian Centre for Research and Development of Community Education (ICRDCE) was launched on September 1 by UGC Chairman Sukhadeo Thorat in the presence of the centre's Chairman Rev. Dr. M. Devadoss

The Centre will continue to serve the community colleges, which seek to reduce school dropout rates through skills development and provide them education for livelihood chances.

ICRDCE's director Xavier Alphonse sketched the milestones of Madras Centre for Research and Development of Community Education (MCRDCE) which is being upgraded to ICRDCE. On the occasion, three books were released: *English Made Easy, Tears into Cheers* and *back to the Villages.* The Centre has also helped 933 Tsunami-affected young men and women through 30 Community Colleges and has shown them the way for permanent livelihood through job placement.

He noted that the Community College movement which began in India 11years ago aimed at empowerment of the disadvantaged through appropriate skills development leading to gainful employment, thus making a qualitative difference in the lives of the urban poor, rural poor, tribal poor and women in collaboration with local industrial establishments, potential employers and community leaders.

MCRDCE, Chennai, an initiative of Madurai Jesuit Province and a unit of Loyola Technical Institute Society (LTI), Madurai, was founded in 1999. It has turned into a facilitating and coordinating agency for community colleges in the country. It has been involved in the preparation, establishment, monitoring and evaluation of 180 Community Colleges in 21 states of India.

Tamil Nadu Open University has recognised 98 Community Colleges as Vocational Programme Centres all over the country. Yashwantrao Chavan Maharashtra Open University, Nashik, is going to recognise the Community colleges in Maharashtra, Goa and Gujarat. The Ministry of Human Resource Development, Government of India, and the various State Governments are considering the possibility of recognition at the local and national levels.

A profile of 33,853 students attending 132 Community Colleges from different parts of India shows that 75 per cent are women, 90 per cent come from socially backward groups (SC, ST, MBC, BC,) 89 per cent are economically poor (monthly family income below Rs. 3,000 and 93 per cent educationally weaker sections (who cannot go for further education school dropouts, below class X, class X passed, class XII passed). The centre will function from October 2006.

ICRDCE launched at Chennai

The Indian Centre for Research and Development of Community Education (ICRDCE) was launched recently by the Prof. Sukhadeo Thorat, Chairman, University Grants Commission in the presence of its Chairman, ICRDCE Dr. Devadoss, S.J., head of the Jesuits of Tamil Nadu Province. The Centre will continue to serve the Community Colleges in India. The guest of honour hoped that the Centre through the Community Colleges will empower the School Dropouts through skill development providing them education for livelihood.

Dr. Palanichamy, Vice-Chancellor, Tamil Nadu Open University (TNOU), Dr. Thangamuthu, Vice Chancellor, Bharathidasan University, Trichy, Prof. Ramamurthy Naidu, Member, UGC, Prof. K. Aludiapillai, Former Secretary to Government of Tamil Nadu, Dr. Sr. Annamma Philip, Principal, Stella Maris College, Mr. Cletus Babu, Chairman, SCAD Group of Institutions, Tirunelveli, Rev. Fr. Boniface Jeyaraj, S.J., Rector, Loyola College, Chennai were felicitated on the occasion.

Dr. Xavier Alphonse, S.J., the Director of the Centre sketched the milestones of MCRDCE which is being upgraded to ICRDCE. On the occasion of the inauguration, three books were released: "*English Made Easy*", *Tears into Cheers*" and "*Back to the Villages*." The Centre has also helped 933 Tsunami affected young men and women through 30 Community Colleges and has shown them the way for permanent livelihood through job placement.

The Community College Movement in India started in 1995. It is eleven years old. It aims at the empowerment of the disadvantaged through appropriate skills development leading to gainful employment, thus making a qualitative difference in the lives of the urban poor, rural poor, tribal poor and women in collaboration with local industrial establishments and potential employers, community leaders after taking into account the opportunities available for employment and self-employment in the local area.

The Madras Centre for Research and Development of Community Education (MCRDCE), Chennai is an initiative of Madurai Jesuit Province and a unit of Loyola Technical Institute Society (LTI), Madurai. It was started in January 1999. It is a facilitating and coordinating agency for Community Colleges in India. It has been involved in the preparation, establishment, monitoring and evaluation of 180 Community Colleges in 21 States of India. It has also trained 1,057 teachers. The Centre has conducted 39 workshops involving 800 NGOs, 1,728 participants and has also organised five important National Consultations and 10 Regional Consultations among Community Colleges. It has also prepared basic curriculum material and supplied to all these Community Colleges. It has published 14 books and 33 articles in the leading educational journals of India and abroad on the concept and implementation of the system. The Centre also has upto date documentation on the movement by way of newspaper clippings, video, audiotapes, photographs, etc. The Tamil Nadu Open University (TNOU) has recognised 98 Community Colleges as Vocational Programme Centres all over the country. The Yashwantrao Chavan Maharashtra Open University (YCMOU), Nashik is going to recognise the Community Colleges in the States of Maharashtra, Goa and Gujarat. The Ministry of Human Resource Development, Government of India and the various State Governments are considering the possibility of recognition at the local national levels.

The unique achievement of the movement is the empowerment of the disadvantaged groups leading to up-gradation of their educational standards resulting in alleviation of 132 Community Colleges from different parts of India shows that 75% are women, 90% come from socially backward groups (SC, ST, MBC, BC), 89% are economically poor (monthly family income below Rs. 3,000 and 93% educationally weaker sections or cannot go for further education (School dropouts, below 10th, 10th passed, 12th passed). A breakup by religions shows that 55% are Hindus, 41% are Christians, 3% are Muslims and 1% are Buddhists. After passing through the Community College System 75% of the students are employed. In most cases their family income has been doubled. It has led to [poverty alleviation through income generation. The concept has become a secular one transcending religions, castes and languages. It is truly a nation and capacity building exercise.

As it is emerging as an Indian, there is a need for larger space for its various activities. The funding agency which has been supporting the movement for the last four years has supported the initiative. The Address of the centre is 'Old No. 23, New No. 30, Veerasamy Street, Egmore, Chennai – 600 008'.

Indian Community Colleges showing Progress

From a humble beginning in the mid 1990s, Madras Community College was one of the first community colleges to be established in India. Today there are 153 community colleges in 17 states. Fr. Xavier Alphonse, director of the Madras Centre for Research and Development of Community Education, states, "The community colleges promote job oriented, work related, skill based and life coping education." The primary beneficiaries of these educational services are urban and rural poor, tribal poor, women and early school leavers. The community colleges report a collective 75 per cent job placement rate.

Observers in India have begun calling attention to an alarming trend. While much has been written about the country's economic development attributed to globalisation, the rate of growth of job creation has declined substantially. There is mounting concern about lack of employment opportunities in rural areas. This may be an opportunity for the community colleges to assist with rural economic growth through work force development.

The community college concept in India is a secular one attempting to break down barriers of region, religion, caste, language and educational qualification. While the community colleges continue to show great progress and promise, they are still operating without recognition of approved education bodies in the country.

However, there appears to be light at the end of the tunnel as a national committee has been established by the Ministry for Human Resource Development to explore the possible recognition of community colleges. The feeling is that if community colleges are indeed recognised, their enrolments will increase and more people will benefit.

Learning for Livelihood

The community college movement, an innovative system of education aimed at empowering the disadvantaged sections of society, has today become a national phenomenon.

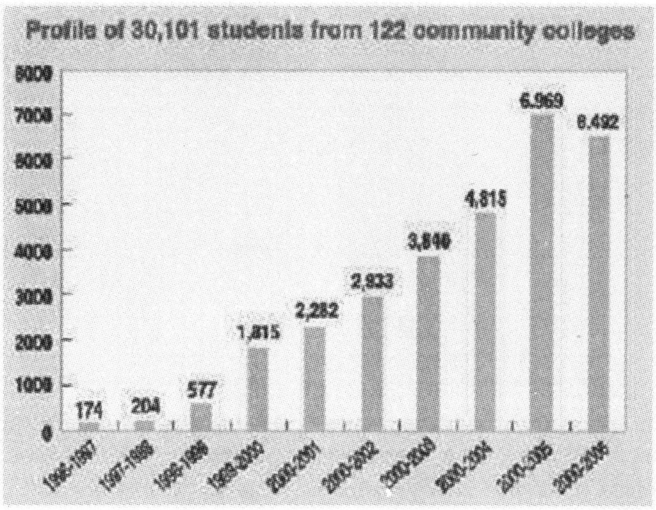

The community college movement has been growing in India ever since it began in 1995 with the opening of the Pondicherry University Community College. The Archdiocese of Madras, Mylapore, was the first non-governmental organization to start a community college, the Madras Community College, in 1996. Today there are 153 community colleges across 17 States. The movement has so far helped 35,000 students from the socially, economically and educationally backward groups. Thus, it has become a national phenomenon.

This innovative alternative system of education is aimed at the empowerment of the disadvantaged and underprivileged sections of society through appropriate skills development leading to gainful employment in collaboration with the local industry and community. The vision of the community college is of the community, for the community and by the community and to produce responsible citizens. In collaboration with the local industry, the community colleges promote job-oriented, work-related, skill-based and life-coping education.

The key words of the community college system are access, flexibility in curriculum and teaching methodology, cost-effectiveness and equal opportunity. In collaboration with the industrial, commercial and service sectors of the local area, in response to the social needs and issues of the local community, the college provides internship and job placement within the local area and promotes self-employment and small business development. There is also an attempt to evolve a profile exclusively for the rural community college.

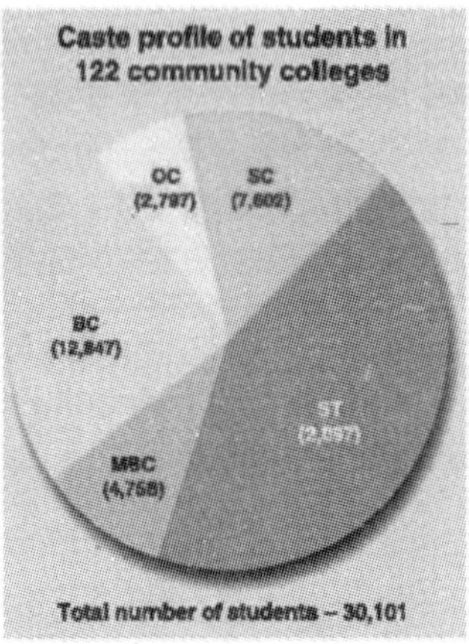

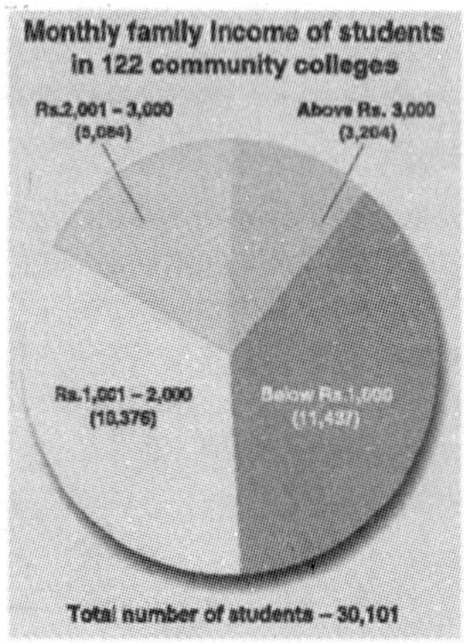

The concept of community colleges has become the need of the hour in view of the elimination and exclusion of children from the education system (154 million of the 160 million who go to the first standard in India are excluded from the formal system); the mismatch between education and employment; the problems of unemployment, under-employment and unemployability (for every 100 workers employed, six are unemployed, 16 are unable to earn $1 per person a day, (*The Hindu* June 28, 2001); and the high rate of dropout.

In September 2002, 939 employment exchanges across the country had registered 4.16 crore candidates of whom 70 per cent are educated. (*Dinamani*, February 28, 2003)

According to data collected by the National Information Centre, Vellore, in December 2001, the dropout rates in Tamil Nadu in 2000-01 was 14.41 per cent at the primary level, 35.59 per cent at the middle school level, 57.59 per cent at the high school level and 82.30 per cent at the higher secondary level. A media report on January 9, 2002, stated that there were around 48 lakh 'non-school going' children (in the 6-14 age groups) in Tamil Nadu. It reported that although 63.04 lakh students got admitted in 31,052 schools across the State, the dropout rate was almost 36 per cent by the time they reached high school, of which 90 per cent are girls. The high percentage of dropouts at the high school and higher secondary levels highlight the need for an alternative system of education like the one offered by community colleges.

It is found that if 100 million students get enrolled in primary school, only about 30 million reach middle school and about 16 million in high/higher secondary school. Of the children in the 6-11 age group about 90-95 per cent are enrolled in primary school. At the secondary stage, that is, age group 11-15, only 48 per cent continue, and at the higher secondary stage, the 15-17 age group, only about 24 per cent are found to pursue their studies. In the 17-23 age group, only about 8 per cent study in the higher education institutions.

From these statistics, it is found that roughly, more than 50 per cent of the school children drop out at every stage. The question is what happens to all those youth in the 11-17 age groups who drop out?

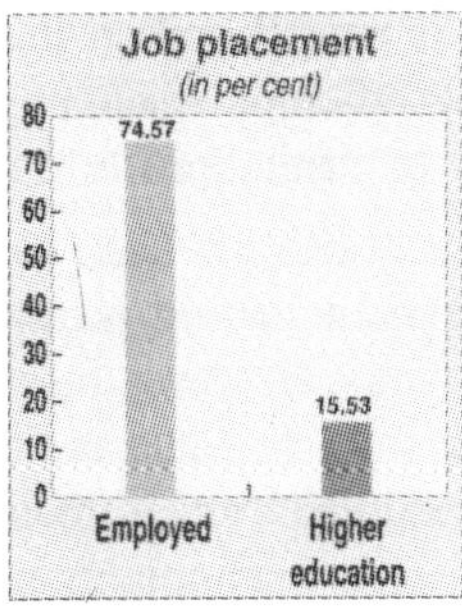

The community colleges in India offer diploma courses in health assistance/nursing assistance; pre-primary teacher training; DTP operation/ computer application; fashion designing and garment manufacture; house electrical/electrical work; air-conditioning and refrigeration; four-wheeler/ automobile mechanism; catering; plumbing technology; tailoring and embroidery; Tally accounting; medical lab technology; computer hardware; sales and marketing management; travel management; bakery and confectionery; cargo management; printing technology; hotel management, rural marketing; community enterprises; Information Technology; business accountancy and chartered accountancy, house keeping, and so on.

Achievements

The unique achievement of the community colleges has been the empowerment of the socially, economically and educationally backward sections of society. The Madras Centre for Research and Development of Community Education (MCRDE) has been able to gather data regarding 30,101 students from 122 community colleges. The break-up gives a complete picture of the target group served.

Women: 76 per cent; **Married** - 8 per cent (16-48 age group).

Qualification: Below Standard X passed - 19 per cent; X passed - 26 per cent; XII passed - 47 per cent; Graduate degree - 8 per cent.

Caste: Scheduled Caste - 25 per cent; Scheduled Tribe - 7 per cent; Most Backward Classes - 16 per cent; Backward Classes - 45 per cent; Other communities - 9 per cent.

Monthly family income: Below Rs.1,000 - 38 per cent; Below Rs. 2,000 - 34 pet cent; Below Rs. 3,000 - 17 per cent; Above Rs. 3,000 - 11 per cent.

Religion: Hindus - 54 per cent; Christians - 43 per cent; Muslims - 3 per cent.

The average percentage of job placement up to 2005 is 75 per cent . Thus, the concept is totally a secular one, breaking all barriers of religion, caste, region, language and educational qualification.

A community college is established on the basis of a thorough need analysis of employment and self-employment opportunities in the local area. The MCRDCE has helped 16 institutions to do their need analysis.

The community college system has been working successfully with 75 per cent job placement without getting recognition from any approved educational bodies of the country. However, most of the community colleges feel the need for recognition from the State and Central governments, which would facilitate the horizontal and vertical mobility of their students. The MCRDCE has succeeded in convincing the State and Central governments to accord recognition and accreditation for the system and approve student-centered funding. The issue of accreditation was examined by the National Institute of Open Schooling (NIOS), under the Ministry of Human Resource Development (MHRD). The NIOS has given accreditation to 18 community colleges. The Tamil Nadu Open University has recognized 80 community colleges as approved vocational programme centres with nine recognized job-oriented courses. The University of Madras has submitted a comprehensive document on the "Indian Community College System" to the MHRD and the University Grants Commission.

The National Committee set up by the MHRD is preparing its recommendations to be submitted to Human Resource Development Minister Arjun Singh. (This writer is a member of the committee.)

The community college system has found a mention in the Tenth Plan. Chapter 2.4 Vocational Education of the Plan document says: "There should be focus on convergence of schemes like the Sarva Shiksha Abhiyan, Adult Education and Vocational Education Programme at Schools, ITIs, Polytechnics, Community Colleges, etc."

The system has reached the shores of the African continent. There were eight representatives from South Africa, Lesotho, Tanzania, Kenya and Uganda for the 15th Teachers Training programme conducted by the MCRDCE in November 2005. The team had plans to start five community colleges by June 2006. The Indian concept has been recognized by the American Association of Community Colleges and the Community Colleges for International Development, U.S. The American Community College teachers have shown keen interest in the Indian community college system.

Chennai at a Glance: Employment and Placement (2001-2005)

Areas of Employment	*Total Number of Units in the Area of Employment*	*Total Number of Jobs up to 2005*
Air-conditioning and Refrigeration	142	909
Automobile Technology	171	992
Beautician and Health care	76	308
Bakery and Confectionery	80	266
Book Publication	129	548
Computer Software	149	13,306
Computer Hardware	89	1,611
Courier Service	148	4,114
Construction Management	118	3,764
Cargo Management	140	1,414
Electrical and Electronics	93	474
Amusement Parks	4	400
Furniture making	175	4,228
Hotel and Hospitality Service	396	16,394
Hospital and allied Services	255	9,626
Interior Decoration	194	2,968
Medical lab technician	63	227
Leather Garments and Export	652	34,425
Multi Mechanism	80	2,232
Printing technology	787	8,027
Commercial Photography	92	478
Retail sales and marketing	474	12,324
Pre-School Teacher	344	4,985
Security management	88	16,773
Travel and Tourism Management	505	6,363
Total		**1,48,156**

The Rural Initiative

More than 72 per cent of the rural population is unable to make a decent living mainly because of the lack of regular employment and income generation. Creating gainful employment opportunities by linking agriculture and rural development with education and livelihood is the biggest challenge facing the community college movement. The emerging trend in areas of agriculture and rural development is to rise up to international standards and it has become necessary to harness the human resource and manpower potential of the rural community to meet this need.

A rural community college, it was felt, could fulfill the requirement of empowering the rural people through skills, education for self-employment as well as through group employment. A rural community college essentially aims at building capacity; improving talents; tapping resources and potentialities; providing skills for self-employment; creating job opportunities; giving more field-oriented training with practical inputs; training rural youth in traditional sectors; enhancing collaboration between the government and the service sector; facilitating self-reliant initiatives; making interested youth upscale their education and skills; transforming the quality of life of the rural poor; initiating sustainable livelihood options for poverty alleviation; and empowering rural people through integrated development.

In this context, the opportunities for regular employment and income generation in rural areas can be grouped into on-farm and off-farm activities. Initially, agro-based activities cannot provide adequate opportunities for landless labourers. But, subsequently, with optimum use of resources and enhanced productivity, demand for labour will rise and even the landless labourers will have increased employment opportunities with improvement in agricultural productivity. Job opportunities for ancillary services will also increase and landless labourers will be able to take advantage of this situation. Based on the above rural development focus, two community colleges were started at Siruganur in Tamil Nadu and Lachragarh in Jharkhand.

The Ertram Rural Community College is situated at the Human Resource Development Training Centre of VOICE Trust at Siruganur village in Mannachanallur Block in Trichy. Siruganur is one of the 38 village panchayats of Mannachanallur Block. VOICE (Voice for the Oppressed through Integrated Community Emancipation) Trust was registered in 1985 as a non-profit and voluntary organisation. The trust is involved in various social action initiatives for the disadvantaged groups, especially, women, children, landless and small farmers, unemployed youth, and the disabled, destitute and aged.

The Ertram College conducts diploma courses in sustainable farming systems for integrated rural development; pre-primary teacher training; house electrician; DTP operator; plumbing technology; fashion designing and garment making.

A Meaningful Partnership

The success of the community college depends on the active participation and collaboration of the industrial, rural, agricultural, commercial and service organisations of the locality concerned. These sectors assist the community college in five different ways: designing the curriculum for various job-oriented courses; deputing their personnel to serve as members on the advisory board; providing part-time instructors; providing training for students in their workplace; and offering job placement service. In some cases a memorandum of understanding is signed with the local industries in all the five areas of collaboration. Representatives from the various sectors could even serve on the governing body of the community college.

Says B.T. Bangera, managing director of Hi-Tech Arai Ltd., Madurai, "There is no dearth of manpower in Madurai. If am not mistaken, more than one lakh youth who have migrated from villages around Madurai, are unemployed. This is in addition to the local youth who pass out from the Industrial Training Institute or senior secondary schools every year.

Hi-Tech Arai has a joint venture with M/s Arai Seisakusho Ltd., Japan, M/s Mitsubishi Corpn, Japan and M/s Japan International Development Organisation Ltd., Tokup. In 1990, the company was a family-owned small-scale business with an annual turn over of Rs. 80 lakhs. In 2001 its turnover touched Rs. 70 crores and the company employed more than 580 persons. "Achieving such phenomenal growth was possible by focussing on human resource development," says Bangera.

"In today's globalised environment with global competition, the only way to survive is by producing world-class products for which we need world-class employees. Unfortunately the regular stream of education, although it imparts knowledge to students, does not impart the appropriate work culture and mind set to produce quality products. By the time the students find employment in the industry it is much too late for them to adapt themselves to the work culture required."

It is in this context that Hi-Tech Arai signed an MoU with the Madurai Community College (MCC), as its industrial partner. "The idea was to associate with an educational institution that was not bogged down with age-old rules and regulations, inflexible teaching content and methods. Being a community college we wanted the institution to impart training that is relevant to the community in and around Madurai. Hi-Tech Arai wanted MCC to help it in two ways:

Convert the mindset of existing employees to fit into TQM [Total Quality Management] philosophy to prepare them to face global competition and get employees at the lowest level who could fit straightaway into the existing work culture in the organisation."

In this context, Hi-Tech Arai uses MCC to conduct tailor-made programmes to the operators so that they think of TQM, zero defect, total productive maintenance, quality control circle movement, good housekeeping, Kaizen [continuous improvement] and develop leadership among workmen. As a result, today one of the four units with about 80 operators runs without any supervisor," Bangera says. "To spread this culture in the industry, we have even developed an employee competence development programme with MCC," he said. According to Senthilnathan, managing director of Premier System and Peripherals, students of MCC are trained to recognise the demands of the industry and function accordingly. "This service of MCC is laudable and industrialists are privileged to be associated with the college," he added.

M. Joseph, proprietor of Zion Refrigeration and a member of the advisory board of MCC since 1998, says, "I see MCC as an extraordinary college for the academically, economically and socially disadvantaged groups."

D. Ramasamy, chief executive officer of 'E Plus Plus' in Madurai, providing sales and services of computers for the past 10 years, is all praise for the "high standard of technical knowledge" and field training provided by the community college.

Other organisations associated with MCC - Susee Car and Trucks Pvt. Ltd, Kalayani Associates Pvt. Ltd. (Group), Sai Engineering Company and Madura Park Inn - are unanimous that MCC promotes systematic acquisition of skills by identifying the students' areas of interest and guiding them in their development.

A Resource Centre

As the community college concept began gaining acceptance, the need for a coordinating agency to help and serve the movement better began to be felt. In response to this need, the Madras Centre for Research and Development of Community Education (MCRDCE), an undertaking of the Jesuits of Tamil Nadu Province, was started in January 1999. The following are the objectives of the MCRDCE: to include the excluded; match education with employment; have close links with industries; promote the participation of the community; develop skills and competencies; and enhance employability. The MCRDCE responds to the dynamism of the community college movement in India; provides a resource centre with books and study materials; helps in the process of curriculum development; offers training programmes for the community college teachers and administrators; evolves methods of evaluation and assessment of skills; publishes books and articles; popularises the concept all over the country; documents the process and evolution of the community college movement; interacts with the State and

Central governments, universities and the University Grants Commission in an effort to make them recognise and accept the community college system as an educational alternative; to replicate the model all over the country with the help of the Union Human Resource Development Ministry; and to enter into international networking of community colleges in the United States, Britain, Germany, Australia, South Africa and Canada.

The MCRDCE has worked with 800 non-governmental organizations in 23 States. The centre is a storehouse of resource material and documentation.

Tsunami-affected Students

Community Colleges have responded to the needs of the tsunami-affected people of Tamil Nadu. As a first step in this direction, consultations were held in different parts of the State in April, May and June with the beneficiary groups.

Thirty community colleges have come forward to enrol the tsunami-affected people. The training cost for 958 students will be provided by the MCRDCE. Special efforts have been made to start community colleges exclusively for the tsunami-affected people.

The Tabor Community College in Mahabalipuram has enrolled 240 students; the Karaikal Community College 410 students; the Karaikal Community College (CEDA TRUST) 76 students; St. Joseph's Community College, Nagapattinam, 100 students; and ALC Community College, Cuddalore, 100 students. These colleges are situated in the tsunami-affected area so that the affected young men and women can have access to skills development.

10

Community Colleges: An Evaluation

Introduction

The Second Convocation of the Tamil Nadu Open University (TNOU) was conducted on the 11th of January 2007 at Chennai, presided over by the Chancellor and Governor of Tamil Nadu His Excellency Surjit Singh Barnala. This was the first time in a Convocation of a University the students from Community Colleges received their diplomas and the rank holders were honoured, even those below 10th Standard qualification.

Association with Tamil Nadu Open University (TNOU)

A milestone in the Community College movement was the recognition given to 67 Community Colleges as Vocational Programme Centres of TNOU in 2005. During the academic year, 4,711 students were enrolled as students of this Open University. They did the following Vocational programmes leading to Skills development and showing the way to earn their livelihood.

1. Diploma in Pre Primary Teachers Training
2. Diploma in Health Assistant Course
3. Diploma in Refrigeration and Air Conditioning Technician Course
4. Diploma in Fashion Design and Garment Making
5. Diploma in Four Wheeler Mechanism.
6. Diploma in Plumbing Technology
7. Diploma in Catering Assistant Course
8. Diploma in House Electrician Course
9. Diploma in DTP Operator Course

During the completion of these skill-based programmes, the students also did Life Coping Skills, Communication Skills and Work Skills. The Diploma was for 36 Credits (Life Coping Skills – 8 Credits, Communication

Skills – 8 Credits and Trade Skills – 20 Credits including Internship – Total Number of Credits – 36 Credits. One Credit – 30 hours. Total Numbers of Hours – 36 × 30 = 1,080 Hours)

The Achievements of the Students

The achievements of these students from the socially, economically, educationally backward and disadvantaged groups cutting across the barriers of religion and caste are marvellous and praiseworthy. We have 87% passed and 12% have gone for higher education. 75% of them are placed in jobs. Among these students there were 933 students doing their programmes in 30 Community Colleges from the Tsunami affected areas. The students have won seven Gold Medals (first ranks) in seven programmes and there have been 38 rank holders from the Community Colleges among the 47 ranks awarded during the Convocation.

Lessons Learnt and Future Direction

1. Opportunity is the key to success. The Urban poor, the rural poor and women can come up in their lives if they are given an opportunity as we have done in the Colleges. The Community Colleges can be called "Opportunity Colleges".
2. The formation given for jobs should be holistic. The training process should not be limited only to trade skills but life coping skills in terms of personal skills, coping mechanisms, preparation for employment, interview skills and communication skills.
3. Through the Community Colleges, the young men and women from the marginalised groups are making an entry into the main stream. They are not the left outs of the society.
4. There is the urgent need to open the doors of Higher Education to these young men and women by building up a system of vertical mobility through Open Universities and Distance learning to make a lateral entry into the Second year degree programme in their respective disciplines.
5. Poverty, Low Economic and Caste Status, being in the rural areas, being women, being affected by disasters like Tsunami are not obstacles to go up the ladder in society.
6. Community College System is emerging as an alternative system of education for all school dropouts in the country.
7. Skills Development in both trade and soft skills will fetch employment in the context of globalization and privatization thus making the Community College as a democratic response to globalization.

8. The Community College should become a national phenomenon since it is already becoming 190 Community Colleges in 19 States of India.

The Process towards National Recognition

The Community College Movement has attracted the attention of the Government of India. Today it has found a place in the working paper of HRD and UGC submitted to the Planning Commission requesting the Community College to be added as a scheme in the XI Five Year Plan. We are requesting the Government for National Recognition, Scholarship to the students of weaker section of society and the possibility of vertical mobility. Such a type of recognition would be a revolutionary measure in the history of Higher Education in India.

The Chairman of UGC has appointed a National Committee on Community Colleges headed by Dr. Xavier Alphonse, S.J., The committee met 125 representatives from 91 Community Colleges and received all their suggestions and recommendations.

The Committee has submitted its report to the UGC incorporating all the suggestions for further action. In the meantime the State Governments of Tamil Nadu and Haryana have come forward to start Community Colleges on their own. Dr. Xavier Alphhonse, S.J., attended the consultation with the Governor of Haryana, Chief Minister, the Finance Minister, the Education Minister and representatives of industry and Vice-President and faculty members of the Montgomery Community College, Maryland on the 2nd of April at Haryana Bhavan, New Delhi with the UGC Chairman, Vice-Chairman of AICTE and the Deputy Secretary of Education, Government of Tamil Nadu with the Vice Chancellor of the Tamil Nadu Open University. The Community College as an alternative system will get the official recognition in the next legislative assembly session of Tamil Nadu in May, 2007. The prospects are very bright for the system to be recognized to benefit the poor and the marginalised.[19]

Bhopal Community College

Bhopal Community College is an alternative system of education, which was launched by Asha Niketan Welfare on July 31, 2004 after conducting the study of "need Analysis" under the guidance of Rev. Dr. Pascal Topno, Archbishop of Bhopal and Fr. Xavier Alphonse, Director of ICRDCE and a member of UGC.

After three years, Fr. Xavier Alphonse had come to review and evaluate Bhopal Community. There were 75 participants, Dr. Pascal Topno, Fr. Xavier Alphonse, Fr. Mathew Vattakuzhy, Director of MP and CG region, Development expert DEFID for MP-USP, Sr. Anna and Sr. Esther from St. Mary's School and Fr. P. Soosai Principal of Bhopal Community College were present on the occasion. The programme commenced with lighting of lamp at 11.30 a.m. by Archbishop, Fr. Dr. Xavier Alphonse and other dignitaries followed by cordial welcome to all.

In the achievement of the college Dr. Palanichamy – Vice Chancellor of Tamil Nadu Open University (TNOU) inspected in colleges on 23rd April 2006 we are going into the process of getting recognition for Health Assistant and fashion designing courses. We have collaborated with many government and NGOs to give a great deal of exposure to our students and developed good and active Industrial partners who give their full cooperation in all the activities of colleges. The placements for our students start as 65 per cent in the first year (2004 – 05), 72 per cent in the second year (2005-06). The students are earning between Rs. 2000 to 3000 per month.

Eight computer hardware students (2005-06) have started" Kaizen Computing Solution.

Fr. Xavier Alphonse in his address appreciated the excellent performance of Bhopal community college and compared the student with "Discovery Channel" because it is in this institute the students with confidence and skill develop them and sustain them during job placement till their life.

Dr. Pascal Topno congratulated the efforts of Bhopal Community college and blessed the students that they come as the shining stars of this country. Dr. Shashi Rai, Member of the UGC too appreciated the effort of the college and promised to get scholarship for the student in future from UGC.

11

Community Colleges : An Interview with Fr. Xavier Alphonse

Fr. Xavier Alphonse, S.J., served as Principal of Loyola College during 92-95 and is currently the Director for ICRDCE which has pioneered the formation of Community Colleges initiating the implementation of an alternative system of education for the poor and downtrodden from 1995. Since then he has been involved in the preparation, establishment, monitoring and evaluation of 214 Community Colleges in 20 States of India. Besides training well over 1200 teachers, he has conducted 48 Workshops involving 950 NGOs, 2179 participants and has also organized 6 important National Consultations and 41 Regional Consultations among Community Colleges. In addition to the basic curriculum material he had prepared and supplied to all the Community Colleges, Fr. Xavier has published 21 books and 35 articles in the leading educational journals of India and abroad on the concept and implementation of the system. He was appointed as Chairman of National Committee on Community Colleges to discuss the concepts and methodology for establishment and functioning of Community Colleges, was appointed by UGC in January 2007 and served as a member of various UGC committees. Considered as an authority on College Autonomy in India, he was appointed as member of UGC and has led many teams to inspect Deemed to be Universities and Colleges all over the country. In recognition of all his achievements and contributions, Dr. Xavier Alphonse has been conferred with thirteen prestigious awards.

What are Community Colleges?

It's an alternative system of education. Why do I call it so? It gives a second chance to those who've dropped out of school. It provides opportunity for those who otherwise would have been excluded. It is empowerment through skills development for the urban, rural and tribal poor.

Basically the motto reads as "Including the Excluded, Giving the best to the Least". In India, exclusion takes place on account of two reasons. One is social exclusion on the basis of caste. Most people belonging to the lower caste do not have opportunity for higher education, skills training or availing decent jobs. Second is economic exclusion, on account of poverty, because of which there's no upward mobility.

We do have a second motto called "Giving the Best to the Least." For example, though India may rank 7th in the terms of software production in the Information technology revolution, more than 70 per cent of people in India are excluded from this revolution. So, part of our response is to give computer training to the least of these left outside. To summarise it, community colleges give access. Access is given by removing blockades such as minimum qualification and age bar. Secondly, what is noteworthy is the flexibility of the curriculum which is designed for the varying aptitude of the students and their ability to grasp and assimilate information. They may be slow or fast learners and categorized as urban or rural learners. Thirdly, if we have to reach out to the poor it has to be at an affordable cost. The course amounts to Rs. 5, 000 for the annual training. Because it is for the poor, quality in training should not be compromised. Finally, the process aims towards providing life and job placement. Essentially, it is education for livelihood. In the past, the national discourse on education was for knowledge but today it is education for livelihood.

How Did the Concept Originate and Establish itself in India?

Community colleges are popular in several Western countries though they may be called by different names. USA had introduced the idea 100 years ago especially for those who came back from war, who were conscripted for military services and training. When they returned, they couldn't fit into schools and colleges as many had not completed school nor enter into colleges for lack of necessary qualifications. It was President Truman who started Land Grant Colleges which later went on to be called Community Colleges.

The scope was enlarged to include all those who could not enter into higher education but who could do so eventually by going through the community colleges as a bridge course. There are at least 1,400 community colleges spread across all the States in the U.S. They are supported one-third by the Federal government grant, one-third by the County and the other one-third by the tuition fees. Universities like Harvard, Yale or Berkeley may charge around 18,000 to 30,000 dollars a year, but for community college students the fees will be as low as 1,100 dollars. The training period is for two years with 66 credits which will be accepted by formal and conventional Universities. They enter into higher education. Some colleges have around

40,000 students in multiple shifts allowing students to work and at the same time, do the training. Hispanics, African-Americans and other communities who want to improve their quality of life choose community colleges. The government is supportive and the movement is big.

What got you Interested in the Concept and Practice of Community Colleges?

I never knew the concept till 1995. Back then I served as the Principal for Loyola College. When we talk about the education scenario in India, we need to address four issues primarily. One is exclusion elimination. Around 160 million children go to standard one, eventually around 153 million drop out and only 7 million make it to higher education. Though today we have 343 Universities and 18,720 colleges in the country. Our enrollment has not even touched 10 per cent. So, what happens to the millions who get excluded in the process? Do they have any alternative? Community Colleges are that alternative system. Secondly, even in the formal colleges which offer engineering, medical, architecture, pharmacy or other professional courses and conventional colleges which with its arts and sciences courses, there is a big mismatch between education and employment. The present statistics point out that nearly 40 million people are unemployed, even after registering themselves in the employment exchanges. These are people who've completed their formal education but remain unemployed because they do not have skills which industries are looking for. With the changing scenario in the industry and job markets, these people do not have the skills that could keep pace with the growing demands in the employment market.

The third problem is capability poverty in India. When you consider 229 million people below the poverty line we have nearly 554 million people without skills in our country. It's such a huge wastage of human resources. We are confronted with 75 per cent of the rural poor. The fourth issue is the number of school dropouts. Among the dropouts, nearly 50 per cent of them drop out from the fifth standard and 30 per cent drop out from eight standard and the other 20 per cent drop out completely out of standard tenth. Even in Tamil Nadu, nearly 83 per cent don't enter colleges after their 12th standard.

In the Past, the National Discourse on Education was for Knowledge but Today it is Education for Livelihood.

After my tenure as Principal of Loyola College, I went to the US for a year to study the community college system, and interacted with the students, staff, industrial partners, the governing boards. I found the system which offered huge opportunities for the poor to be excellent. It then dawned on me to introduce the system in India.

How do you Categorize your Target Groups?

We have identified four target groups – tenth failed, tenth passed, twelfth failed and twelfth passed. We offer them a certificate programme in a particular skill like electrical, carpentry, masons, plumbing etc. For the tenth passed, twelfth failed and passed, we give a diploma. The certificate is for 22 weeks whereas the diploma is for 54 weeks. The courses offered are on various trades that are wanted in the local area.

What are Some Prerequisites for the Success of Community College?

In order to start a community college, the most important step is the need analysis of employment and self employment opportunities in the local area. This is the backbone. Only then can the courses be fixed and training be offered.

A vital aspect in the community colleges is the industry – institution linkages. Community colleges have around 200 industrial partners from hospitals, mechanic workshops, hotels, DTP centres, computer hardware and several other industry trades.

For this, a need analysis is so vital without which you cannot address the employment needs in the local area. In the final analysis one cannot orient the training programmes toward those needs.

In the last 13 years, there are now around 220 community colleges. With the primary aim of job placement, these colleges have trained around 60,000 students with 90 per cent employment placement. The rest have pursued higher education.

How are Community Colleges Different from Vocational Training Institutes?

Where we differ from the ITIs, Polytechnics and other vocational training institutes is that we've got clear-cut differences in our training methodology. There are four parts in our training modules. The first part is what we call Life Skills which is further divided into five segments. The first one is Life-Coping Skills, where personal transformation takes place. Areas like self respect, positive thinking, decision-making, problem-solving, stress management and time management are handled. Modules dealing with coping with fear, loneliness, sexuality, HIV/AIDS, substance abuse, anger, including interview skills and presentation skills are also taught. These are covered in seven weeks time.

Apart from this we cover a course on Communication skills. We have created uniquely designed textbooks to deal with different skills like Spoken English, Computer hardware. We are now preparing materials on entrepreneurship. We must not only raise skilled job seekers but job creators and thereby promote self employment.

The 22 weeks really help the student who has gone through social, economical, psychological disadvantages or is suffering from deep seated inferiority complex or a sense of failure, disappointment and disillusionment. In fact, after the life skills programme, the student is able to channelize all their disadvantages into advantages and become self motivated to achieve in life. Whereas vocational training institutes do not touch this personal dimension in people. We believe that the person has to be transformed before we impart skills. Training skills without the necessary change in mindset and attitude will not produce well rounded human beings.

So in the community college systems we have three components – Attitude, Skills and Knowledge. Attitudinal formation is critical, secondly is the theoretical aspect of the work skills and thirdly the hands on experience in terms of internship. A nursing assistant must spend two months in a hospital. Similarly, a mechanic must work two months in a mechanic workshop.

We have the onsite supervisor to help the students in the internship. Since there are good tie ups with the industry, our college teachers are able to monitor and assist the students, after which the students come back for evaluation and prepare themselves for employment. Evaluation is done by the life skills teacher, work skills teacher and onsite supervisor and the individual student. If the student is not confident and needs further training, we provide them this facility with the sole aim that the student will find job placement. Vocational institutes don't provide this level of training.

What is the Role of the Industry in Community Colleges?

The active and dynamic ongoing relationship with the industry is of immense advantage. In several community colleges across India, many industry representatives themselves volunteer to teach and they take the students for onsite training. Because it provides a win-win situation for the industry, the community colleges and the poor who need employment. Industries feel socially responsible in such collaboration. They don't have to train people afresh since we do that. Several students in the rural community colleges display levels of talent and skills, so much so they are inducted during the internship process itself.

As someone pointed out, the community colleges are a democratic response to globalization. Globalization is inevitable and our community colleges can equip the poor with the required skills to face it.

They help community colleges in five primary areas. They help in the development of the curriculum. The industry requirement is spelt out by them. Secondly, they serve as members of the advisory boards in several community colleges. Thirdly, they come to teach as regular or part-time guest lecturers. Then, they take our students for internship and finally they place them in jobs. Many colleges have Memorandum of Understanding with the industries. For example, the Madurai Community College has an MOU with SUSI Autos, which services around 450 vehicles a month. The students from the college are absorbed in their services. In the recent past, we had organized a conference of around 200 delegates from the community colleges across India and around 100 delegates representing several industries. These industry delegates presented their requirements and interacted with colleges.

You serve as the Director for Indian Centre for Research and Development of Community Education (ICRDCE). What are its functions?

Our job is to facilitate and coordinate with over 200 community colleges. We identify the colleges. Usually, church congregations, diocesans and NGOs apply in our institute. If one is desirous of starting a community college, we first study the organization and its capabilities. We then help them to do the Need Analysis and the feasibility study. We recruit teachers and train them. We have conducted around 21 training programmes for 2000 teachers across India. It's critical to teach them curriculum on the changing and emerging needs in the market. ICRDCE involves in curriculum designing and publishes various text books and other publications. We also do the evaluation of the community colleges, the students and staff.

What Factors Led to its Formation?

Madras Community College in Chennai was the first community college in India. Many didn't understand the concept initially. After introducing the one year diploma programmes, the momentum picked up really well. When the movement grew to around hundred institutions or so, there was a great need for co-ordinating and facilitating in terms of establishing and monitoring, orientation, curriculum development, resource preparation, evaluation etc. Thus, ICRDCE was created as a co-ordinating agency and has played a vital role since its inception in the creation and monitoring of colleges, establishing linkages with industries, providing job placement. There is also an ongoing research done in the institute, through its documentation centre which collects relevant information from colleges. From 1993 we have documented the evolution of the colleges in terms of newspaper clippings, video tapes, details of each college with its history and growth. So the Institute was created out of a felt need among community colleges.

The ICRDCE has Crossed Several Milestones. What are its Greatest Achievements?

An important work that we do is to lobby with the State and the Central Governments for recognition and accreditation. We have succeeded with the TN government as they have passed a GO which states that community colleges have been recognized as centres for job training under TN Open University. The Indian Centre was instrumental in the composition and promulgation of the Tamil Nadu Government Order (G.O.) on community colleges. 118 colleges are under the TN Open University. The Chief Minister has apportioned Rs, 1 crore in the budget from which Rs. 1000 will be given to each student. Though the amount is small, the recognition is historic for the movement.

But where we've actually succeeded in implementing the scheme is the role played by service minded NGOs and Christian organizations as many of them have the vision/mission and the infrastructure to implement the schemes. However, we are secular in our approach in that we offer our services to anyone wanting to serve humanity. We have offered our services to Hindu, Muslim and Sikh organizations. The movement is now a national phenomenon.

Initially, we were called Madras Centre but after growing to a national level movement in 20 States in India, we changed our name to Indian Centre. But now we've expanded into the international arena with community colleges established in Papua New Guinea and other parts of Africa. We're expecting the President of Papua New Guinea to arrive here with around 53 teachers. When that takes place, we'll be called the International Centre. There are invitations from Thailand and Indonesia as well. The economic deprivation is similar in these places. As someone pointed out the community colleges are a democratic response to globalization. Globalization is inevitable and our community colleges can equip the poor with the required skills to face it.

Community Colleges haven't been Recognized yet in the Mainstream. What are some Roadblocks in the Way?

In the past the Government's priority has always been on primary, secondary and higher education. The Government never thought about or factored in the reality of drop outs in the previous 10 plans. But with the growing awareness of the community college model and its potential to help the poor, it is now finding its place in the 11th Plan. As a member in the UGC and chairman of the National Committee, we've been lobbying for the Central Government to recognize our system. The Knowledge Commission has indicated that at least 210 colleges need to be formed. Union Grants Commission has shown interest.

We follow a democratic process in our dealings with the government and others. We have, at least once in six months a meeting with all the community colleges. Decisions on directions are taken collectively through consultations and workshops. For example, we had dialogued with the colleges and only then joined the Tamil Nadu Open University. We are careful that our original spirit and ethos of community colleges and its vision for the poor are not lost in unwise decisions. There are risks of such a movement like ours getting in the wrong direction with the wrong people who'd want to commercialize on the idea.

How do you see Churches and Mission Organizations Realizing the Potential of Community Colleges and Starting them?

I think they'll play a significant role. If you look at history, it was the missionaries who bought the primary school to villages and started colleges. We need to relook at how our churches and missions need to get involved in nation-building today.

2009

Community College an Alternative to Include the Excluded in Higher Education

Education is the manifestation of knowledge already inherent in man. It is also a continuous process of perfecting the inherited as well asc learnt knowledge and skills to serve the society. It could be much better and useful when provided at a right stage. The number of schools, colleges and universities have increased manifold. Hcwever, the right type of education is not being imparted as students coming out of these institutions are unable to find suitable employment not being fully equipped to face life and its challenges.

It is necessary to ask the question, for whom these educational institutions exist if they do not prepare young men and women for life in the real world. Unemployment is persisting in all the developing countries and is increasing over the years. Indeed, education which is provided both through the formal as well as non-formal education centers has nct created confidence in the student community. On the other hand, they have made them depend upon the outside agencies. We need education which is not only competitive, but also seen to be fair, and closely linked to employment opportunities. Combating the two may satisfy better requirements of both ability and aspiration of the school leaving students.

Therefore, it is felt necessary to respond to the deficiencies of the vocational education system through proper industry-institutional linkage, competence assessment, on-the-job training on the basis of local needs. Hence, community college can be an alternative system of education to liberate and empower such desperate groups of society and to include the excluded in employment opportunities by imparting the needed skills for their livelihood.

The concept of community college is an innovative and recent phenomenon. Philosophically, community college is one that accept the responsibility for providing students both transfer to higher education regardless of financial resources and also prepare for some occupation. It is an institution which satisfies the demands of the community for post-higher secondary education and for middle-level manpower of the nation.

Community college is an American concept, but is not new to Indian education because it was already recommended by Sampurnananda Committee way back in 1962 to provide skills and work-oriented education to meet the needs of the students who have finished school. The original concept was according to Indian situation. However, it was started in India only in 1995.

Community college system specially focuses on the education for livelihood. It is expected to promote job-oriented, work-related, skills-based and life-coping education to the unreached section of the society. Therefore, it attempts to include the poor of both rural and urban areas and women.

Moreover, the idea of community college is considered to be an important part of restructuring Indian education. It has gained the international significance already, for dealing with large numbers and training of middle-level manpower for the economic and social needs of the nation. It is a new social invention to intervene structurally, between the school and the university though it is a part of the higher education and not of the school.

In India, it is intended to serve the students of the adolescent age-group, but it is open to everyone in the community including the very aged. Courses of study and duration are formulated in relation to the demands of the community, vocational choices and individual aptitudes and manpower requirements at different levels.

Need for the Study

Community colleges are spread over in Tamil Nadu State and of these Madras and Madurai Community colleges get due importance. Besides, the concentration of such colleges is found to be more in southern districts of Tamil Nadu. At present, there are a total of 32 community colleges functioning in Tirunelveli, Tuticorin and Kanyakumari districts. Of the total colleges found in these districts 46.9% are in Kanniyakumari, followed by Tirunelveli (37.5%), and Tuticorin (15.6%).

It is the right to recognize that the community college has an identity of its own though it is a part of the totality of education. IT occupies a strategic position and has productive relationship with higher secondary schools and college and university system. Hence, an attempt has been made to conduct an evaluative study on these colleges, and therefore, the present study was carried out on community colleges of these districts.

Objectives

The present study of community colleges was carried out with the following objectives:

(a) To understand the social-economic background of the students studying in community colleges;

(b) To assess the infrastructure facilities made available at the community colleges;

(c) To know the students' attitude towards such colleges;

(d) To elicit their opinion about the courses offered at community colleges; and

(e) To know the students' plan for future.

Research Design

Of the total of 32 community colleges found in these three districts, four of them were randomly selected as sample for the present study. From these four colleges, 100 students were selected as sample from a total of 220 students. Efforts were made to include the respondents from all the courses offered by these colleges.

The required data were collected from the selected 100 student-respondents by using structured interview schedule prepared for the purpose of the present study.

In addition to the interview schedule each college office was approached for collecting details regarding its origin, structure, composition, functioning, infrastructure, assets and governance by making personal visits.

The collected data were processed properly, analysed and interpreted to arrive at general conclusion by using descriptive methods. No attempt has been made to form hypotheses since the sample was too small.

Findings

Among the four community colleges studied, two of them are run by Christian institutions and the remaining two are run by non-government organisation (NGO) and a community's trust, each respectively. These organisations, which have ventured into community colleges, run many educational institutions like schools, polytechnics, I.T.I., and colleges. They were started between 1998 and 2000. They offer one-year Diploma programme in Female Nursing Assistance, Four Wheeler Mechanism, Medical Laboratory Technology, Computer Applications, Printing Technology, Computer Technology, and Pre-school Teachers Education. They admit 30 students in each course and offer four of these courses at the maximum. Three of them are located in rural areas while the remaining one is an urban centre.

More than half of the total strength (60.9%) of the community colleges were girls. Hence, the same truth was reflected in the sample (62%) also. It is found that 56 % out of the total respondents were hailing from rural areas. Community colleges attract mostly fresh candidates who were below 20 years of age. It is evidenced that a large majority (90%) of the total student-respondents have joined the colleges after plus 2 course while there are some graduates as well as those who discontinued their degree courses, and about three-fourth of the total pursuing Diploma in Four Wheeler Mechanism

(28%), Computer Applications (26%), and Medical Laboratory Technology (19%), show their interest in professional courses.

The concept of 'including the excluded' has been realised through the fact that nearly three-fifths (59%) of the total respondents belonged to Backward Castes whereas Scheduled Castes and most Backward Castes constitute 21% and 19%, each respectively.

Though at least two colleges under study were run by Christian affiliated institutions, Hindus (65%) have joined in large number. Christians (29%) constituted a sizeable part.

It is clear from the study that community colleges provided chance for candidates with varied background from all walks of life. The respondents hailed from Government service (27%), Business (26%), Agriculture (25%), and daily wagers (22%). Therefore, it is understood that the concept of equality of opportunity has been achieved through community colleges.

That the Community Colleges are being utilized by the poor and the needy is evident from the students' parental income. They earn Rs. 3,840 per month on an average. The concept has reached smaller families where there was an average of five and among them the second child has the maximum chance to make use of community colleges.

It is found that 85% of the total students selected the course themselves and were not forced. A large number of them sought admission in these colleges because of short duration of courses, employment-oriented courses, and affordable fee structure.

All the community colleges under the study were equipped to run computer-based courses and have atleast one computer for two students.

Nearly three-fourths of the total students lived within an average of 6.3 kilometres radius from their colleges, but the distance was not a major problem to commute to their colleges for some students. Among them nearly half of the students came to college either by bicycle or by foot. The proximity of these colleges to their place of residence was found to be one of the important factors for the selection of a particular community college for study by the students.

However, none of the selected colleges provided the chance for the students to form "Students Union". Of course, the majority of the students strongly felt for it both to press their demands and express themselves whereas some opined that the short duration of the course did not accommodate student union.

It is to be noted that nearly one-third (31%) of the total did not know the difference between polytechnic, I.T.I, and community colleges while nearly two-thirds of the total knew the distinction among these three and also about the courses offered, their duration, fees and teaching etc. Very few knew the nature and duration of their courses.

Table 1: Mean of Selected Variables

Variable	*Mean (N=100)*
Parental monthly Income (in Rs.)	3,840
Household Size	5
Students' Birth Order	2
Distance to College (in kms.)	6.3
Student-Computer ratio	2.1

Two-thirds of the total students agreed that special classes were conducted in their colleges by outside experts. Most of them said that internship is arranged by their college managements from time to time and nearly three-fourths (73%) of them were satisfied with the usefulness of the practicals/internships made by their colleges.

Most of the students are satisfied about the classroom, facilities provided for practicals and qualification of teachers, and expect more as far as laboratory facility is concerned. All the students of Four Wheeler Mechanism expressed their satisfaction for their colleges.

When analysing the infrastructure facilities provided at the community colleges, sports, retiring, and hostel facilities were in progress; all of them provided drinking water adequately. Most of the students were satisfied about the facilities viz., drinking water, lavatory, cycle stand, and library.

None of the students paid capitation fee for their admission. A vast majority of the students (94%) were satisfied about the fee structure for the courses. Likewise, the perception of the majority of these students (84%) about expenditure for the course was that of moderate one and more than half of them felt that studying in community colleges was worthy for time and expenditure.

For many students specially designed courses, positive image about community college, parent's wish, and absence of nearby college were the important factors for the preference towards community colleges.

It is found that a large number of students were not ready for entrepreneurship risk as it is costly experiment, and therefore, they prefer experience in job before venturing into anything new. More than one-third of the total students said that they do not have the necessary capital for starting self-employment avenues. However, many of them are positive that they could arrange money either from their parents or banks and most of them have positive perception about their parental support to self-employment openings.

The fact that more than half of the total students (58%) are sure that the community college could alleviate the problem of unemployment whereas another one-fourth of the total has no idea regarding this.

However, all the colleges are making arrangements for on-the-campus interview for their students job-placement, since almost all of them would like to have it. Of course, nearly half of the students (48%) know about the prospects of getting attractive jobs with community college's certificates.

It is significant to note that about half of the students (49%) did not have any idea about the university's role in running the community colleges. However, they opined that universities should take over community colleges for proper administration, lesser fees, recruitment of efficient teachers and safeguarding them from capitation fee in future.

While asking the students' perception about the positive changes in the functioning of community colleges more than half of them (53 %) did not have any idea regarding what kind of changes are possible for the effective functioning of such colleges.

It is important to note that almost all the students want the teaching language to be their mother tongue.

We may conclude from the present study that the community college has come a long way and is going to stay as a viable alternative to empower the disadvantaged, underprivileged, and excluded by imparting them appropriate skills and making them gainfully employed than the conventional with transfer courses offered by a large number of colleges and universities across the country. It is necessary to encourage community colleges to offer skills, and work-oriented education to meet the needs of the students who have finished formal school education and hence, it would be a multi-campus reality for skill-based education. The students' community can make use of these job oriented courses, instead of moving towards transfer kind of education. Therefore, all universities of the State as well the Country should take necessary steps both to start and supervise these colleges for the prescribed infrastructure facilities, fee being collected and other facilities necessary for the course, students and teachers. The Access, equity, and Relevance can be achieved by establishing more community colleges in India. Then only community college would become the "College for Community".

References

1. Theresa Novak and Michael Moffett, "Community Colleges – Academic and Professional Success", *Studying in America.* 2 (2), 1999.
2. Audree M. Chase, "Attending Community College can really Launch Your Career", *Educational Courses in Britain and America.* 19 and 20 (4 and 6), 1999.

3. "The Community College System – An Educational Alternative: Perspective, Philosophy, Recognition and Affiliation", First Consultation of Community College in Tamil Nadu, 04, July 1998.
4. National Seminar on "Framework of Education for the Indian Context", Trichirappalli, 04.06, Dec.1997.
5. Xavier Alphonse, S.J., *Changing Track: Community Colleges in India.* New Delhi: AIACHE Publication, 1996.
6. Joshi, K.L. *Problems of Higher Education in India.* Bombay: Popular Prakashan, 1997.
7. Government of India. *Report of the Sampurnanda Committee on Emotional Integration.* New Delhi: Ministry of Education, 1962.

12

Community College Movement at a Glance (1995-2009)

The Origin of Community College

The Community College Movement started in 1996 at Chennai with the starting of Madras Community College. It was decided to concentrate on one year diploma programme in the community college system. It was promoted as an alternative system of education based on inspiration and model of US Community Colleges. The whole concept was evolved because of the interaction with more than 30 professors of US Community College and by the visit of Dr. Xavier Alphonse, S.J., in 1995-96 to 18 Community Colleges. Right from the beginning conscious efforts were made to create and formulate an Indian Community College system to respond to the needs of the people of India. The Community College system aims at empowering the marginalized and disadvantaged sections of the society. It has become a National phenomenon with the clear articulation of Urban, Rural, Tribal, and Women Community Colleges.

It has spread its wings to 18 states of India with 234 Community Colleges associating with Indian Centre for Research and Development of Community Education (ICRDCE). Which is a pioneering institute to develop the concept to help in the establishment and monitoring of all the Community Colleges.

The Formulation and Articulation of the Concept: Local and Indigenous

The Community College aims at the Empowerment of the Disadvantaged through appropriate skills development leading to gainful employment, thus making a qualitative difference in the lives of the urban poor, rural poor, tribal poor and women in collaboration with local industrial establishments and potential employers, community leaders after taking into account the opportunities available for employment and self-employment in the local area.

Types of Community Colleges

There are four types of community colleges evolved so far in India. They are:

- Urban Community Colleges for Urban development and placement.
- Rural Community Colleges for Rural Development / Urban Placement
- Women Community Colleges for Women Development and Rural/ Urban Placement.
- Tribal Community Colleges for Tribal Community Development.

The Two Experiments

- Madras Community College, Santhome, Chennai (August, 1996).
- Madurai Community College, Gnanavolivupuram, Madurai (July, 1997).

Consolidation

The spread of the Movement among the NGOs and Universities in Tamil Nadu and Andhra Pradesh (M.S.University, Avinashilingam Deemed University and Tenali, Andhra Pradesh etc.).

The Community College Movement has become a National Phenomenon spreading its wings to many states of India. We have 234 Community Colleges in 18 states of India. The table below demonstrates the growth of the Community College movement in India.

1	Tamil Nadu	147	2	Pondicherry	03	3	Andhra Pradesh	11
4	Karnataka	26	5	Kerala	11	6	Maharas-htra	06
7	Madhya Pradesh	05	8	Gujarat	01	9	Jharkhand	09
10	Chhattisgarh	01	11	Goa	02	12	Orissa	04
13	Himachal Pradesh	01	14	Uttar Pradesh	02	15	West Bengal	01
16	Haryana	02	17	Punjab	01	18	Assam	01
Grand Total 234								

The Growth and Development of the Movement

Number of Community Colleges

Year	*Total Number of Community Colleges*
1995 - 1996	1
1996 – 1997	2
1997 – 1998	3
1998 – 1999	8
1999 – 2000	25
2000 – 2001	33
2001 – 2002	43
2002 – 2003	57
2003 – 2004	75
2004 – 2005	88
2005 – 2006	125
2006 – 2007	160
2007 – 2008	188
2008 – 2009	207
2009 - 2010	234

Unique Achievement of the Movement

Target Group Served

The unique achievement of the movement is the empowerment of the disadvantaged groups leading to the up gradation of their educational standards resulting in alleviation of poverty. A profile of 58,566 students attending 190 Community Colleges from different parts of India shows that women 72%, Married, 10%, Widows and Deserted women 2%, have so far benefited from the movement. Eighty Eight per cent come from socially backward groups (SC, ST, MBC, BC). Ninety per cent are economically poor (monthly family income is below Rs.3,000/) and Ninety Five per cent educationally weaker sections or cannot go for further education (School dropouts, below 10th, 10th passed, 12th passed). A breakup by way of religion shows that 55% are Hindus, 38% are Christians, 6% are Muslims and 1% belong to Other Religions (Buddhists, Sikhs and Jainism). Two hundred and seventy three physically challenged students have passed through this system and come out with flying colours. We have 2622 industries that have tie up with 152 Community Colleges. After Passing through the Community College System, 75% of the students are employed. In most cases their family income has been doubled. It has led to poverty alleviation through income generation. The concept has become a secular one transcending religions, castes and languages. It is truly a nation - building and capacity building exercise. ICRDCE has achieved a significant networking of all groups: Christians, Muslims, Hindus and all other service minded NGOs and organizations.

Distinction Obtained

TNOU GOLD MEDAL WINNERS and RANK HOLDERS - TNOU EXAMS - (2005 - 2006) - A SUMMARY

I Ranks With Gold Medal	10
II Ranks	07
III Ranks	08
IV Ranks	04
V Ranks	06
VI Ranks	04
VII Ranks	02
Total	38

Total Number of Students – 38
Total Number of Community Colleges - 21

TNOU GOLD MEDAL WINNERS and RANK HOLDERS - TNOU EXAMS - (2006 - 2007) - A SUMMARY

I Ranks With Gold Medal	10
II Ranks	10
III Ranks	13
IV Ranks	09
V Ranks	11
Total	53

Total Number of Students – 53

Total Number of Community Colleges - **38**

Tsunami Services

The most valuable contribution, ICRDCE has made is to educate 1230 Tsunami affected students and help them to have a bright future with God's blessings.

The Role of Industrial Partners

The Community College cannot succeed without the active participation and collaboration of the industrial, rural, agricultural, commercial and service organisations of the locality. The above sectors come to assist the Community College in the following five ways:

- Designing the curriculum for various job oriented courses.
- Serving as members of the advisory board.
- Being part time instructors for teaching and assessment in the college.
- On the job training for the students in the work place.
- Job placement for students who have been trained in the Community Colleges.
    - Memorandum of Understanding (MoU) could be signed with the industries for all the above five areas of collaboration.
    - A few representatives from the above sectors industrial, commerce and service sectors could also serve as the members of the governing body of the College.

2622 Industries that have tie-up with 152 Community Colleges

Job Placement from 135 Community Colleges

Total No. of Students from

135 Community Colleges (1996 - 2008)	= 40,057
No. of Students Placed in Job	= 31,746
No. of Students yet to be Placed	= 04,477
No. of Students gone for Higher Education	= 03,816
Job Placement (in Percentage)	= 31,746 / 40,057 = 79.25%
Yet to be Placed (in Percentage)	= 04,477 / 40,057 = 11.17%
Moved to Higher Education (in Percentage)	= 03,816 / 40,057 = 09.52%

Governing Board

The Community College will ensure the participation of the members of the agency that establishes the Community College (Board of Management), Administrators, Representatives of the faculty of the Community College, Industrial Partners, Community Leaders, Consultants to the Community College and Representatives nominated by the Government.

The authorities of the College will make sure of the proper management of Life Skills, Work Skills, Placement for Training, Financial and General administrative matters and also the needed infrastructural facilities necessary for training.

Statutory Bodies

(I) Board of Management (II) Governing Body of the College (III) Advisory Boards (IV) Director (Head), Programme Co-ordinators, Placement Officer, Members of the College, Life Skill Staff, Work Skill Staff, Guest Faculty and Supportive Staff.

Networking of the Agencies in India

S. No.	*Name of the Agency*	*No*
1.	Congregations – Priests	5
2.	Congregations - Brothers	2
3.	Congregations – Sisters	28
4.	Catholic Dioceses	16
5.	Community Colleges Run by Other Churches	11
6.	Community Colleges Run by Hindu Agencies	6
7.	Community Colleges Run by Muslim Agencies	9
8.	Community Colleges Run by NGOs	56
9.	Community Colleges Run by Government / Universities	5
	Grand Total	**138**

Secular Aspect of the Community College Movement

The concept has become a secular one transcending religions, castes and languages. It is truly a nation - building and capacity building exercise. ICRDCE has achieved a significant networking of all groups: Christians, Muslims, Hindus and all other service minded NGOs and organizations in India and abroad.

Religious Status

Religions	*Total*	*Per Cent*
Hindus	32,323	55
Muslims	3,313	06
Christians	22,120	38
Others	810	01
Grand Total	58,566	100

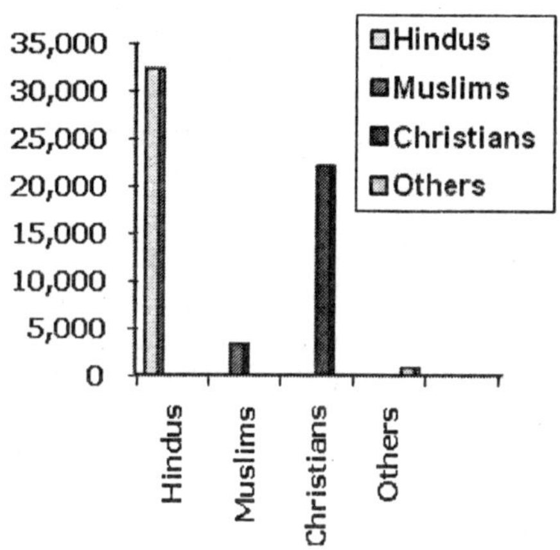

Story of the Recognition from 1996

Efforts of Recognitions

Consultations

- The Community College System has been working successfully with 75% Job Placement without getting recognition from any approved educational body of the country. However, most of the Community Colleges felt there is the need for recognition from the State and Central Governments to facilitate the horizontal mobility and the vertical mobility of the students of the Community College.
- The ICRDCE has conducted twelve Consultations to further this cause. It is for the first time in the educational history of the country, that nagencies that run Community Colleges have devised Self-Regulatory and Autonomous Guidelines to ensure credibility and accountability of the system.

National Institute of Open Schooling (NIOS)

- The ICRDCE has succeeded in influencing the State and Central Governments for recognition and accreditation of the system and for student centered funding. The issue of Accreditation was examined closely by the NIOS, New Delhi at the direction of the MHRD, Government of India, New Delhi.
- The NIOS has given accreditation so far to 18 Community Colleges in the country.

Ministry of Human Resources Development (MHRD)

- Letter dated 26th of July 1999, Mr. Champak Chatterji, Joint Secretary (HE) and CVO, Ref No. D.O. No. F. 3-13 / 99 - U.I.

  Content: To discuss the concept of Community Colleges in India and replication of the same elsewhere in the country.
- The meeting was held at the Education Secretary Government of India Shri. M.K. Kaw's Chamber on 6th of August 1999 from 11.20 a.m. - 1.15 p.m.
- Letter dated 16th of August 1999, Mr. Maharaj Krishen Kaw, Secretary, Department of Education, MHRD, Ref. No. F.3-13/99-U.I.
- Presentation to the Ministry of Human Resource Development, Government of India on 7th of September 1999.
- Letter dated 4th of October 1999, Record of discussion held during the presentations by experts on Vocational Education on 07.09.1999.
- 18th and 19th of February 2000, National Workshop on Community

College system as an alternative system of education in collaboration with the Ministry of Human Resource Development, New Delhi.

- 22nd, 23rd and 24th of February 2000, Workshop on National Qualification Framework organized by NIEPA, New Delhi.
- Letter dated 18th of February 2005, Committee constituted to go into various issues concerning role for Community Colleges in Indian Education system - notice for first meeting. Ref. No. F.5.2/2005 - U.3.
- 20th of September 2006, Working Paper from MHRD submitted to the planning commission in which community college is included.

University Grants Commission (UGC) Role (2006-2009)

- 14th of November 2006, Meeting of Dr. Arjun Singh, Minister for MHRD at the UGC Commission in which the Honourable Minister refers to the Community College system that merits the attention of UGC.
- 5th of January 2007, UGC finalises the working paper to the Planning Commission in which Community College System is included. Dr. Xavier Alphonse, S.J., is appointed Chairman of the National Committee on Community Colleges.
- 31st of March 2007, The National Committee on Community Colleges appointed by the UGC Chairman to draw up guidelines for the implementation of the Community College scheme headed by Dr. Xavier Alphonse S.J. The Committee interacted with the participants from 100 Community Colleges all over the country.
- 2nd of April 2007, The report of the committee was submitted to Prof. Thorat, Chairman, UGC by Dr. Xavier Alphonse, S.J.
- 27th of June 2007, The Chairman of UGC requested Prof. (Dr.) Xavier Alphonse, S.J., to make a presentation on "Community Colleges" on 2nd of July 2007.
- 2nd of July 2007, Dr. Xavier Alphonse, SJ., made a presentation to the UGC members and the Officials of UGC
- 10th of September 2007, The Chairman of the UGC constituted the second Expert Committee to deliberate on the issue regarding concept and methodology for establishment and functioning and funding of Community College - Eight Member Team.
- 19th of September 2007, The Committee met at UGC and discussed recognition and funding to the Community College.
- February 2008, The Members of the Committee submitted the Report to UGC.

- 21st May 2008, The UGC has constituted an Expert Committee to formulate the guidelines for establishment and functioning of Community Colleges. - 7 Member Committee.
- 18th and 19th of June 2008, the 448th meeting of the University Grants Commission discussed the proposals.
- 1st of September 2008, The Commission finally decided that the same Committee by request to work out the operational mechanism taking into account the above dated discussion - 9 Member Committee - D.O.No.F.1-2/2007 (CPP - II).
- 18th September 2008 - UGC Expert Committee on Community Colleges- No. F1-2/2007 (CPP - II).
- 5th of February 2009 - Meeting at IGNOU about Community Colleges and Associate Degree
- 6th of February 2009 - Meeting with the Honourable Minister Dr. Arjun Singh at his office in New Delhi

Government of Tamil Nadu

- The State Government of Tamil Nadu has issued a Government Order (GO) recognizing the system in May 2008.

Tamil Nadu Budget 2008 - 2009

Higher Education - Announcement No. 48

- Having regard to the fact that Community Colleges are playing a very important role in imparting employment oriented skills to poor dropouts who could not continue their education, Government will extend its support to them. From the coming academic year onwards, these Community Colleges will be given student grant at the rate of Rs.1,000 per student through Tamil Nadu Open University. A sum of Rupees One Crore is allocated in the Budget for this purpose. 10,000 students will benefit from this scheme.

Tamil Nadu Open University

Tamil Nadu Open University has recognised Community Colleges in Tamil Nadu as Vocational Programme Centres. The following nine courses have been recognised as Diploma Courses to be conducted by Community Colleges from this year including Life Coping Skills and Communication Skills.

- Early Childhood Care Education (Pre School Teaching)
- Health Assistant
- Fashion Design and Garment Making

- DTP Operator
- Refrigeration and Air Conditioning Technician
- House Electrician
- Plumbing Technician
- Catering Assistant
- Four Wheeler Mechanism
- Beautician
- Computer Hardware Servicing
- Computer Applications
- Multimedia Systems
- Animation
- Home Appliances Repairing and Servicing
- Mobile Phone Servicing.
- The Tamil Nadu Open University (TNOU) has recognized 118 Community Colleges as Vocational Programme Centres all over the country and it has extended its recognition to the Community Colleges in other States of India.
- 84 Community Colleges from Tamil Nadu have submitted their application forms to the TNOU and are waiting to be approved as Community Colleges.

Indira Gandhi Open University (IGNOU)

The Associate Degree of IGNOU

It is a welcome change that the IGNOU starts associate degree through Community Colleges for 64 credits and each credit carrying 15 working hours.

Suggestions:

Some of the important concerns regarding the Associate degree are:

(i) The fee structure of the programme.

(ii) The individual student's fee.

(iii) Collaboration with Industrial partners and Employers.

(iv) The scheme of evaluation Internal as well as External.

(v) The development of resource materials and popularization of the concept and careful selection of voluntary organizations who are service minded than making the Associate degree as their business using the poor and the underprivileged.

Planning Commission Document

Ninth Five Year Plan (1997- 2001)

Concerted efforts were made to make higher education relevant by introducing career-oriented courses as a part of the first degree programme. Further restructuring of courses was undertaken to provide an application component to university education. A study was undertaken to examine the concept of community colleges.

Volume II, Education, p. 95

Tenth Five Year Plan (2002 - 2007)

- There should be focus on convergence of schemes like the Sarva Shiksha Abhiyan, Adult Education and Vocational Education Programme at Schools, Industrial Technical Institutes (ITIs), Polytechnics, Community Colleges etc.

Chapter 2.4 Vocational Education p. 51.

Eleventh Five Year Plan (2008 - 2012)

1.3.71 Setting up of additional 210 community colleges, mainly in northern, western, and eastern parts of the country will be supported on placement based funding. Existing 190 community colleges (largely in southern States, some of which offer diploma courses) will also be supported for capacity building, training cost (equipment, faculty development, TLM, stipend, etc., but not for civil works and other capital costs). Funding will based on MoU between community colleges, States, and MHRD.

Volume II, Education, p. 34

The Problems and Challenges

1. Sustainability and self sustainability of each Community College
2. National recognition of the Community College System
3. Vertical mobility

4. Government funding
5. Financial constraints of the Community College
6. Sustaining motivation of the student/staff
7. Inspiration (Vision), dedication and commitment of the staff.
8. Evaluation of institutions, courses, teachers and students.
9. Difficulty in training cost of the students - need for subsidy of tuition fee.
10. The need for infrastructural development and equipment in individual Community Colleges.
11. International Collaborations.
    - ICRDCE has created ten Community Colleges in East Africa and South Africa. The book on Life-coping skills "*We Shall Overcome*" written by Fr. Xavier Alphonse has been translated into Afrikaners language with the title "*ONS SAL OORWIN*" *Vaardighede om die lewe te hanteer* (433 pages) and prescribed as a textbook approved by the Government of South Africa.
    - ICRDCE and the Director have been appointed as Consulting Agency to the Honourable Prime Minister of Papua New Guinea (PNG) for the creation of 13 Community Colleges in 2008 under the scheme "Inclusiveness in Education for National Development through the Community Colleges".

Contribution of the ICRDCE Movement

The Indian Centre for Research and Development of Community Education (ICRDCE), Chennai is an initiative of Madurai Jesuit Province and a unit of Chengai Jesuit Society of Chennai Mission. It was started in January 1999. It is a facilitating and coordinating agency for Community Colleges in India. It has been involved in the preparation, establishment, monitoring and evaluation of 234 Community Colleges in 18 States of India. It has also trained 1318 teachers. The Centre has conducted 48 Workshops involving 950 NGOs, 2179 participants and has also organised six important National Consultations and 41 Regional Consultations among Community Colleges. It has also prepared basic curriculum material and supplied to all these Community Colleges. It has published 21 books and 35 articles in the leading educational journals of India and abroad on the concept and implementation of the system. The Centre also has an uptodate documentation on the movement by way of newspaper clippings, video, audiotapes, photographs, etc. The Tamil Nadu Open University (TNOU) has recognized 102 Community Colleges as Vocational Programme Centres all over the country. The Yashwantrao Chavan Maharashtra Open University (YCMOU),

Nashik is going to recognize the Community Colleges in the States of Maharashtra, Goa and Gujarat.

The Community College movement merits the attention of the Government of India from the year 1999. Dr. Xavier Alphonse has made a few presentations to the Ministry of Human Resource Development. The system has been mentioned in the Union Planning Commission Tenth Five Year Plan document. It has been included in the Eleventh Five Year Plan for establishment and funding recommended by the Ministry of Human Resource Development and the University Grants Commission (UGC). Dr. Xavier Alphonse has been appointed as the Chairman of National Committee on Community Colleges to discuss the concepts and methodology for establishment and functioning of Community Colleges, appointed by UGC in January 2007. The document has been submitted to the UGC. The State Governments of Haryana and Tamil Nadu have come forward to recognize the system.

Future Directions

1. ICRDCE will try to minimize the difficulties Community Colleges are facing with Tamil Nadu Open University (TNOU).
2. ICRDCE will continue to consolidate and strengthen the one year diploma programme through TNOU Recognition in Tamil Nadu and National Skill Development Mission at the Central Government. It also prepares the profile of New Community Colleges for the year 2009 - 2010 and helps them for the recognition.
3. ICRDCE will continue to promote the scheme of Associate Community Colleges with IGNOU.
4. ICRDCE will continue with the training programme for the teachers of Community Colleges in June and November.
5. ICRDCE will prepare the books on work skills.
6. ICRDCE will help IGNOU to promote Associate Degree through Community Colleges.
7. ICRDCE will help to prepare text books and training programme at the State, Regional and National level with IGNOU.
8. ICRDCE will help its Associate Community Colleges to participate in National Workshop on the Institutionalization of Community Colleges on 22nd and 23rd of June 2009 and it will encourage the member colleges to take up the programme as value addition.
9. ICRDCE will join with Indira Gandhi National Open University (IGNOU) for the whole scheme of credit transfer like Certificate Course, Degree Course, Associate Degree Course and one year Diploma Course.

10. ICRDCE will consider associate degree colleges as value addition not an essential component of Community Colleges.
11. ICRDCE will help University Grants Commission (UGC) to implement Associate Degree Community Colleges in conventional colleges by UGC's scheme of credit transfer.
12. ICRDCE will continue its international mission by helping the African, Papua New Guinea (PNG) and Nepal Community Colleges both in establishment as well as monitoring of the system.
13. ICRDCE will help to organize workshops, seminars in North India and Propagate the concept far and wide.
14. ICRDCE will take stock and critically review the evolution and development of Community Colleges.
15. ICRDCE will once again submit the document to Ministry of Human Resources Development (MHRD) on Community College System.
16. ICRDCE will request Ministry of Human Resources Development (MHRD) and Indira Gandhi National Open University (IGNOU) to recognise ICRDCE as a Resource Centre for the Community Colleges in India.

"Community College is a new educational system wherein you enable the least to acquire the best skills suited to an individual in the shortest period to sustain oneself for the longest period - life". (Prof. V. Joachim, Loyola College, Chennai).

13

Community College–
The Scope for the Disadvantaged

Introduction

The Community College Movement started in 1996 at Chennai with the starting of Madras Community College. It was decided to concentrate on one year diploma programme in the community college system. It was promoted as an alternative system of education based on inspiration and model of the US Community Colleges. The whole concept was evolved because of the interaction with more than 30 professors of US Community College and by the visit of Dr. Xavier Alphonse, S.J., in 1995-96 to 18 Community Colleges. Right from the beginning conscious efforts were made to create and formulate an Indian Community College system to respond to the needs of the people of India. The Community College system aims at empowering the marginalised and the disadvantaged sections of the society. It has become a National phenomenon with the clear articulation of urban, rural, tribal, and women Community Colleges.

It has spread its wings to 18 states of India with 234 Community Colleges associating with Indian Centre for Research and Development of Community Education (ICRDCE). This is a pioneering institute to develop the concept and to help in the establishment and monitoring of all the Community Colleges. The Community College aims at the empowerment of the disadvantaged through appropriate skills development leading to gainful employment, thus making a qualitative difference in the lives of the urban poor, rural poor, tribal poor and women in collaboration with local industrial establishments and potential employers, community leaders after taking into account the opportunities available for employment and self-employment in the local area.

State-wise List

The Community College Movement has become a national phenomenon spreading its wings to many states of India. We have 234 Community Colleges in 18 states of India. The table below demonstrates the growth of the Community College movement in India:

1.	Tamil Nadu	147
2.	Pondicherry	03
3.	Andhra Pradesh	11
4.	Karnataka	26
5.	Kerala	11
6.	Maharashtra	06
7.	Madhya Pradesh	05
8.	Gujarat	01
9.	Jharkhand	09
10.	Chhattisgarh	01
11.	Goa	02
12.	Orissa	04
13.	Himachal Pradesh	01
14.	Uttar Pradesh	02
15.	West Bengal	01
16.	Haryana	02
17.	Punjab	01
18.	Assam	01
	Grand Total	234

Types of Community Colleges

There are four types of community colleges evolved so far in India. They are:

- Urban Community Colleges for Urban development and placement.
- Rural Community Colleges for Rural Development / Urban Placement
- Women Community Colleges for Women Development and Rural / Urban Placement
- Tribal Community Colleges for Tribal Community Development

Research Study

The Indian Centre for Research and Development of Community Colleges undertook a research study to focus on the Impact of the Community College movement on the society for the last 14 years during 2008 -2009.

Objectives of the Research Study

- A comprehensive evaluation of the Community College movement as well as individual Community Colleges all over India.

- To take stock of our quality service to the poor and the marginalized
- To chalkout new directions and to face adequately the challenges with innovative methods.

Profile of Students

The unique achievement of the movement is the empowerment of the disadvantaged groups leading to the up gradation of their educational standards resulting in the alleviation of poverty. A profile of 58,566 students attending 190 Community Colleges from different parts of India shows that women 72%, Married, 10%, Widows and Deserted women 2%, have so far benefitted from the movement. Eighty Eight per cent come from the socially backward groups (SC, ST, MBC, BC). Ninety per cent are economically poor (monthly family income is below Rs.3,000/) and Ninety Five per cent educationally weaker sections or cannot go for further education (School dropouts, below 10th, 10th passed, 12th passed). A breakup by way of religion shows that 55% are Hindus, 38% are Christians, 6% are Muslims and 1% are Other Religions (Buddhists, Sikhs and Jainism). Two hundred and seventy nine physically challenged students have passed through this system and come out with flying colours. We have 2622 industries that have tie up with 152 Community Colleges. After passing through the Community College System, 75% of the students are employed. In most cases their family income has been doubled. It has led to poverty alleviation through income generation. The concept has become a secular one transcending religions, castes and languages. It is truly a nation - building and capacity building exercise. ICRDCE has achieved a significant networking of all groups: Christians, Muslims, Hindus and all other service minded NGOs and organizations in India and Abroad.

The Findings of the Research Study is tabulated below

Total Number of Students – 58, 566	*Urban*	*Per cent*	*Rural*	*Per cent*	*Women*	*Per cent*	*Tribal*	*Per cent*	*Total Per cent*
Number of Community College	37	19	90	42	58	31	15	8	100
Number of Students	13,325	23	25,614	44	13,626	23	6,001	10	100
Gender									
Male	4,842	8	8,467	15	0	0	2,958	5	100
Female	8,483	15	17,147	29	13,626	23	3,043	5	
	13,325		25,614		13,626		6,001		
Marital Status									
Unmarried	12,452	21	22,336	33	12,053	20	5,488	9	
Married	854	2	3,233	5	1,531	2	510	1	
Widows	13	1	39	1	19	1	3	1	100
Divorced	06	1	6	1	23	1	0	0	
	13,325		25,614		13,626		6,001		
Age Group									
18 – 22	10,438	17	20,311	34	10,315	17	3,000	5	
23 – 26	1,821	3	3,457	6	2,051	4	2,050	4	
26 – 30	724	1	1,129	2	863	2	694	1	100
31 – Above	324	1	717	1	367	1	257	1	
	13,325		25,614		13,626		6,001		
Education Status									
Below 10th	2,776	5	4,776	8	1,471	3	1,967	4	
10th Passed	3,970	7	6,469	11	3,695	6	1,692	3	
12th Passed	5,863	10	12,862	22	7,451	13	1,274	2	100
Degree	716	1	1,480	3	793	1	565	1	
	13,325		25,614		13,626		6,001		

contd...

Total Number of Students – 58, 566	*Urban*	*Per cent*	*Rural*	*Per cent*	*Women*	*Per cent*	*Tribal*	*Per cent*	*Total Per cent*
Economic Status									
Below – Rs.1,000	4,030	7	9,463	16	4,615	8	2,042	3	100
Rs. 1,001 – 2,000	4,485	8	9,486	16	5,207	9	2,120	4	
Rs. 2,001 – 3,000	2,720	5	5,253	9	2,180	4	1,274	2	
Rs. 3,001 – Above	2,090	3	1,480	2	1,624	3	565	1	
	13,325		25,614		13,626		6,001		
Social Status									
SC	3,468	6	6,969	11	4,504	8	482	1	100
ST	440	1	519	1	375	1	5,116	8	
MBC	1,871	3	5,032	9	1,772	3	71	1	
BC	5,159	8	11,067	18	4,828	8	40	1	
OC	2,387	4	2,028	3	2,147	4	289	1	
	13,325		25,614		13,626		6,001		
Religious Status									
Hindus	8,293	14	15,171	25	7,643	13	1,216	2	100
Christians	974	1	1,406	2	644	1	289	1	
Muslims	4,042	7	9,022	15	5,304	9	3,752	6	
Others	16	1	15	1	35	1	744	1	
	13,325		25,614		13,626		6,001		
Physically Challenged									
Physically Challenged	17		157		81		18		

Status of Placement

Types of Community Colleges	*Total Number of Community Colleges*	*Total Number of Students*	*Number of Students Placed*	*Students yet to be Placed*	*Moved to Higher Education*
Urban	34	10,800	09,110	1,251	0,439
Rural	67	17,660	14,419	1,821	1,420
Women	50	10,515	07,730	1,266	1,516
Tribal	10	04,552	02,747	1,119	0,686
Grand Total	**161**	**40,057**	**31,764**	**4,477**	**3,816**

The Associate Degree of IGNOU

It is a welcome change that the IGNOU started associate degree through Community Colleges for 64 credits and each credit carrying 15 working hours.

We would like to make the following suggestions:

Content	*Credit*	*Total no. of hours*
I Year		
Foundation course	16 Credits X 15 Hours	240 Hours
Application oriented course	8 Credits X 15 Hours	120 Hours
Basic Electives	8 Credits X 15 Hours	120 Hours
II Year		
Application oriented course	8 Credits X 15 Hours	120 Hours
Basic Electives	8 Credits X 15 Hours	120 Hours
Internship	8 Credits X 15 Hours	120 Hours
Project Work	8 Credits X 15 Hours	120 Hours
Total	**64 Credits X 15 Hours**	**960 Hours**

Some of the important concerns regarding the Associate degree are:

- The fee structure of the programme.
- The individual student's fee.
- Collaboration with ndustrial partners and Employers.
- The scheme of evaluation Internal as well as External.
- The development of resource materials and popularisation of the concept and careful selection of voluntary organisations who are service minded than making the Associate degree as their business using the poor and the underprivileged.

5. Future Directions

(i) National recognition of Community College system throughout the country.

(ii) The functional implementation and the target group served.

(iii) The financial aid to committed and voluntary organizations.

(iv) Paying the training cost by way of scholarship to the students.

(v) Salary of the Community College teachers and their service conditions as well as the training of all the teachers and administrators to understand the concept and implementation.

(vi) The challenge is the vertical mobility of the students through associate degree and development of resource material for each trade according to the local needs.

(vii) Collaboration of Industrial Partners / employers for internship and for placement.

The Community College is truly a national building exercise. It is transforming the individual life and improving the socio economic and educational background of the individual student. It is also causing social changes in the life of the individual as well as the community with its mission of Including the excluded and giving best to the least.

Initiative to recognize the system for the last two years on the insistence of the Honourable Minister for Human Resource Development Dr. Arjun Singh. The first committee was constituted in January 2007. The Committee explored the following issues:

- The nature of lateral entry of students admitted in the Community Colleges need to be elaborated further.

(ii)

The role of AICTE and UGC needs to be spelt out clearly.

- How this system is different in comparison with the ITI and polytechnics?
- The system and experiences of Association of the Community Colleges in USA and Australia may also be studied and appropriately included in our scheme.
- The committee also met 125 representatives from 98 Community Colleges at Chennai in March 2007.

The second committee was constituted in October 2007. It produced a draft document. It was submitted to the UGC. The third committee was constituted in May 2008 with the members from the Knowledge Commission, Distance Education Council, Open University Vice – Chancellor, and UGC members. The committee made a few useful suggestions in terms of establishment and funding of Community Colleges in the XI Five Year Plan. The suggestions are under the consideration of the University Grants

Commission. Dr. Xavier Alphonse, a member of the UGC and a member of DEC and the Director of ICRDCE, Chennai was the Chairman of all the three national Committees constituted by the Chairman of UGC Prof. Thorat. Being a new and innovative scheme of skills Development for the disadvantaged, the UGC is keen to work out a mechanism that is acceptable to the whole country. The Community College scheme fits into the agenda of the XI Five Year Plan of promoting inclusiveness, equity, access and expansion in Higher Education. The day is not far off when the Community College will be announced as a scheme for the poor and the marginalized in India by the Ministry of Human Resource Development. It is a great boon to millions of young men and women who cannot continue their Higher Education and who are searching for a way to have meaningful livelihood and quality of life.

Decennial Celebration of ICRDCE

Indian Centre for Research and Development of Community Education (ICRDCE), Chennai is an initiative of Madurai Jesuit Province and a unit of Chengai Jesuit Society of Chennai Mission. It was started in January 1999. It is a facilitating and coordinating agency for Community Colleges in India. It has been involved in the preparation, establishment, monitoring and evaluation of 207 Community Colleges in 18 States of India. It has also trained 1275 teachers. The Centre has conducted 48 workshops involving 950 NGOs, 2179 participants and has also organised six important National Consultations and 41 Regional Consultations among Community Colleges. It has also prepared the basic curriculum material and supplied to all these Community Colleges. IT has published 25 books and 55 articles in the leading educational journals of India and abroad on the concept and implementation of the system. The Centre also has an up-to-date documentation on the movement by way of newspaper clippings, video, audiotapes, CDs, photographs, etc.

The Tamil Nadu Open University (TNOU) has recognised 118 Community Colleges as Vocational Programme Centres all over the country. The Yashwantrao Chavan Maharashtra Open University (YCMOU), Nashik is likely to recognize the Community Colleges in the States of Maharashtra, Goa and Gujarat. The State Government of Tamil Nadu has issued a Government Order (GO No. 163) recognising the system in May 2008. It has also sanctioned Rs. 10 million Indian Rupees by way of scholarship to 10,000 students of Community Colleges in Tamil Nadu. The Government of India is considering the proposal for national recognition and funding to Community Colleges all over India. It is also discussing the vertical mobility of these students to the mainstream of higher education through credit transfer.

The Community College movement has drawn the attention of the Government of India from the year 1999. Dr. Xavier Alphonse has made a few presentations to the Ministry of Human Resource Development. The system has been mentioned in the Union Planning Commission (2007-2012) Tenth Five Year Plan document. It has been included in the Eleventh Five Year Plan for establishment and funding recommended by the Ministry of Human Resource Development and University Grants Commission (UGC). Dr. Xavier Alphonse has been appointed as the Chairman of National Committee on Community Colleges to discuss the concept and methodology for establishment and functioning of Community Colleges, appointed by UGC in January 2007. The document has been submitted to the UGC. The State Government of Haryana also has come forward to recognise the system.

The unique achievement of the movement is the empowerment of the disadvantaged groups leading to the upgradation of their educational standards resulting in alleviation of poverty. A profile of 54, 519 students attending 184 Community Colleges from different parts of India shows that 75% are women. 90% of the students come from socially and economically backward groups. After passing through the Community College System, 75% of the students are employed. In most cases their family income has been doubled. It has led to poverty alleviation through income generation. The concept has become a secular one transcending religions, castes and languages. It is a nation and capacity building exercise. ICRDCE has achieved a significant networking of all groups: Christians, Muslims, Hindus and all other service minded NGOs and organisations.

ICRDCE has created ten Community Colleges in East Africa and South Africa. The book on Life–Coping skills "*We Shall Overcome* written by Fr. Xavier Alphonse has been translated into Afrikaners language with the title "ONS SAL OORWIN" and prescribed as a textbook approved by the Government of South Africa. The ICRDCE has trained 50 teachers from South Africa and East Africa from June 2005.

ICRDCE and the Director have been appointed as the Consulting Agency to the Honourable Prime Minister of Papua New Guinea (PNG) for the creation of 13 Community Colleges in 2008 under the scheme "Inclusiveness in Education for National Development through the Community Colleges". It has so far trained 22 teachers from PNG in June and November 2008.

Recognition for Community Colleges Likely by Year-end

ICRDCE Urged to Bring Community Colleges into Election Manifestos

The Ministry of Human Resource Development (MHRD) is likely to clear a proposal to grant recognition to community colleges, Xavier Alphonse, director, Indian Centre for Research and Development of Community Education (ICRDCE), said.

Speaking at the 10th anniversary of the ICRDCE, Fr. Alphonse said that the Community College movement has received a major fillip with Tamil Nadu Open University (TNOU) recognising 118 colleges as vocational programme centres all over the country. This has allowed vertical mobility of students from Community Colleges to the mainstream of higher education through credit transfer.

He said the Community College system has been included in the 11th Five Year Plan. He has been appointed by the University Grants Commission as Chairman of the National Committee on Community Colleges to discuss the concept and methodology to establish community colleges. The document has been submitted to the Ministry by the UGC. Over the past decade, ICRDCE has taken in nearly 70,000 drop-out students. The Centre, an initiative of the Madurai Jesuit Province, and a unit of the Chengai Jesuit Society of the Christian Mission, was started in January 1999. It has been involved in the preparation, establishment, monitoring and evaluation of 207 community colleges in 18 States. Over 1,380 teachers have been trained and workshop conducted for NGOs, N. Ram, Editor-in-Chief, and *The Hindu*, expressed his admiration for the clear focus of community colleges in facilitating skill development leading to employment. The base of the Indian education system was far too narrow and the proportion of high school students who reach college was low. This would be the primary social challenge of anyone who sought to remedy the situation.

Mr. Ram urged ICRDCE to bring Community Colleges into election manifestos of different political parties. The Prince of Arcot, Nawab Mohammed Abdul Ali, said the Christian community that had done so much in the field of education had to be admired instead of being targeted by divisive forces. He urged Christian educational institutions to provide a quota for Muslim students in order to enable more Muslim youngsters to move ahead.

Kalyani Annies, TNOU Vice-Chancellor, said the focus of education should be on training and re-training of youth, as “employability,” rather than “unemployment”, was the issue. The Community college system had emerged as an effective complementary system of education to train youth and make them “job-fit”.

M.S.Palanichamy, former Vice-Chancellor, TNOU, said the Community Colleges were able to transform underprivileged youth into employable persons. J.A.K. Tarren, Vice-Chancellor, Central University Pondicherry, said the difference between the Community College and university system was that while in a university college the intake had to increase, the target should be to reduce the intake of community colleges by reducing the drop-out rate in the mainstream.

A. Selvaraj, Chief executive, Sri Jeyarekha Industries, also one of the first industrial collaborators of the Community College system, said employers must consider hiring these students as wise investment.

Three books *Beyond Margins Believing in Miracles* (Two Volumes) and *Change is Certain*, authored by Fr. Alphonse, were released on the occasion.

Community Colleges Groomed to Work

The Government is all set to grant National recognition to community colleges in India. The Indian education system has so far explored the idea of making a person employable after senior secondary education or higher education. Open school and open universities, too, offer an opportunity to those who want to continue their education while working. But then, there are millions who are below the poverty line or who come from the underprivileged sections of society with no access to any form of education and hence not eligible to be employable in any formal sector. The lack of sufficient education, despite the talent, makes them unemployable. This is where community colleges step in.

A community college aims to empower members of underprivileged sections of society with employment skills. Internationally, education through community colleges has been successful as well as accepted by governments. "In India, the Community College system came into being in 1996, with the establishment of Madras Community College. Though we adopted the US model of awarding points through certificates and diplomas, we changed the model in keeping with the needs of people in our country. In the US, the emphasis is more on work skills. Here, the emphasis is on job as well as life skills," says Xavier Alphonse, Founder of the first community colleges in India and Director, Indian Centre for Research and Development of Community Education. (ICRDCE).

As per the figures quoted by ICRDCE, there are 206 community colleges existing in 17 states. "The government is not yet involved. Most community colleges are the result of initiatives taken by private organisations or NGOs," says Alphonse.

The Need

"As the name suggests, a Community College does not offer academic or professional programmes that are offered by a university or a polytechnic. Instead, it offers skill-based programmes, addressing the needs of a community – especially the underprivileged sections of society. Four aspects that sum up the idea of Community Colleges are access, flexibility in curriculum, equal opportunity and quality in training," Alphonse explains.

"It aims to empower those who are economically and socially deprived. Out of the age group between 16 and 24, a maximum number of people can't make it to colleges. They remain unemployed because they lack in the area of skill. A community college makes sure that more people get employment," says Mani Jacob, General Secretary, All Indian Association for Christian Higher Education (AIACHE) and head of the Community College for women in Delhi, which equips girls from the nearby villages in stitching work. "There are four types of Community Colleges – for the urban poor, the rural poor, people belonging to the tribal areas and women. We start by training them in life skills that include language, computing, fluency in speaking and writing English. Then, we impart work skills in 40 different areas," informs Alphonse.

There is no age bar or minimum qualification for joining a community college. Any person earning 16 credits is awarded a certificate. With 32 credits, one gets a diploma. "The National Institute of Open Schooling (NIOS) has given accreditation to many community colleges. Also diplomas offered by Community Colleges in Tamil Nadu is recognised by Tamil Nadu Open University for enrolment in higher education," Alphonse says.

A class VII dropout, Reema Singh joined the Delhi Community College due to lower family income. "During the first phase, I learned about communication, English writing and calculations before I went for stitching classes. I got internship with an export house. After earning a diploma, I got myself enrolled in NIOS. I completed my class X and XII and now I have applied for a degree course from an Open University," Singh says.

Latest development

An important milestone, has been achieved recently with IGNOU's decisions to offer associate degrees to students of Community Colleges. "Our academic council has passed the decision to introduce an associate degree, which may not be a complete qualification but it enables students to get into a university. With IGNOU's associate degree, one will be able to get a lateral entry into the third year of the degree programme," says VN. Rajasekharan Pillai, Vice Chancellor, IGNOU. Also, UGC has appointed as many as five committees under the chairmanship of Alphonse for promotion of community colleges.

"The UGC is keen that the system of community colleges is promoted as a parallel system within the existing infrastructure of arts and science colleges in India. A report to develop a mechanism for providing national recognition has already been submitted to the HRD Ministry," concludes Alphonse.

National Workshop on the Institutionalization of the Community College System in India held on 22nd and 23rd, June, 2009.

The National Workshop on the institutionalisation of Community College system in India was started with a theme prayer on "Unity in Diversity" led by Fr. M.S. Jacob, S.J. in Esthell Hotel, Adayar, Chennai from 22nd morning to 23rd evening. There were 182 participants from 19 states across India who attended and benefited from this workshop. Fr. Xavier Alphonse welcomed the dignitaries and the gathering. Dr. Rajasekharan Pillai, the Honourable Vice Chancellor of the IGNOU and its Pro Vice Chancellor, Dr. Latha Pillai,

Dr. Kalyani Annie, the Vice Chancellor of TNOU and the other officials Dr. Paneer Selvam, the Regional Director, Chennai from IGNOU and Mr.Manickam, the Registrar and Dr. Thiyagarajan, the Head, SOCE from TNOU were also present in the inauguration of the workshop. ICRDCE Industrial Partner and outside expert, Mr. Selvaraj and ICRDCE master trainer Mr. Anto Vincent were among those present for the workshop.

Dr. Rajasekharpillai in his inaugural address highlighted the activities of the IGNOU and its contribution in serving the disadvantaged sections of the society. IGNOU was started as an alternative foundation for Degree Colleges not only for the rural area but also for the urban area with an adaptation of Gandhian Philosophy of Education that is always working well with the rural as well as the urban communities. It has got 2.2 million learners basing themselves on Community Education. It has got an open entry into the system and flexibility of the system. He also emphasized the need for institutionalizing the Community college system in our country as there are a large number of students pushed out of the formal education system. 1200 Community Colleges are effectively functioning in the USA and Canada, and each district in USA has got a Community College. Knowledge and skills are being imparted to the students through Community Colleges.

He also touched upon the knowledge and skill network, modern technology, IIT and ICT through which the Community Colleges can reach out to so many millions of students. M.S. Swaminathan Institute which is reaching out to the villages through Broadband and ISRO which is also reaching out to 33 countries in the world and Ramachandra Medical University is reaching out to the rural poor through teleconference. The immense capabilities of our advanced and modern infrastructure should be optimally utilized and the facilities from Multimedia will definitely contribute to the local communities.

While he mentioned about the dropouts, he said, out of ten, only three of them pass the school and seven of them remain dropouts. In order to look at the large number of dropouts, he highlighted the following things:

1. Functional literacy, only 5% has Certificate in our country.
2. Welfare schemes on various programmes of the Central Government wherein ordinary people can go for bridge courses.
3. Policy for dropouts: Bachelor Preparatory Programme.
4. National Schooling System.
5. Community Colleges can implement Modular skills development.
6. 2-year Associate Degree Programme through Community Colleges.

7. Certificate model – Credit transfer between universities and educational institutions. Here a large number of dropouts could be benefited.
8. IGNOU networks with the Federation of Rural NGOs, Civil Society Organizations and gives sustainable and livelihood development programmes to the rural poor. It also provides technology for the rural people.
9. Common Wealth of Learning for the grass root level workers.
10. IGNOU is the best in facilitating qualitative changes in the lives of the rural poor and urban poor.

He also added that IGNOU is not a funding agency. He has given full freedom to the Community College system in the formation of the curriculum. Community Colleges can come out with new trades based on the needs of the communities and industries. Curriculum can be devised based on the teachers' experience. Get materials from IGNOU and tailor it and send it back to IGNOU for approval.

Dr. Kalyani Anbuchelvan the Vice Chancellor of TNOU felicitated the dignitaries and narrated the historical association of TNOU with IGNOU and ICRDCE. The Tamil Nadu Open University (TNOU) is honoured to associate itself with the world's largest Open University, the Indira Gandhi National Open University, on the Community College initiative. Tamil Nadu remains the pioneer in the Community College initiative. She was happy to share that the present Government at the State not only encouraged the Community College system, but also has in its last budget allocated INR 1 crore for student scholarships for those who study through the Community Colleges.

As on date, the Tamil Nadu Open University has 124 Community Colleges, which have enrolled a little more than 40,000 students. Of this, about 70 per cent of the students are employed in the relevant industries. The Tamil Nadu Open University itself has employed more than 55 students who have successfully completed the Diploma Programme from the Tamil Nadu Open University through the Community Colleges. The community college concept has created motivation among the faculty members and other officials in the university and many industrial partners have come forward to help the learners for employment.

Pro Vice Chancellor of IGNOU, Dr. Latha Pillai's presentation focussed on the relevance of the alternative educational model in India. She also mentioned that only this type of alternative and Community college education would serve all segments of society through an open - access admissions policy that offers equal and fair treatment to all students. She also stressed that Community colleges will serve as community – based institutions of higher education and the teaching will be focussed on the skill development.

There was an interactive session between the participants with Dr. Rajasekharan Pillai and Dr. Latha Pillai in which the following points were raised and clarified:

Eligibility level for the Associate Degree (AD) is +2 pass since it is a University programme, and 10th pass for Certificate programme. IGNOU will register the Community Colleges as it can not give affiliation to any college. It gives importance for the functional literacy which has to be the catch word for Community Colleges.

The participants were grouped state-wise to work on the following:

1. What changes would you like to suggest in the Associate Degree programme.
2. Evolve a model for Office Management Associate Degree.
3. What are the Associate Degrees we can provide through our Community Colleges?

The reports of the Group work were presented to the floor and submitted to Fr. Jacob and a few observations were made by Mr. Anto Vincent based on the Group reports. The observations are the following:

1. The Community Colleges are doing good work and serving the target groups.
2. Community Colleges should continue the same mission with much more zeal and vigour.
3. Should not dilute the Community College concept.
4. Internal Auditing for Community Colleges is a must (quality check).
5. Reduction of the Registration fees for the Community Colleges.
6. Institutionalization should not take away the freedom and flexibility of Community Colleges.
7. Opportunity for making self-responsibility as a tool for empowerment.
8. Number of Committees have to be formed.
9. Community Colleges should continue to do the power of bargaining with the state and central governments.

Day-2

Prayer service was led by Fr. Jacob on the theme Energy is Within. Fr. Xavier Alphonse kick started the second day by mentioning that consolidating our Diploma Programme is our topmost priority before plunging into the Associate Degree. Associate Degree is not the main issue for the Community colleges. Only the Diploma Programmes for the school dropouts will effectively work and Associate Degree will come as the enhancement of knowledge and for our Community college students.

Dr. Selvaraj made his presentation and it was wonderful and very informative. He was very passionate and involved in the Community College movement for the past 13 years. He spoke about the growth and genesis of the whole movement from its inception. He stressed the need for the industrial collaboration without which community college system in India would become a failure.

Fr. Xavier Alphonse highlighted the efforts taken in the last 13 years for this Community College movement. He posed the following questions to the participants to be discussed in the Groups based on four types of Community colleges such as Rural, Tribal, Urban and Women Community colleges.

(a) Nature of the Community College

(b) 10 Features of the Community Colleges

(c) 5 points for the improvement of the Community College system.

Mr. Anto's presentation highlighted the importance of the Institutionalization of the system for the sake of serving the target groups. Dr. Thyagarajan's presentation was informative and stressed the TNOU collaboration with the Community colleges and the contribution of TNOU in the growth of the community college movement in India. Interactive session was held between the TNOU officials and the participants in the afternoon. The entire team of officials of the TNOU was present. Fr. Xavier Alphonse introduced the officials and requested the participants to be precise and stick to the following questions:

1. ID cards.
2. Supply of study materials.
3. Examination Center and Hall Tickets.
4. Certificates.

Points were raised by the participants regarding the delay in issue of ID cards, Hall tickets etc. and the need for a receipt for payment made to TNOU.

The Controller and VC of TNOU responded positively and VC promised that the Recognition will be issued to 84 Colleges once the amendment of the GO is made by the Government. The scholarship will be issued at the end of July. The cheques will be issued in the name of students and sent to the respective Community Colleges. Concluding remarks and observations were made by Mr. Anto Vincent. Both the officials and the participants were highly complimented for being soft on the people and hard on the issues, articulating clearly the difficulties faced with the TNOU. We expect the single window system from TNOU. The Community Colleges too should adhere to the rules and regulations of the TNOU and make use of the Cyberlink. Community Colleges must often check the website of TNOU, IGNOU and ICRDCE for the various needs and updates. Vote of thanks was delivered by Fr. Xavier Alphonse and the workshop ended fruitfully with the National Anthem.

2010 - May

A People's Movement

Interview with Xavier Alphonse

Founder Director, Indian Centre for Research and Development of Community College (ICRDCE), Chennai, Reverend Dr. Xavier Alphonse, talks to EDU about the idea of community colleges.

You are one of the pioneers of the community college concept in India. It has not picked up yet. Why?

The concept is new to our country which is home to a variety of educational systems. This one is an alternative system which addresses the needs of those at the bottom of the pyramid. It will take a people's movement and like any other movement it will take time to build. There have been pockets of success and it has huge potential. So far 80,000 people have benefited from this system and 90 per cent of them have been gainfully employed. I believe that the movement will gain momentum as more people begin to comprehend its benefits and more volunteers – NGOs, self help groups join in. It requires tremendous institutional and civil society support. We have to bring together like-minded people and talk about it. Teachers and the communities benefiting from it require orientation. I am no sure how many of the 406 community colleges would survive but we have to make a concerted effort to make this a roaring success.

Do you think the Concept will see a high Push, with IGNOU coming into the Picture?

After IGNOU was made the nodal agency last year, the idea of community colleges has received a big institutional push with national recognition. With IGNOU's footprints in 56 commonwealth countries, community colleges have also got an international recognition. There is lot of in-built flexibility in the programmes which is core to IGNOU's philosophy. The associate degree programme, a distinctive tool for future progression into higher education, has been introduced for the first time in the country.

What are the Challenges you Foresee?

One of the biggest challenges is to ensure that all the participating agencies understand the philosophy inherent in the concept. We need to ensure strict mechanisms are in place to filter the agencies that are merely driven by commercial interest and keep only those that are rooted in community-based action and driven by the philosophy of social transformation. Another challenge is to ensure curriculum is relevant and teachers are trained adequately to meet the particular needs of communities. The fee structure should also be in sync with the philosophy of serving the communities.

How is our system Different from that in the USA?

There are definite differences and we must be alert to these. Our system is people oriented unlike the USA's which is market-oriented. In our system there is a lot of emphasis on teaching life-skills- personality development, communication, computing, linguistics – while in US there is no such particular emphasis. It will still be a while before we reach the stage as in US to enable learners' achieve vertical mobility via credit transfers. Today our emphasis is more on creating a workforce to meet the unique challenges of the new and emerging economy. Our system is more akin to one which can be termed education for livelihood unlike in the US.

What has your Centre been doing to take this Movement Forward?

Since we began in 1995, centre has helped establish 280 colleges across Tamil Nadu. We have also assisted these colleges create systems- curriculum, pedagogy, evaluation, monitoring- besides carrying out constant research. We have also trained over 1800 teachers through our 24 programmes. Significantly, we have taken the movement to Kenya, Tanzania, Uganda and Papua New Guinea.

July – September 2010

TNOU Community College Model in Collaboration with ICRDCE – Chennai

The Community College movement for the empowerment of the disadvantaged and underprivileged began in 1996. The Community Colleges grew over the next ten years all over the country. In 2006 this model was observed by the Tamil Nadu Open University (TNOU) and the Community Colleges were declared as Vocational Programme Centers (VPCs) in 2006.

In the year 2008 with the issue of G.O 163 by the Tamil Nadu Government, this system was recognized and accepted as an alternative system of education, and the Community Colleges were affiliated to TNOU. Today TNOU has recognized 164 Community Colleges in Tamil Nadu as well as in Andhra Pradesh and Himachal Pradesh.

This article traces the concept, history and evolution of Community College system with TNOU in collaboration with ICRDCE Chennai over the period of last 6 years.

<u>Abstract</u>

Announcement made by the Hon'ble Minister for Higher Education - Establishment of Community Colleges in Tamil Nadu - Orders - Issued.

<u>Higher Education (K2) Department</u>

G.O.(Ms).No:163

Dated: 22-5-2008
Thiruvalluvar Aandu-2039
Vaikasi-9

<u>Read:-</u>

1. From the Director of Collegiate Education, Chennai-6, Letter Rc. No.15767/Q2/2007 dt.22.6.2007.
2. From the Joint Secretary, University Grants Commission, Bahadur Shah Zafar Marg, New Delhi-110 002, Letter F.1- 2/2000 (CPP-II) dt.27.9.2007.
3. From the Registrar, Tamil Nadu Open University, DOTE Campus, Guindy, Chennai-25, Letter F/No.11-10(3)/Estt/2007 dt.19.11.2007 and 2.4.2008.
4. From the Director of Medical Education, Kilpauk, Chennai- 10, Letter No.6406/PME/3/2008, dated 14.2.2008.

<u>Order:-</u>

The Community College system in India aims at the empowerment of the disadvantaged through appropriate skills development leading to gainful employment thus making a qualitative difference in the lives of the urban poor, rural poor, tribal poor and women in collaboration with local industrial establishments and potential employers, voluntary organizations after taking into account the opportunities available for employment and self employment in the local area. This has been included in the Eleventh Five Year Plan for establishment and funding recommended by the Ministry of Human Resource Development and University Grants Commission.

2. The Hon'ble Minister for Higher Education during the demand for Higher Education (2007-2008) in the Tamil Nadu Legislative Assembly has announced that the Government will encourage the establishment of Community Colleges and take steps for their integration with the University System by providing Vertical Mobility to those who complete their study in the Community Colleges.

3. The following proposal for implementation of Community Colleges in the State has been arrived at tentatively, so as to provide vertical mobility to such candidates to enable them to pursue higher studies in affiliated college and universities as follows:-

<u>Level – I:</u>

Below 10th Std. candidates (School drop-outs) : They are eligible for admission in certificate programmes in Community Colleges with 16 credits – 6 month duration

After completion of the above Certificate Course, students can take up a bridge course of 16 credits in Community Colleges, which will make them eligible to pursue courses for which 10th Std pass is minimum qualification.

2

Level – II:

10th Std. pass candidates : They are eligible to take one year Diploma Programme of 32 credits in Community Colleges.

After completion of the above Diploma Course, students can take up a Bridge course of 32 credits, which will make them eligible to pursue courses for which +2 pass is the minimum qualification.

Therefore they become eligible to enter into first year Degree Course in affiliated colleges of Conventional Universities / Open Universities and Distance Education Institutions.

4. The views of the Vice-Chancellors of the Universities under the control of Higher Education Department and University Grants Commission have been obtained. Considering the fact that Tamil Nadu Open University is presently offering different programmes of study through Distance Education Mode and only, Tamil Nadu Open University will be offering the Open University courses (Non-formal Distance Education programme) to all those who have completed 18 years, the Government considered that the Tamil Nadu Open University will give recognition to Community Colleges for offering job oriented programmes and the Tamil Nadu Open University will be empowered to frame Norms, Rules and Regulations to maintain quality and standard in the Community College System.

5. Accordingly, the Registrar, Tamil Nadu Open University has submitted proposals for the establishment of Community Colleges system in Tamil Nadu in Polytechnics, Industries, Hospitals, Hotels and Voluntary Organisations.

6. The Government have examined the proposals of Registrar, Tamil Nadu Open University in detail and they have decided to establish the community colleges in Polytechnics, Industries, Hotels and in Voluntary Organisations excluding the scheme in Hospitals. They accordingly issue the following orders for the establishment of community colleges in Tamil Nadu:-

(i) Following types of community colleges can be established.

(a). POLYTECHNICS:

Polytechnics can start the Community Colleges in their own campus itself in the specialized vocational programmes required by the industries in their locality for the development of skills, utilizing the infrastructure and faculty available in the Polytechnics in the evenings and weak end holidays. The practical training can be offered in the workshops / laboratories, related to the skills.

(b).INDUSTIRES:

Industries can start Community Colleges to offer courses related to their area of operation, so that the skilled labours working in the Industry without proper qualifications and certifications can take up these courses for the enhancement of their skills and for certification. In this connection, they have to attend only theory classes during the evening or week ends in the Community Colleges, set up by the Industries within their premises. Practicals can be exempted for them, as they are already working in the same trade in the Industry.

(c). HOTELS :

Hotels with 100 rooms and restaurants in semi urban / rural & 150 rooms in Municipal Corporation area and 200 rooms with restaurants in Chennai can start the Community Colleges to offer courses related to the hotel industry for the enhancement of the skilled labour working in the industry for certification and also for the development of skills

3

elated to the Hotel Industry for the students in their locality. Both theoretical classes and practical training can be given in the hotel and the restaurants.

d). VOLUNTARY ORGANIZATIONS (NGOS)

Voluntary Organizations, who have already established Community Colleges and offering skill development programme with industrial tie-up for providing practical training can also apply for recognition.

ii) The non - industrial agencies should have a strong tie-up with industries, where nternship and hands on experience will be provided and the evidence of tie-up should be submitted to Tamil Nadu Open University along with the application. No Community College other than Industries and Hotels shall be given recognition without ndustrial tie-up.

iii) Tamil Nadu Open University will give recognition to Community Colleges for offering Job Oriented Programmes. The recognized Community Colleges will conduct any of the following Vocational Education Programmes offered by Tamil Nadu Open University.

- DTP Operator
- Early childhood care education
- Fashion Designing and Garment Making
- Diploma in Apparel and Fashion Design
- Refrigeration and Air Conditioning Technician
- House Electrician
- Catering Assistant
- Four Wheeler Mechanism
- Beautician
- Plumbing

Additional Certificate / Diploma courses in other trades in consultation with Industries and Voluntary Organisations can also be offered by Tamil Nadu Open University.

iv) The Tamil Nadu Open University will supply study materials, conduct examinations, evaluation and award Diploma / Certificates .

Community Colleges will carry out activities related to publicity of the courses, conduct of theory classes and practical training.

v) The following infrastructure and other facilities are to be provided by Community Colleges:-

A). FOR COMMUNITY COLLEGES IN INDUSTRIES / HOTELS

Infrastructure

i. Class Rooms
ii. Laboratory / Workshop / Equipments and instruments for offering practical training.
iii. Small Library / Computer Centre / Office

I. Faculty:

i. Co-ordinator / Principal

ii. Work skilled teachers one per course based on requirement.
iii. Lab Assistant for offering practical training based on requirement.

III. Equipments

Equipments required for offering practical training in the relevant trade

IV. Furniture

Minimum Furniture required in Class rooms / Laboratory/ Workshop / Computer Centre

(B) FOR COMMUNITY COLLEGES ESTABLISHED BY THE VOLUNTARY ORGANISATIONS:

I. Infrastructure

1.	Office cum Principal and Staff room	-	500 sqft.
2.	Class rooms per course based on requirement.	-	250 sqft.
3.	Laboratory per course based on requirement.	-	300 sqft.
4.	Library	-	300 sqft.
5.	Computer Centre (required only for Computer related Courses)	-	300 sqft.
6.	Toilets	-	300 sqft.

II. Faculty

1. Principal or Co-ordinator with Degree / Diploma qualification
2. Work skill Teacher with Diploma / Degree / ITI Certificate in the Trade 1 per Course based on requirement.
3. Lab Assistant – 1 in each Lab based on requirement.
4. Assistant / Data Entry Operator – 1.

III. Equipments

As prescribed by Tamil Nadu Open University for each course.

IV. Furniture

Required number of furniture for Class Rooms, Laboratories, Library, Computer Centres, Office, Staff Rooms & Principal's Room should be provided.

(vi) Tamil Nadu Open University, which gives recognition to the Community Colleges is empowered to frame Norms, Rules and Regulations to maintain quality and standard in the Community Colleges System.

(vii) The fee structure for giving approval by Tamil Nadu Open University shall be fixed as follows:-

Application / Processing / Inspection Fee	-	Rs. 5000/-
Recognition Fee	-	Rs.25000/-
Refundable Deposit	-	Rs.50000/-

7. The Government also direct that Community Colleges Development Council be formed with the following composition:-

1.	Minister for Higher Education	Chairman
2.	Vice-Chancellor, Tamil Nadu Open University	Member
3.	The Secretary, Higher Education, Government of Tamil Nadu	Member
4.	Director of Technical Education	Member
5.	Member-Secretary, Tamil Nadu State Council for Higher Education	Member
6.	Two Industrial establishment representatives	
7.	Three Government Representatives [One from Employment & Training, One from Polytechnic Colleges and One from Government ITI)	
8.	Two Representatives from Community Colleges.	

8. The modalities for integration of Community Colleges with the University system by providing vertical mobility to the students who complete their studies in the community colleges will be examined on the lines indicated by the University Grants Commission and orders will be issued separately.

(BY ORDER OF THE GOVERNOR)

K.GANESAN
SECRETARY TO GOVERNMENT.

To
The Registrar of all Universities,
(Under the Control of Higher Education Department.
The Director of Collegiate Education, Chennai-6.
The Commissioner of Technical Education, Chennai-25.
The Director of School Education, Chennai-6.
The Director of Government Examinations, Chennai-6.
The Secretary, University Grants Commission, New Delhi.
The Secretary to Government of India,
Ministry of Human Resource Development,
Department of Higher Education, New Delhi.
The Vice-Chairman, Tamil Nadu State Council for Higher Education, Chennai-5.
The Director of Medical Education, Chennai-10.
The Accountant General, Chennai-18/35.

<u>Copy to:</u>
The Chief Minister's Office, Chennai-9.
The Sr.P.A. to Hon'ble Minister for Higher Education, Chennai-9.
The Health and Family Welfare/ Industries/Finance/School Education Department,. Chennai-9.
All Sections in Higher Education Department.

//forwarded/by order//

Sd/xx
Section Officer.

G.O. – II

Abstract

Tamil Nadu Open University, Chennai-25 Waiving of Refundable Deposit of Rs. 50,000 for Community College run by voluntary organisation – Orders – issued

Higher Education (K1) Department

G.O. (Ms) No. 362

Dated 8-10-2009
Purattasi-22
Thiruvaliuvar Aandu-2040
Read:-

1. G.O. (Ms) No. 163 Higher Education (K2) Department, dated 22.5.2008
2. From the Director, Indian Centre for Research and Development of Community Education, Chennai Letter dated 21.12.2009
3. From the Registrar, Tamil Nadu Open University, Chennai-25, Letter No. TNOU/SOCF/CC/2009-02, DATED 2.4.2009

ORDER

In the Government order first read above, the Government among other things have ordered that Tamil Nadu Open University shall give recognition to Community College for offering job oriented programmes. For granting recognition, the following fees structure has been prescribed:

S. No.	*Description*		*Amount*
1.	Application/Processing/Inspection Fee	-	Rs. 5000/-
2.	Recognition Fee	-	Rs. 25000/-
3.	Refundable Deposit	-	Rs. 50,000/-

2. In the letter second read above, the Director, Indian Centre for Research and Development of community Education has stated that in the consultation held on 3rd of July, 2008 between the Community Colleges and Tamil Nadu Open University, Chennai, it was agreed that the Community Colleges may be exempted from the payment of refundable deposit of Rs. 50,000/- ordered in the Government order first read above.

3. Accordingly, the Registrar, Tamil Nadu Open University, Chennai-25 in his letter third read above has submitted proposal for waiving of collection of refundable deposit of Rs. 50,000/- for community Colleges run by voluntary organisations, since it is difficult for them to mobilize the amount and keeping in mind the target group they are serving.

He has therefore requested the Government to issue an amendment to the G.O. Ms. No. 163, Higher Education (K2) Department, dated 22.5.2008.

4. The Government have examined the proposal of the Registrar, Tamil Nadu Open University, Chennai-25 in detail and they have decided that refundable deposit of Rs. 50,000/- need not be collected from the Community Colleges run by the voluntary organisation since they impart vocational and the coping skills to poor students belonging to disadvantaged sections of the society.

(BY ORDER OF THE GOVERNOR)

K. GANESAN
Principal Secretary to Government

To
The Registrar, Tamil Nadu Open University, Chennai-25
The Director, Indian Centre for Research and Department of Community Education, Chennai
The Director of Collegiate Education, Chennai-6
The Registrars of all Universities.
The Finance (Edn. I Department, Chennai-9
All Sectors in Higher Education Department

//forwarded/by order//

Section Officer

References

1. Alphonse, Xavier, "Community Colleges: A National Phenomenon", Extracts from *University News*, Vol. 39, No. 26, June 25 – July 1, 2001, p. 8.
2. Alphonse, Xavier, "Best to the Least: Community College Movement in India – An Update", Extracts from *New Frontiers in Education*, Vol. 32, No. 2, April – June, 2002, p. 83.
3. "Developing Community Colleges", *Southern Economist*, Bangalore, October 1, 2003, p. 26.
4. Alphonse, Xavier, and James C., "Best to the Least: Education for Livelihood – Community Colleges in India", Extracts from *University News*, New Delhi, Vol. 42(14), April 5-11, 2004, p. 11.
5. "Fit for Life", *The New Indian Express, City Express*, June 16, 2004.
6. Alphonse, Xavier, "Integration of Community College System With TNOU" *New Frontiers in Education*, New Delhi, Vol. XXXV, No. 3, July-September, 2005, pp. 216-247
7. Alphonse, Xavier, "Empowerment of Socio-Economic Weaker Sections through the Community College System and the support of the Universities in India" *University News*, New Delhi, 43, (47), November 21-27, 2005. pp. 35 - 40.
8. Alphonse, Xavier, "Community College System and its Future in India", *New Frontiers in Education, New Delhi,* Vol. XXXVI, No. 3, July-September, 2005, pp. 294-300.
9. S. Muthukumaran, "*Best to the Least – An Eye Opener"News,* New Delhi, 43 (47), November 21-27, 2005 p. 41.
10. Alphonse, Xavier, "Marching with the Marginalized", *The Hindu, Education Plus,* December, 19, 2005.
11. Alphonse, Xavier, "Education for Livelihood", *The Hindu,* Wednesday, December, 21, 2005.
12. Aludiapillai. K., *"Marching with the Marginalized"* Tamil Nadu State Council for Higher Education and Former Vice Chancellor, Madurai Kamaraj University, TSCHE, lady Wellington Campus, Kamaraj Salai, Chennai-600 005.
13. Mohanty, Ajay Kumar, "Community College Empowerment Endorsed – A Well Planned BooK", *University News*, New Delhi, 44 (37), September 11-17, 2006.
14. "Inauguration of ICRDCE" *News Today*, Chennai, Saturday, 2 September 2006.
15. "ICRDCE lunched in Chennai", *The Hindu, Education Plus*, Monday, September 11, 2006.
16. Alphonse, Xavier, "ICRDCE launched in Chennai", *University News*, New Delhi, Volume 44, No. 42, October 16-22, 2006.
17. Keener, Bob, "Indian Community Colleges", CCID, *International News*, Spring 2006.

18. Alphonse, Xavier., "Learning for Livelihood" *Frontline*, Volume 23, No. 2, January 28-February 10, 2006.

19. Alphonse, Xavier., "Community Colleges: Opportunity is the key to Success", *New Frontiers in Education*, New Delhi Vol. XXXVII, No.1, January – March, 2007, pp. 56-63.

20. Bhopal Community College Evaluated, *Central Chronicle*, Bhopal, Sunday, July 15, 2007.

21. Interview of Fr. Xavier Alphonse, S.J., Director, ICRDCE, Chennai. *Christian Manager*, Volume 8, Issue 6, August–September 2008, pp. 20-24.

22. Gandhi, Arumuga, "Community College an Alternative to Include the Excluded in Higher Education", *New Frontiers in Education,* New Delhi, Vol. 42, No. 1, January-March, 2009, pp. 32-36.

23. Alphonse, Xavier , *Community College Movement at a Glance (1995 - 2009),* ICRDCE, Chennai.

24. Alphonse, Xavier, "Community College – the scope and space for the disadvantaged for Education and Employment" *New Frontiers of Education,* New Delhi, Volume 42, No. 3, July – September 2009. pp. 285-291.

25. Alphonse, Xavier, *"Decennial celebration of ICRDCE" University News,* New Delhi, Volume 47, No. 5, February 2-8, 2009, p. 18.

26. "Recognition for Community Colleges likely by year end" *The Hindu*, Sunday, March 08, 2009.

27. Bhatia, Surbhi, "Community Colleges Groomed to Work" *Times of India, Education Times*, Chennai, Monday 23, February 2009.

28. Alphonse, Xavier, "National workshop on the Institutionalization of the Community college System", *New Frontiers in Education,* New Delhi, Vol. 42, No.3, July-September, 2009.

29. People's Movement, *Edu Tech*, May 2010.

30. *Alphonse, Xavier,* "TNOU Community College Model in Collaboration with ICRDCE - Chennai", *New Frontiers in Education*, New Delhi. Vol. 43, No. 3, July-Sep, 2010 and Alphonse, Xavier, "TNOU-ICRDCE Consultation Meeting on Community College", *University News,* New Delhi. Vol. 48, No. 31, August 2-8, 2010.

14

Total Quality Management of the Community Colleges (2011)

Part I

TOTAL QUALITY MANAGEMENT OF THE COMMUNITY COLLEGES

1. Introduction

The aim of this section is to clarify for ourselves the concept of Total Quality Management (TQM) and also its relevance and application to the running of the community colleges.

A definition of Total Quality Management (TQM) has been taken and it has been analyzed in the context of functioning of community colleges.

The following is the outline of the presentation:

(a) Definition of Total Quality Management (TQM)

(b) Its application to the Community Colleges

(c) Analysis and application to the community colleges

1.1 The Definition of Quality

Quality is "the totality of characteristics and features of a product or process, which facilitate the realization of given requirements".

1.2 Definition of Total Quality Management (TQM):

Total Quality Management (TQM) is a positive attempt by the organization concerned to improve the structural, infrastructural, attitudinal, behavioural and methodological ways of delivering to the end customers, with emphasis on consistency, improvement in quality, competitive enhancement, all with the aim of satisfying or delighting the end customer.

- Total Quality Management (TQM) means a total operational philosophy, which covers every aspect of the organization and a set of guiding principles that represent the foundation of a continuously improving organization.

2. The Definition to be Analysed and its Application to the Community Colleges

"A planned proactive process approach to facilitate change by aligning people with processes and technology to achieve an organisation's vision and performance objectives".

3. Analysis and Application to Community Colleges:

3.1 Proactive process approach

- To establish and secure social justice and equality of opportunity.
- To overcome social exclusion, educational exclusion and economic exclusion.
- To convert disadvantage into advantage (personal and societal transformation).
- To empower the marginalized.
- To make positive intervention in the lives of young men and women who are looking for hope.
- To serve as catalysts for personal and social change.
- To enhance the community with skills required for jobs.
- To make the poor share the fruits of development and technological revolution.
- To achieve the objectives of development process
  - (a) Alleviation of poverty
  - (b) Enrichment of human resources and potential.
- To promote social equilibrium in a growing economy.
- To respond democratically to globalization
- To find suitable employment with appropriate skills
- To answer the call of the territory.
- To discover the latent and hidden individual potential.
- To create better, self confident, self supporting individuals.

3.2 Facilitating Change

- Personal Change
- Familial Change

- Communitarian Change
- Social Change
- National Change

"Day By Day Everyday Better And Better".

Creating a positive climate and environment for individual and societal growth.

3.3 Aligning people, processes and technology

Stake holders: students, teachers, parents, industrial partners, employers, community leaders, service organizations, state and central government bring them all together to achieve positive results.

3.4 Planned Processes

(1) Understanding the concept of the community college.

(2) Seven stages of preparation.

(3) Need analysis.

(4) Identifying enthusiastic industrial partners.

(5) Identifying the least, the most disadvantaged push-outs, left-outs and the marginalized.

(6) Using different teaching methodologies

(7) No profit motivation

(8) Facilitating the learning process

(9) Counseling the disadvantaged, problematic and those struggling to discover their roots and to move forward in life.

(10) Ongoing dynamic relationship with industrial partners.

(11) Knowledge of the family situation of the students.

(12) Feedback mechanism from students, community, parents and employers.

(13) The ongoing process of evaluation and assessment and portfolio of our students.

(14) Meaningful and fruitful internship of the students.

(15) Positive efforts to place students in jobs that are income generating.

3.5 Technology

Using computers, e-mail, internet, adequate infrastructural facilities including modest labs for learning and reasonably comfortable classes.

3.6 To achieve an organisation's vision and mission

1. Urban Community College - Vision

- Committed to the Community
- People, all our stake holders, are treated as our community College's greatest assets. Our primary value is relationship among the stake-holders based on sensitivity, compassion, trust and respect. With relationship as the base we believe we can bring out people's potential and help realize their talents towards our unified purpose, namely to equip our students "Fit for Life", and "Fit for Job". We believe in giving "Best to the Least". We believe in integrating character formation of our students along with development of their competencies. We value in harmonizing *work and faith.*

2. Rural Community College – Vision

- The vision of **Swami Vivekananda Rural Community College** is to give to our country every year 500 – 600 young men and women for a place in the industrial advancement of India as active, result – oriented and positive powerhouses. To be counted among the best community colleges in the sub-continent. To replicate the model through more, newer NGO's and create multiplier effect.
- RUSHA Community College is to include the excluded economically and socially disadvantaged groups and to give the best to the least.

3. Tribal Community College - Vision

- "To be of the community for the community and by the community and to produce responsible citizens".
- "Empowerment of the tribal women through skilled education".

4. Community College for Women – Vision

- "Education and empowerment, life to the least".
- "To empower women at all levels to struggle for justice"

5. Community College for Prisoners – Vision

- To make the prisoners fully human and skilled persons -fit for life and fit for job.

6. Community College for HIV infected – Vision

- Improve the quality of life of the HIV infected and affected persons we wish to improve the quality of life of the deprived youth so that they may enjoy a fuller life in the society.

3.7 Performance, Objectives/Quality Parameters

1. Target Group
    - Educational exclusion
    - Economic exclusion
    - Social exclusion
2. Minimum input and Maximum output
3. Industrial partners and internship
4. Job Placement – impact on the community
5. Subsidy and scholarship to poor students
6. Well defined administrative structure
7. Committed and qualified staff
8. Impact on the community in terms of alleviation poverty and income generating
9. Motivation for higher education and vertical mobility
10. Teaching of life skills – to make better human beings
11. Responses to the employment and social needs of the local community
12. Consistency in the preservation of documentation and registers
13. Meaningful and periodic interaction with the parents and community leaders
14. Innovative and facilitating teaching methodologies
15. The measurable and quantifiable results: learning of knowledge, growing attitude and mastery of skills leading to gainful employment.

Overall view of the Evaluation from the data collected from 135 colleges for the last 15 years

15

Pan Indian Scenario of Community Colleges

Evaluation done in Academic/Administration/Financial/Impact on the Community/Vertical Mobility of individual Community Colleges

Part – I ACADEMIC (135 Community Colleges)

1. Total Number of Students covered - 62008

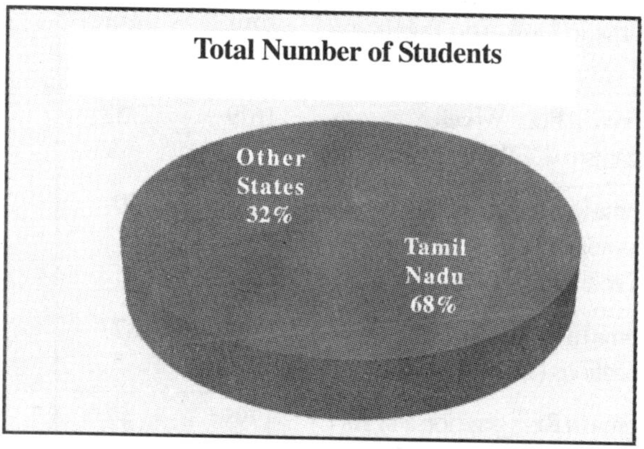

Gender Status

	TN	*OS*	*Total*	*Percentage*
Male	11417	5032	**16449**	27 %
Female	30832	14727	**45559**	73 %
Total	**42249**	**19759**	**62008**	**100 %**

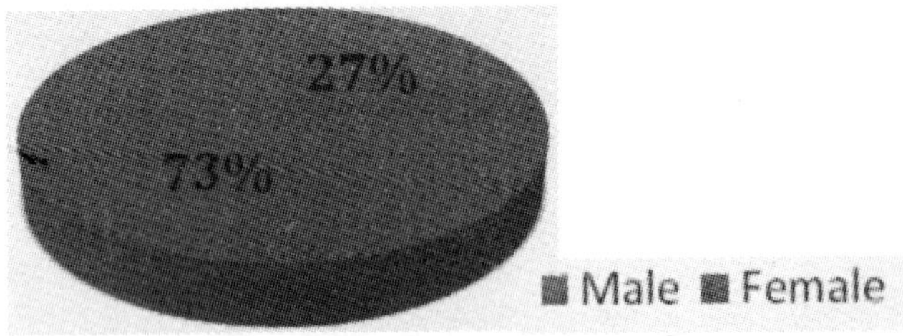

Gender Status

2. Course wise Students

S. No.	Name of the Course	Tamil Nadu	Other States	Total
1.	Diploma in Health Assistant (DHA/DFNA)	11607	1982	13589
2.	Diploma in Early Childhood Care and Education/ Diploma in Pre-Primary Teacher Training (DECE/DPTT)	5806	1302	7108
3.	Diploma in Fashion Designing and Garment Making (DFGM)	3588	2932	6520
4.	Diploma in Desk Top Publishing (DDTP)	5791	461	6252
5.	Diploma in Four Wheeler Mechanism (DFWM)	1619	753	2372
6.	Diploma in Medical Lab Technology/Diploma in Clinical Lab Technology (DMLT/DCLT)	1656	507	2163
7	Diploma in Computer Applications (DCAS)	1264	877	2141
8	Diploma in Refrigeration and Air Conditioning Technician (DRAT)	1795	47	1842
9	Diploma in Office Management (DOM)	270	1536	1806
10	Diploma in House Electrician (DHE)	1501	225	1726

contd..

contd..

S. No.	*Name of the Course*	*Tamil Nadu*	*Other States*	*Total*
11.	Short Course/Spoken English	259	845	1104
12.	Diploma in Two Wheeler Mechanism (DTWM)	491	0	491
13.	Diploma in Masonary, Carpending, Tile and Water Proofing	0	449	449
14.	Diploma in Computer Hardware Servicing (DCHS)	311	108	419
15.	Diploma in Computerized Financial Accounting (DCFA)	405	0	405
16.	Diploma in Hospitality Management	0	382	382
17.	Diploma in Catering Assistant	346	0	346
18.	Diploma in Beautician	153	192	345
19.	Diploma in Fitter and Welding (DFWELDE)	82	220	302
20.	Diploma in CT Scan / X0Ray / CHN	295	0	295
21.	Costume Jewellery Making/Paper Cups and Office Cover Making/Glass Painting (CJM / PU andOCM/ GL.P)	230	0	230
22.	Diploma in M.S. Office	85	140	225
23.	Diploma in Retail Management	0	217	217
24.	Diploma in Home Appliances and Radio and Television Servicing (DMS of HOME / RADIO)	215	0	215
25.	Diploma in Business Oriented Computer Application (DBOCA)	197	0	197
26.	Diploma in Foreign Trade and Import-Export Documentation(DFTIED)	180	0	180
27.	Diploma in Geriatric Nursing (DGN)	165	0	165
28.	Diploma in Plumbing	0	148	148
29.	Diploma in Varma and Massage (DVM)	131	0	131
30.	Diploma in Typing	38	86	124

contd..

S.No.	*Name of the Course*	*Tamil Nadu*	*Other States*	*Total*
31.	Diploma in Tally/Corporate	112	10	122
32.	Diploma in Physical and Rehabilitation (DPR)	115	0	115
33.	Diploma in Physiotherapy (DPT)	110	0	110
34.	Diploma in Hotel Management	0	75	75
35.	Diploma in Computer Usage and Management Accountancy (DCOMA)	71	0	71
36.	Diploma in Textile	0	69	69
37.	Diploma in Digital Video and Photography	0	67	67
38.	Diploma in CARD	0	53	53
39.	Diploma in Agro Business	0	43	43
40.	Diploma in Information Technology (DIT)	41	0	41
41.	Diploma in Communication English (DCE)	24	0	24
42.	Diploma in Community Health Worker (DCHW)	20	0	20
43.	Diploma in Driving	0	18	18
44.	Diploma in Computerized Accounting Management (DCAM)	14	0	14
45.	Diploma in Hospital Administration (DHoA)	13	0	13
46.	Diploma in Animation (DIA)	12	0	12
47.	Diploma in Marketing Management (DMM)	9	0	9
48.	Diploma in Mobile Phone Servicing (DMPS)	7	0	7
49.	Diploma in Barbending	5	0	5
50.	Diploma in Web Designing	0	3	3
	Total	**39225**	**13747**	**52972**

3. Profile of the Students

Marital Status

	Tamil Nadu	*Other States*	*Total*	*Percentage*
Unmarried	36369	17226	53595	86
Married	5475	2485	7960	12.5
Widows	294	24	318	1
Divorced	111	24	135	0.5
Total	**42249**	**19759**	**62008**	**100**

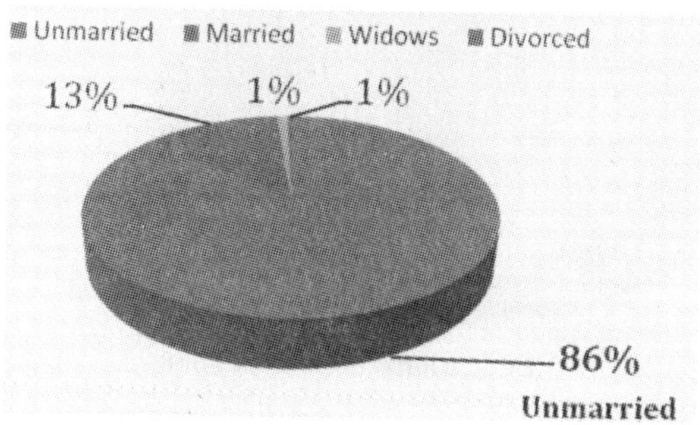

Marital Status

Age

	Tamil Nadu	*Other States*	*Total*	*Percentage*
18 – 22	31676	12426	44102	71
23 – 26	6342	4701	11043	18
26 – 30	2371	1864	4235	7
31 - Above	1860	768	2628	4
Total	**42249**	**19759**	**62008**	**100**

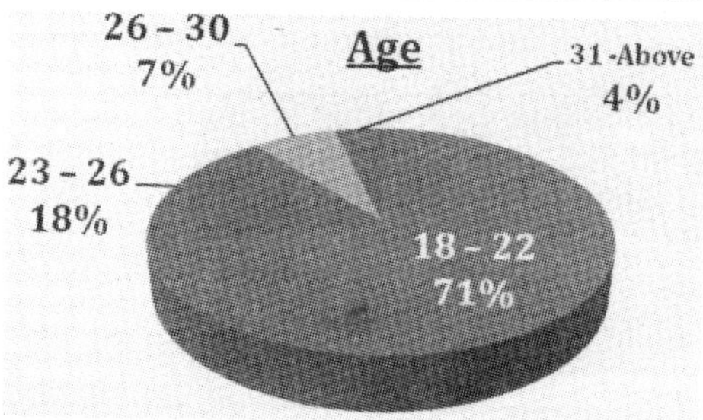

Age

Educational Status (Qualification)

	Tamil Nadu	*Other States*	*Total*	*Percentage*
Below 10th	7722	4903	12625	20
10th Passed	11596	7751	19347	32
12th Passed	20883	5797	26680	43
Degree	2048	1308	3356	5
Total	**42249**	**19759**	**62008**	**100**

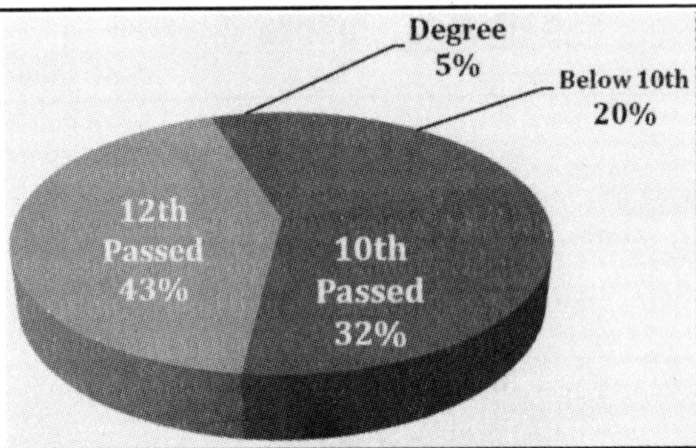

Educational Qualification

Social Status (Caste)

	Tamil Nadu	*Other State*	*Total*	*Percentage*
SC	14868	3758	18626	30
ST	626	7402	8028	13
MBC	9145	1130	10275	17
BC	15949	2743	18692	30
OC	1661	4726	6387	10
Total	**42249**	**19759**	**62008**	**100**

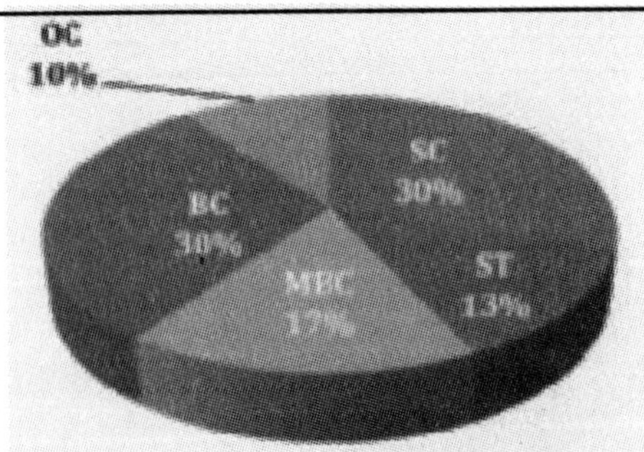

Social Status

Economic Status (Family Monthly Income)

	Tamil Nadu	*Other State*	*Total*	*Percentage*
Below-1,000	13353	7569	20922	34
1,001-2,000	15278	6422	21700	35
2,001-3,000	8667	3223	11890	19
3,001-above	4951	2545	7496	12
Total	**42249**	**19759**	**62008**	**100**

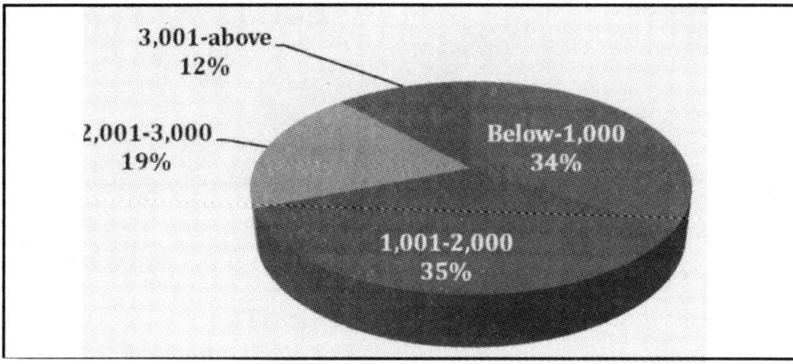

Economic Status

Religious Status

	Tamil Nadu	*Other States*	*Total*	*Percentage*
Hindus	26926	8640	35566	57
Christians	12678	9597	22275	36
Muslims	2613	801	3414	6
Others	32	721	753	1
Total	**42249**	**19759**	**62008**	**100**

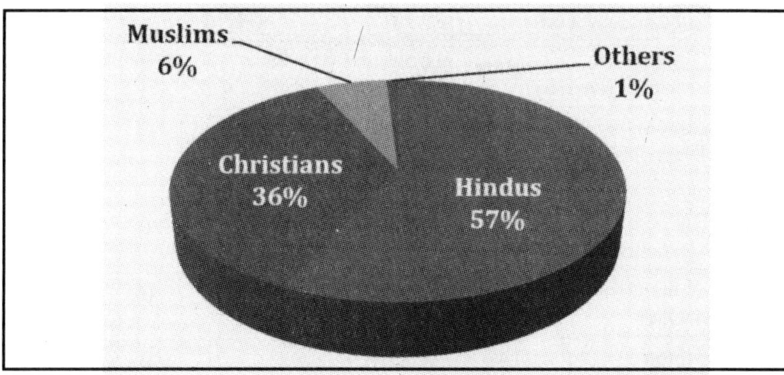

Religious Status

Physically Challenged

	Tamil Nadu	*Other States*	*Total*	*Percentage*
Physically Challenged	469	148	**617**	1
Others	41780	19611	**61391**	99
Total	**42249**	**19759**	**62008**	**100**

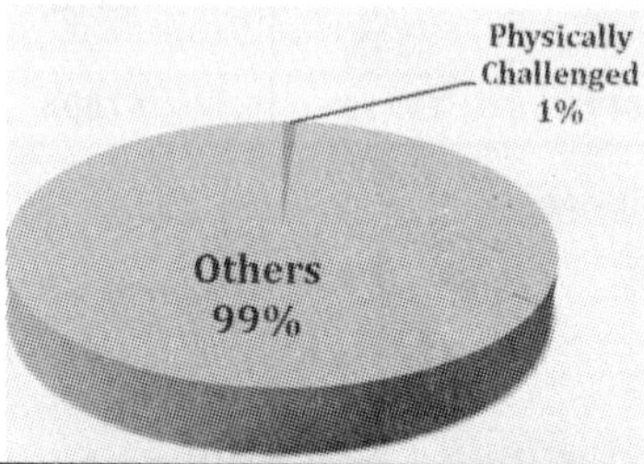

Physically Challenged

4. Industrial Partners

4.1 Course Wise

Sl. No.	*Name of the Course*	*Tamil Nadu*	*Other States*	*Total*
1.	Diploma in Health Assistant (DHA)	521	107	628
2.	Diploma in Desk top Publishing (DTP)	500	20	520
3.	Diploma in Early Childhood Care and Education (DECE)	376	39	415
4.	Diploma in Fashion Designing and Garment Making (DFGM)	320	23	343
5.	Diploma in House Electrician (DHE)	141	03	144
6.	Diploma in Refrigeration and Air Conditioning Technician (DRAT)	87	3	90
7.	Diploma in Computer Hardware Servicing (DCHS)	76	10	86
8.	Diploma in Medical Lab Technology/Diploma in Clinical Lab Technology (DMLT/DCLT)	52	14	66
9.	Diploma in Four Wheeler Mechanism (DFWM)	67	6	73
10.	Diploma in Office Management (DOM)	33	16	49
11.	Diploma in Two Wheeler Mechanism (DTWM)	33	0	33

contd...

Sl. No.	*Name of the Course*	*Tamil Nadu*	*Other States*	*Total*
12.	Diploma in Computerized Financial Accounting (DCFA)	28	0	28
13.	Diploma in Tally	25	2	27
14.	Diploma in Catering Assistant (DCA)	49	2	51
15.	Diploma in Hospital Administration (DHoA)	12	2	14
16.	Diploma in Computer Applications (DCAS)	25	3	28
17.	Diploma in Beautician	13	7	20
18.	Diploma in Mobile Phone Servicing (DMPS)	10	0	10
19.	Agro Business	0	7	7
20.	Hospitality Management	0	7	7
21.	Diploma in Foreign Trade & Import-Export Documentation (DFTIED)	6	0	6
22.	Diploma in Fittering and Welding (DF WELDE)	6	0	6
23.	Diploma in Business Oriented Computer Application (DBOCA)	5	0	5
24.	Call Centers	0	5	5
25.	Diploma in Computerized Accounting Management (DCAM)	4	0	4
26.	Diploma in Retail Management	0	4	4
27.	Diploma in Bartending	2	0	2
28.	Diploma in Animation (DIA)	2	0	2
29.	Diploma in Digital Video and Photography	0	3	3
30.	Diploma in Physical Rehabilitation (DPR)	2	0	2
31.	Diploma in Varma and Massage	2	0	2
		2397	**283**	**2680**

4.2 Duration of Internship

Sl. No.	*Duration*	*Tamil Nadu*	*Other States*	*Total*
1	Every Week End	2	0	2
2	Two Weeks	0	2	2
3	One Month	7	5	12
4	Two Months	71	38	109
5	Two and half Months	1	0	1
6	Three Months	5	0	5
7	Six Months	3	3	131

5. Recognition

S.No.	*Recognition*	*Tamil Nadu*	*Other States*	*Total*
1.	Tamil Nadu Open University (TNOU)	94	3	97
2.	Indira Gandhi National Open University (IGNOU)	21	10	31
3.	Manomanian Sundarnar University, Tirunelveli (MSU)	11	0	11
4.	Other Recognition (NIOS)	5	2	7
5.	Without Recognition	0	31	31

Part – II ADMINISTRATION (135 Community Colleges)

1. Infrastructure Facilities

	Tamil Nadu	*Other States*	*Total*
Adequate	74	36	110
Not Adequate	15	10	25

2. Building

	Tamil Nadu	***Other States***	*Total*
Owned	72	42	114
Rented	17	2	19

3. Types of Organisations

	Tamil Nadu	*Other States*	*Total*
NGOs	31	3	34
Trust/Society (Religious congregation, Catholic Dioceses, C.S.I Dioceses and others)	58	42	100

4. Administration Structure

4.1. Governing Boards

	Tamil Nadu	*Other States*	*Total*
Governing Boards	85	46	131
Without Governing Boards	4	-	4

4.2. Advisory Boards

Sl. No	*Name of the Course*	*Tamil Nadu*	*Other States*	*Total*
1	Diploma in Health Assistant (DHA)	21	5	26
2	Diploma in Desk Top Publishing (DDTP)	14	1	15
3	Diploma in Fashion Designing and Garment Making (DFGM)	10	3	13
4	Diploma in Early Childhood Care and Education (DECE)	11	8	19
5	Diploma in Four wheeler Mechanism (DFWM)	3	0	3
6	Diploma in House Electrician (DHE)	4	0	4

4.3. Directors/Principals

	Directors / Principals	*Life Skills Teachers*	*Work Skills Teachers*	*Guest Lectures*	*Support-ive Staff*
Tamil Nadu	89	151	383	6	17
Other States	45	100	225	31	7
Total	**134**	**251**	**608**	**37**	**24**

5. Salary Range of the Staff (Number of Teachers)

Salary	*Tamil Nadu*	*Other States*	*Total*
1001 -2000	42	39	81
2001- 3000	97	48	145
3001- 4000	97	37	134
4001-5000	59	23	82
5001- 6000	28	12	40
6001- 7000	18	6	24
7001- 8000	14	4	18
8001- 9000	5	1	6
9001- 10000	9	1	10
10,000 and Above	19	0	19

Part – III Financial (82 Community Colleges)

1. Income Over Expenditure/Deficit

Income (In Rupees)			
	2007-2008	*2008 –2009*	*2009 –2010*
Tamil Nadu	1,89,00,747 (41 Colleges)	2,41,71,146 (49 Colleges)	2,80,06,634 (57 Colleges)
Other States	70,67,169 (20 Colleges)	1,12,43,280 (23 Colleges)	98,71,043 (25 Colleges)
Total	**2,59,67,916 (61 Colleges)**	**3,54,14,426 (72 Colleges)**	**3,78,77,677 (82 Colleges)**

Expenditure (In Rupees)			
	2007-2008	*2008 –2009*	*2009 –2010*
Tamil Nadu	1,93,13,501 (41 Colleges)	2,56,49,956 (49 Colleges)	2,61,37,505 (57 Colleges)
Other States	66,86,107 (20 Colleges)	1,26,71,694 (23 Colleges)	1,11,77,713 (25 Colleges)
Total	**2,59,99,608 (61 Colleges)**	**3,83,21,650 (72 Colleges)**	**4,07,41,009 (82 Colleges)**

Deficit (In Rupees)			
	2007-2008	*2008 –2009*	*2009 –2010*
Tamil Nadu	25,07,675 (18 Colleges)	36,59,507 (23 Colleges)	37,91,321 (28 Colleges)
Other States	20,01,853 (8 Colleges)	53,18,409 (11 Colleges)	44,81,399 (10 Colleges)
Total	**45,09,528 (26 Colleges)**	**89,77,916 (34 Colleges)**	**84,68,585 (38 Colleges)**

Deficit			
	2007-2008	*2008 – 2009*	*2009 – 2010*
Number of Colleges	26 Colleges	34 Colleges	38 Colleges

1. Subsidies/Scholarships (82 Community Colleges)

	Total Number of Colleges
Scholarship	54
Local Contribution	70
Congregation and Diocese	29
Foreign Funds	25
Government Funding from the Department of Social Welfare	16
Scholarship given by the Tamil Nadu Government	81

3. Fee Charged from the students from Rs. 2000 to Rs. 9000

Part – IV Impact on the Community (126 Community Colleges)

1. Total number of students employed - 40763
2. Total number of students gone for Higher Education - 7710
3. Educational Qualification (87 Colleges)

	Tamil Nadu	*Other States*	*Total*
Below 10th to 10th Pass	2329	743	**3072**
Below 12th to 12th Pass	3287	934	**4221**
12 to Degree Level	2343	500	**2843**
Total			**10136**

4. Salary Range Job Placement From 32 Colleges (Highest Salary Rs. 32,000)

	Below - 1000	*1000- 2000*	*2001 - 3000*	*3001 - 4000*	*4001- 5000*	*5001- 6000*	*6001 - 7000*	*7000 and above*
Total Number students	**155**	**987**	**1246**	[illegible]	**326**	**170**	**149**	**195**

5.6 Students sent to US Community Colleges by the US Consulate

S. No.	Name of the Student	Community College Name	Year
1.	Ms. Elizabeth Beena Netto	Sacred Heart Community College, Villupuram	2010
2.	Ms. Jancy Lourdhu Mary	Sacred Heart Community College, Villupuram	2010
3.	Ms. Rajendran Jayabharathi	Tarbes community College, Bangalore	2011
4.	Mr. Anthony Dass Christopher	Bangalore Community College, Bangalore	2011
5.	Mr. Lazar Sajan	Hindustan Community College, Padur	2011
6.	Ms. E. Gomathi	YWCA Community College, Chennai	2011

Part – V. Contribution of ICRDCE to the Movement

1. Established number of Community Colleges - 293 (from 20 States)
2. Number of Teachers Training Programme conducted - 25
3. Number of Teachers Trained
   (a) India - 1365
   (b) Other Countries - 129
4. Publications - 23
5. Regional Workshops - 55
   1. Samudaya Kalluri Oir Arimugam
   2. Changing Track
   3. Mismatch
   4. Back to the Villages
   5. Community Colleges in India, Education for Livelihood.
6. National workshops and Conferences - 6
7. Consultations - 43
8. International Conferences - Presentations - 28
9. International Networking (Papua New Guinea (PNG), East Africa and Other Countries)
   - PNG - 10 Community Colleges started in parallel stream to Vocational centres.
   - 25 Community Colleges to be established before 2012
   - 10 Community Colleges are functioning in East Africa

10. Scholarships to the students given by ICRDCE

Year	*Number of Community Colleges*	*Total Number of Students*	*Amount*
2006 - 2007	23	443	Rs. 4,65,000
2007 - 2008	30	518	Rs. 5,00,000

11. Financial assistance to children affected by Tsunami
    - BATCH - I - 933
    - BATCH - II - 625

    Total 1558
12. Special service to prisoners through Local Community Colleges in collaboration with TNOU and Jail Department.
    (a) 13 Centres - 220 Prisoners

Part III : Observations on the Data and Suggestions to MHRD

1. The Community Colleges have definitely served the Target Group
    (a) Economically
    (b) Socially
    (c) Educationally backward sections of the society
2. The Community Colleges maintain the secular character. The Target group served goes beyond caste, religion, language and region
3. The Community Colleges have helped not only individuals but also the families and they have become catalysts for social upliftment and empowerment.
4. The Community Colleges help in the alleviation of poverty and enrichment of human resources thus paving the way for National development.
5. The Community Colleges are the joint effort of the service minded organizations dedicated and committed Administrators/Directors/ Teachers, socially responsible Industrial partners and the Community Leaders.
6. Vertical Mobility

TNOU Diploma holders for the last 6 years

(a)	Computer based Courses	-	5213
(b)	Electrical Courses	-	1389
(c)	Mechanical Courses	-	3024
(d)	Catering Courses	-	542
(e)	Health Related Courses	-	11916
(f)	Education Related Courses	-	9383
(g)	Fashion Designing Courses	-	1418
Total			**32885**

There is a possibility of Vertical Mobility of providing associate degrees of both TNOU & IGNOU credit through transfer and also the facility to complete Community College certificate programme below 10th Standard, 10th Standard Bridge Course, 12th Standard Bridge Course to become eligible to take the diploma and degree programmes of TNOU and IGNOU. This will also increase enrollment ratio in Higher Education.

Conclusion

Considering the above I would like to make the following suggestions to MHRD, New Delhi as per the proposal submitted to the ministry:

1. All India recognition for the alternative system of education based on Quality parameters.
2. The training cost given to the students by way of scholarships for skill development. Rs. 10000 in order to reach out poorest of the poor in the society and to create social equilibrium in growing economy.

This funding should be administrated in a relative manner ensuring accountability and responsibility fixed on the individual Institution.

- Rs. 5000 at the time of admission
- Rs. 3000 after the completion of work skills
- Rs. 2000 after the Job placement

3. The Community Colleges should be given institutional grant by way of financial assistance not for the buildings but for the enhancement of equipment and quality training.
4. Colleges serving the Urban poor 10 lakhs

   Colleges serving the Rural poor 15 lakhs

   College serving the Tribal poor 15 lakhs

   Colleges serving the women 15 lakhs

Special Groups

Like prisoners, HIV, Trans genders and physically challenged 20 lakhs

5. This is one time grant given to the institutions to promote the Quality of Community Colleges.
6. In the XIth plan 100 crores have been allotted for the purpose of Community Colleges - skills development. So I request the MHRD to guide us with the funding mechanism to help these Institutions.

Given below is the extract from the document of XI th PLAN

"Setting up of additional 210 Community Colleges, mainly in northern, western and eastern parts of the country will be supported on placement based funding. Existing 190 community colleges (largely in southern States, some of which offer diploma courses) will also be supported for capacity building, training cost (equipment, faculty development, TLM, stipend, etc., but not for civil works and other capital costs). Funding will be based on MoU between community colleges, states and MHRD."

XIth Plan Document , Volume II- Page 51 Extract from the speech of President Barack Obama Sept. 27, 2010

Another priority Obama wants to fulfill is training a strong workforce that may be ready for the occupations in the future. He sees Community Colleges playing a large role in such training.

"Community Colleges are going to play a critical role in getting there, and I've asked Dr. Jill Biden to hold the first-ever White House Summit on Community College," Obama said. "That way stakeholder are going to be able to discuss how community colleges can make sure we've got the most educated workforce in the world in relevant subjects that help people get jobs."[1]

Reference

1. Alphonse, Xavier, "Total Quality Management of Community Colleges", New Frontiers in Education, New Delhi. Vol. 44, No.1, January – March, 2011.

16

The Curriculum of a Community College

1. Introduction

There has been a lot of struggle during the last six years in discovering the relevant and the needed curriculum to be given to the students of the Community College. So what is offered as the curriculum taught in the Community Colleges is a result of the collective search and it is based on the actual teaching experience of many of the Community College teachers.

2. General Curriculum

PART – I : LIFE SKILLS

Sl. No.	*Programme*	*Duration*	*Hours*	*Credits*
1.	Students Orientation	1 Week	30 Hours	1 Credit
2.	Life Coping Skills	6 Weeks	180 Hours	6 Credits
3.	Interpersonal Relationship and Communication Skills	4 Weeks	120 Hours	4 Credits
4.	Developmental English	6 Weeks	180 Hours	6 Credits
5.	Basic Computer Applications	4 Weeks	120 Hours	4 Credits
Total		**21 Weeks**	**630 Hours**	**21 Credits**

PART – II : WORK SKILLS

Sl. No.	*Programme*	*Duration*	*Hours*	*Credits*
1.	Career Guidance and Counselling	1 Week	30 Hours	1 Credit
2.	Work Skills	20 Weeks	600 Hours	20 Credit
Total		**21 Weeks**	**630 Hours**	**21 Credit**

PART – III : INTERNSHIP AND HANDS ON EXPERIENCE

Sl. No.	*Programme*	*Duration*	*Hours*	*Credits*
1.	Internship and Hands on Experience	8 Weeks	390 Hours	13 Credits
Total		**8 Weeks**	**390 Hours**	**13 Credits**

PART – IV: PREPARATION FOR EMPLOYMENT AND EVALUATION

Curriculum – Elaboration

Sl.No.	*Programme*	*Duration*	*Hours*	*Credits*
1.	Preparation for Employment and Evaluation	2 Weeks	60 Hours	2 Credits
Total		**2 Weeks**	**60 Hours**	**2 Credits**

The Life Coping Skills: aim at the development of the personality in terms of sharpening person skills and learning coping mechanisms and making oneself fit for job and work environment.

Interpersonal Relations: aims at empowering the student to express and articulate his/her ideas, opinions and to talk about oneself boldly before the interview board and to participate in group discussion and also to speak in public with confidence.

Computing Skills: aims at developing their basic computing skills so that the students are introduced to the basic knowledge of computer operations.

Developmental English: as a part of life skill has been beneficial to thousands of students. We start with the basic and go up to the level of gaining efficiency in composing letters, paragraphs and their own bio-data.

Work Skills: Subject related which is based on the particular needs of the society. The curriculum combinations of practical and theory. (60% of Practical and 40% of Theory). It is purely skill oriented.

Internship: On the spot training testing both Life skills and Work Skills in the industries

Life Skills in terms of personality and Work Skills in terms of Skills which will be tested by the industrial supervisors.

Preparation of Employment: To Train the students, how to prepare their bio data and face the interview and how to get the job and keep it.

TOTAL NUMBER OF CREDITS

Category	*Programme*	*Weeks*	*Hours*	*Credits*
PART I	Life Skills	21 Weeks	630 Hours	21 Credits
PART II	Work Skills	21 Weeks	630 Hours	21 Credits
PART III	Internship and Hands on Experience	8 Weeks	390 Hours	13 Credits
PART IV	Preparation for Employment and Evaluation	2 Weeks	60 Hours	2 Credits
Total		**52 Weeks**	**1710 Hours**	**57 Credits**

- One Credit = 30 Hours of work.
- Depending on the learning level of the target groups in the local areas, the college could conduct classes from the minimum of three hours (for part timers) to maximum of six hours per day (for full timers).
- The curriculum for every day Job-Oriented Programme should be designed in collaboration with the practitioners of the Industry / Commerce / Agricultural / Rural Sectors.
- The college should help the students to attain their Entry-Level Skills required for the Job-Oriented Programmes.
- For the Certificate Courses, the Life Skills should be compulsory and the duration of the Work skill Courses could be modified according to the job requirements.
- For all the students of the Community College whatever might be their specialised programmers, Courses on Life skills are mandatory.
- It is advisable to have 25 to 30 students maximum for skills development in specific Job-oriented Programmes.
- The presence of Job Placement Cell Placement Officer is a must in every Community College for effective internship training and subsequent Job Placement.

1. Course Outline

DACUM Process

The Job-Oriented Programmes for different fields of specialisation have to be designed with the collaboration of experts from the fields. They become the members of the advisory boards of the Community Colleges.

The Community College follows the DACUM (Developing a Curriculum) with the following stages.

1. The exact Job Description – Example – Financial Assistant, Community Development Organiser, Nursing Assistant, Office Assistant, Construction supervisor.
2. The responsibilities and tasks the persons should fulfil.
3. The skills required to fulfil these tasks
4. The courses needed to equip them with the skills.

17

Evaluation and Assessment of Skills

1. Introduction

The Evaluation and Assessment of the Skills of the incumbents of the Community College at present is completely internal and done by the Community College with the help of technical and field experts. The evaluation is aimed at the testing of the skills rather than the absorption of information. The evaluation is jointly done by the Life Skill Instructor, Work Skills Instructor, Industrial Supervisor supplemented by the self-assessment of the student of the Community College, thus making the evaluation comprehensive and purposeful, determining the attainment of skills.

The knowledge and skills component should be given equal weightage. This evaluation is to be continuous, transparent and should contain checks and balances within the system to ensure credibility.

The Diploma or the certificate is signed by the Director of the college as well as the Industrial Partner who has trained the students in the particular fields of specialisation.

2. Scheme of Evaluation of Life Skills and Work Skills Programme in the Community Colleges

I. LIFE SKILLS

1. Life Coping Skills

1.	Assignments	4x5 = 20 marks
2.	Two Tests	2x5 = 10 marks
3.	Oral Presentation	10 marks
4.	Group Discussion	10 marks
5.	Poster Presentation	10 marks
6.	Final Examination	40 marks
	Total	**100 marks**

2. Interpersonal Relations and Communication Skills

1.	Two Assignments	$10 \times 5 = 20$ marks
2.	Two Tests	$5 \times 2 = 10$ marks
3.	Group Discussion	10 marks
4.	Public Speaking	10 marks
5.	Just a Minute	10 marks
6.	Final Examination	40 marks
	Total	**100 marks**

3. Developmental English

1.	Ten Letters and Ten Paragraphs Writing	10 marks
2.	20 Exercises (News Paper Clippings)	10 marks
3.	20 Categories (Flowers, towns etc.)	10 marks
4.	200 words from the dictionary	10 marks
5.	Two Tests	20 marks
6.	Final Examination	40 marks
	Total	**100 marks**

4. Basic Computer Applications

1. Theory – 80 Marks

1.	Assignment	5 marks
2.	Seminar	5 marks
3.	Six Tests	$6 \times 5 = 30$ marks
4.	Final Examination	40 marks
	TOTAL	**80 marks**

2. Practical – 120 Marks

1.	Six Tests	$6 \times 10 = 60$ marks
2.	Final Examination	60 marks
	TOTAL	**120 marks**

II. WORK SKILLS

Each Paper will be evaluated for 200 Marks

Internal Assessment	100 marks
Final Assessment	100 marks
Total	**200 marks**

Internal Assessment

1.	Two Written Tests	$2 \times 10 = 20$ marks
2.	Two Oral Presentations	$2 \times 10 = 20$ marks
3.	Two Group Discussions	$2 \times 10 = 20$ marks
4.	Two Assignments	$2 \times 10 = 20$ marks
5.	Two Quizzes or Objective Tests or Two Practical Tests or Two Field Visits	$2 \times 10 = 20$ marks
	TOTAL	**100 marks**

Final Assessment

1.	Theory Three Hour Examination	40 marks
2.	Practical Three Hour Test Examination	60 marks
	Total	**100 marks**

Dr. Xavier Alphonse, S.J.,

18

Industrial and Community Partnership

1. Industrial and Community Partnership

Industrial Collaboration

The Community College cannot succeed without the active participation and collaboration of the industrial, rural, agricultural, commercial and service organisations of the locality. The above sectors come to assist the Community College in the following five ways:

1. Designing the curriculum for various job oriented courses.
2. Serving as members of the advisory board.
3. Being part time instructors for teaching and assessment in the College.
4. On the job training for the students in the work place.
5. Job placement for students who have been trained in the Community Colleges.

- Memorandum of Understanding could be signed with the industries for all the above five areas of collaboration.
- A few representatives form the above sectors industrial, commerce and service sectors could also serve as the members of the governing body of the College.

Industrial Collaboration and Community Colleges – A Key to Employability

Community College is a college with a difference. The difference lies in the way the formation is imparted to the excluded only. This difference in the college is presented to the Public, Academicians, NGOs, Management Professional Bank Officials, Commercial and Business Sectors and Industrial Partners and Executives at different dates and in different ways.

This introduction facilitated them to understand better the "Need Analysis" and then they realised the importance of such college as Alternative System to the Existing System of Education. It is this alternative system that makes the excluded (the school drop-outs, the early school leavers, and the drop-outs from various other educational institutions) to match education with employment.

Expectation of Industry

Employers today are interested in well-informed graduates or professionals. They are in need of skilled persons who are integrated and who have more common sense and practical mind-set to do a job. They are also looking for candidates with total involvement, greater enthusiasm, better commitment and desire to persevere and to learn more and more.

Measures To Meet Their Expectations

1. Clear presentation of the Concept of Community College to the Industrialists.
2. Representing the same concept to Industrial Trainers / Supervisors in the presence of their bosses.
3. Involving them in the formulation of syllabus and assessment of students' performance.
4. Regular visit and contacts with them.
5. Association of the Industrial Trainers in teaching the subjects.
6. At specified intervals, visit to industries with students during internship.
7. Sending the excluded to Field Placement according to the learning speed and according to the three-tier assessment.
8. Follow up of the candidate at every phase of the training-on campus, outside the campus, in-house training and in other places.
9. Memorandum of Understanding (MoU) or Letter of exchange can be obtained from Industrialists, depending upon the association of the College, the Quality of Training and their involvement.
10. Openness to change the procedure and classes as per the advice of the partners and in accordance with the advancement of skills in each trade.
11. Updating the Laboratories and Library at the advice of Industrial Collaborators.
12. Accommodating the work skill classes to the time suited to Industrial Trainers and part time faculty members.
13. There must be a staff in the Community College to assist the Industrial Trainers to carry out Work Skill Programmes.

14. Neither student nor the college staff should count the time and duration of the classes or Work Skill Programmes, since this training is learner centred, flexible and totally dependent on the need of the community in which it is located.
15. Community College staff carry out the follow-up of the training in the college and in the industry very closely.
16. Community College should not count the cost, labour and pain but rather count the benefit of the excluded trainees in all aspects.
17. Parents' Meet is essential and is to be periodical to make the field placement a success and make the trainers really become employable.
18. Regular board of studies meeting is necessary and they are composed of Industrialists and Industrial Trainers.

What is to be done? And what is not to be done?

Community College efforts do not stop with one-time contacts or association. The Collaboration is continuous and college should never lose sight of the Role of Industrial and other related organisations. Genuineness, Truthfulness, Promptness, Regularity, Mutual Respect and Regular and Clear Communication are to be carefully attended with details, omitting anyone of these would result in strained relationship. Straining relationship in this collaboration will cost the employability of the excluded. Ultimately it will not serve the trainee and the Community.

Community College cannot function in strict frame of mind. Staff should update themselves to suit the need of the Community. Management should be prepared to invest in the up-gradation of the faculty and in the welfare of the industrial trainers.

Conclusion

Community College is for people and people are to be motivated to understand the role of this College at regular intervals. Such association of the college with parents, trainers and partners from industries make the programmes relevant to the Industry, Community and to the Large Society, i.e. Nation. This Community College is built on Relationship, Collaboration and Co-ordination from Promotion of Employment, Entrepreneurs and Small-Scale Industrialists, Finally the goal of Community College "Empowerment of the Excluded" is achieved through the above measures.

(Dr. G. Pushparaj. S.J., Director, Madurai Community College, Tamil Nadu)

A Partnership with a Difference

One way to give a quality output is partnering with quality people. It is always a mutual beneficial ideology of betterment. The partnership of the Immaculate Community College of Cuddalore and Musee Educational group towards the unmatched contribution towards the unreached has a successful running of a year by now.

This model of an Educational Institution and an NGO working in the field of community enrichment using training as the major tool has come together to make this conceptual dream a real one.

This model makes the following ideology come true:

- A Partnership with community consciousness
- A tie-up to break the religious fencing towards the community
- A model of institutional and NGO tie-up
- A perfect blend of Educational experience and Real Time experience

How the Concept was well Blended?

It had a simple truth in it, an Institution-Immaculate Sisters, with a legendry experience in conventional education, could understand the other side of the existing system of education.

The NGO reaching the grassroots people using its Training tool, which has an experience in moulding the people for living and not just existing, jointly tried various aspects of giving the "Best to the Least".

And exactly this blend started to work out. It exactly absorbed the concept of Community College System in India. This would certainly stand has a successful model in the system.

What are the other Features of this Model?

This would have also an Interesting answer in it, apart from the training partnership, the Musee Educational Group in its commercial expansion had a turn out of Industrial Partner also.

The Group has expanded in the areas of Computer Training Division – Targeting K-12 Business and Software Development. This expansion also very well helped in putting the real – time expectation of the market.

What is More Innovative from us?

The other most ideal support is the Skill School Division of the Group. It works on Personality Development program for K-12 and for Colleges also. This wide experience had worked out in giving all the latest modules in the Soft Skill Development program to the Community College Students.

Since the group was working for quite a long time on Entrepreneurial Development program along with the Government agencies, it has made the group to introduce EDP programs to the students of Community College. It is also working on a tie-up along with the District Industries Centre to consider the students with that appropriate training as beneficiaries also.

First time ever the group is working in the simulated program which is quite costly in the market and which is designed for MBA students.

The group also has designed management programs, which is likely to be introduced from the coming year of training.

The Purpose of this Study

Even though the paper has talked about the group at the outset, the inner urge towards this study is the, recognition of the work of the force that has taken part in this movement all over the country.

Any thing in this world that matters would certainly need recognition in reaching the people. It might be an innovative concept on the shoulders of the western country, but this is more Indian-the traditional Gurukul System that has been poisoned by the western system needs an emerging out energy from the authorities for the simple reason of a result-oriented education.

This system with a technological backup could turn round the Indian scenario, which is now making the world to look up on us. With one more blend of entrepreneurship we could also support the individual by which the Indian economy could slowly balance itself.

(Paper presented to the Evaluation Team to Community College by Mr. S. Pugazhendhi, Concept Architect of Visions, Cuddalore, Tamil Nadu)[3]

1.8. The Administration and Governance of Community College Movement

The Community College will ensure the participation of the members of the agency that establishes the Community College (Board of Management), Administrators, Representatives of the faculty of the Community College, Industrial Partners, Community Leaders, Consultants to the Community College and Representatives nominated by the Government.

The authorities of the College will make sure of the proper management of Life Skills, Work Skills Development, Placement for Training, Financial and General administrative matters and also the needed infrastructural facilities necessary for training. The structure of the Governance of the Community Colleges will be the following:

STATUTORY BODIES

Community College will have the following three Statutory Bodies.

(i) Board of Management

(ii) Governing Body of the College

(iii) Advisory Council

Board of Management

The agency that owns and establishes the Community College.

Functions

1. It ensures the specific identity and orientation of Community College
2. It lays down policies and guidelines.

3. It undertakes planning and funding and allocation of resources.
4. Monitors the functioning of the Community College according to the philosophy of the Community College System.

Governing Body

Representatives of Board of Management, Industrial Partners, Faculty Members, Administrators, Community Leaders and Consultants to the Community College and one representative appointed by the State Government.

Functions

1. Approves the budget
2. Obtains an appraisal of the functioning of the college.
3. Awards Diplomas and Certificates to the candidates declared eligible by the College.

Advisory Council

It consists of Community Leaders, Industrial Partners and Faculty Members of the College.

Functions

1. It helps in the need analysis.
2. It designs the curriculum.
3. It validates the Evaluation and assessment of skills.
4. It helps in the planning of the relevant courses.
5. It advises on the job placement.
6. It suggests means of fund-raising.

Administrative Structure - Day to Day Administration

(A Suggested Model)

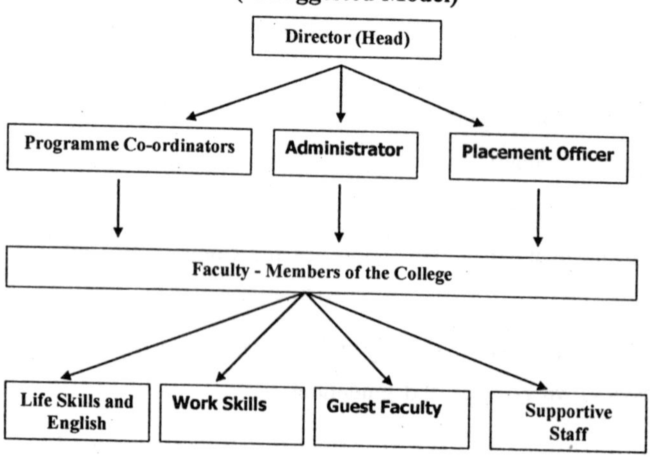

- Each Community College will function as an autonomus unit, supervised by the Community College Development Agency.
- What is envisaged in the Governance of the Community College is Minimum Control, Maximum Room and Freedom for Growth and Innovation in response to the local needs of the community towards the promotion of skills for the underprivileged and in catering to the excluded target groups eliminated from the formal system.

The Qualification of the Instructors, Salary of the Instructors and Service Conditions

Faculty members of the Community College can be divided into three categories, Full Time Instructors, Part Time Instructors and Guest Faculty.

- Qualified Post-graduates and Under Graduates are selected on the basis of aptitude test.
- They will be chosen on the basis of their competence and commitment to the mission of the Community College.
- They are given special training with a Diploma in Community College Teaching with a minimum of 12 weeks of training conducted by the Madras Centre for Research and Development of Community Education (MCRDCE), Chennai.
- They will undergo periodical performance appraisal and on going training.

The above conditions are applicable to the Full Time Instructors.

(a) Full - Time Instructors

They work for a minimum of eight hours a day. They will serve as the "Anchor Faculty". They will be fixed on a scale in keeping with the qualification and experiences. They will be paid Rs. 3,500 as the Basic Pay with DA, PF, CCA and HRA according to the rules of the State Government. Their continuation in service as well as increment in pay will depend on the performance appraisal earlier mentioned.

(b) Part - Time Instructors

Part - Time Instructors will be from the respective fields of specialisation with the years of experience in the field and with the knowledge of the skills required for the jobs for which the Community College trains its students even though they may not have formal academic degrees.

They will be paid on an hourly basis. They will also go through periodic training in the imparting of skills.

(c) Guest Faculty

They will be invited to take special sessions in their areas of expertise and they will be paid according to the local conditions.

(d) Supporting Staff

Supporting Staff will provide the management the necessary service for efficient administration and delivery of the Community College System.

They will start with Rs. 2,000 as their Basic Pay with the DA, PF, CCA and HRA according to the State Government Rules.[5]

Registers and Information to be kept by the Community College

The following registers and information is to be maintained by the Community College:

1. Document of the need analysis of the local area
2. Admission register of the college.
3. Attendance register of the students and the staff.
4. Acquaintance register of the teaching staff and the non-teaching staff.
5. Master mark register of all the skills and work skills courses and the certification from the Industrial supervisors.
6. Portfolio of every individual student with all the details about the student and his or her career.
7. Inventory register of all the equipment and library books.
8. The list of successful candidates and the job placement directory of every batch.
9. The detailed curriculum of Life Skills and Job oriented Programmes.
10. The accounts register of the college.
11. The list of industrial partners and the bio-data of the industrial partners.
12. The Memorandum of Understanding or Letters of Consent for collaboration with the Industrial Partners.
13. The minutes of the Governing Board and The Advisory Board meetings.
14. The diary of events of the college.

Expectations from the Government

1. Recognition and Approval of the Community College System and the courses offered by the Community Colleges.

2. Indirect Financial Assistance could be had from:

(i) Rural Development Department

(ii) Social Welfare Department

(iii) Health Department

(iv) Women Welfare / Empowerment Department

(v) Youth Welfare and Sports Department

(vi) The Quasi Government Organisations / Public Sector Agencies to ensure placements.

(vii) Funds of the Special Component Plan Programmes for the welfare of the SC / ST Population.

3. Direct Financial Assistance

(i) Institution of Scholarships and subsidised tuition fees

(ii) Issue of free Bus/Railway Passes

(iii) Subsidised Canteen Facility

(iv) Provision of learning Aids/Equipment to students

4. Maintenance of Separate Employment Register/Placement Register.

5. Creation of an Autonomous Community Development Board to ensure quality and monitoring.

6. Abstaining from imposing Direct Governmental Restrictions.

19

Testimony of the Students

1. Melapudur St. Anne's Community College, Trichy

Name: Ms. Pushpa Latha

Course: Pre-School Teacher Training

I am handicapped girl from a slum area. My father is a drunkard and my mother earns money by preparing garlands with flowers. Teachers from the community college visited my house and I had interview in my home and I was given the opportunity to join in Pre-school teacher training. Now I am working as a teacher and earning money which is sufficient for our family.

It is the principal and the teachers who have made my life fruitful and they have given me a thought that "I too can lead a happy and contented life inspite of disability".

2. Kanyakumari Community College, Kanyakumari

Name: Mr. L. A. Stalin Rex

Course: Computerized Financial Accounting

After completion of XII examination I decided to enjoy the college life in any one of the Arts Colleges. But unfortunately my father heard about Kanyakumari Community College courses and its scheme of three years integrated course. On completion, I joined the college for the three years integrated course.

First year I studied Diploma in Computer Application, a course for application of computers in the different fields of business like accounting, marketing, management reports, advertising, etc. This practical knowledge attracted me too and induced me to become a qualified computer designer.

In the second year, I studied DCFA. Even though this course is very useful to a student to become a qualified accountant, I was not able to concentrate in DCFA course. I studied the course only from the examination point of view. During my second year of study I had an opportunity of participating at the computer based competitions in college level and won the first prize.

And then I studied Diploma in Foreign Trade and Import-Export Documentation, which gained me a lot of knowledge in Import and Export areas. During the three years, the college provided many skill-training programmes. I attended all the programmes.

I really enjoyed my college life in Kanyakumari Community College with my practical studies with the computer. Now I have full confidence of setting up of my own employment in any kind of business organization. But I aim to become a proprietor of an advertising company for providing employment at least to 10 unemployed youth.

3. Ravel Community College, Coimbatore

Name: Ms. Rani

Course: Health Assistant

After completing my 12th std, I planned to do my Nurse Course. So I applied to Sakthi Hospital. They called me for an interview, but I was not selected. I was very much worried. Then I came to know about Ravel Community College. I got a chance to join the DHA Course. Here I had a good coaching in life coping skills and community skills because of which I could cope with my life very well.

We had spoken English class because of which I improved my English knowledge. By luck I got a chance to do my internship in Sakthi Hospital which made me very happy. I came to know about my hidden talents after joining this college.

Now after completing my Diploma in Health Assistant Course (DHA). I got a seat in B.Sc Nursing, I am very much thankful to the Director and the staff of Ravel Community College.

4. Udhayam Rural Community College, Thuraiyur

Name: Ms. K. Elavarasi

Course: Desk Top Publishing Operator (DTP)

I am Elavarasi. I have completed my Diploma in Desk Top Publishing Operator (DDTP) Course in Udhayam Rural Community College. When I came to the community college, I had a lot of unnecessary fear which prevented me to do anything worthwhile. I was given the life skills. Through the skills, I have learnt to be confident in whatever I do.

I have learnt to take critical decisions. The friendly atmosphere that is prevalent in the community college helps me overcome my loneliness. I have gained a good number of friends. I have learnt how to face the problems and put up with problems. I have picked up the communication skills and now I am able to communicate to people properly and effectively. I have learnt to make best use of my time.

I have learnt to cope with my anger. Before joining the community college, I used to get angry for anything and everything but after the life skills, I could find myself getting angry very rarely. This is very visible and all my friends appreciate me for this. I am thankful to the Udhayam Rural Community College for making me grow a better person everyday.

5. St. Joseph's Community College, Vishakhapatnam

Name: Ms. Ventata Adhilakshmi

Course: Health Assistant

Family History: she is the eldest daughter of the parents. She has one younger sister. Father is a degree holder. According to family situation he could not get the job. Neither her parents could educate the girls. She was married to her first cousin. She has two daughters. Her husband is a mason. She suffered a lot by her husband due to his drinking habit. She is not loyal to her husband after getting two children.

Personal History: since she was young girl she has no responsibility as a mother or a wife. She was more interested in enjoyment of her youth. She is not interested in looking after her family. She had a great desire to study and enjoy her youth. She was more interested in others than in her life partner.

Success story: once she came to college she showed her domineering character and interest in studies. She was not regular to college though she was coming from home. By repeated counseling and guidance, she learned a lot and took interest in life coping skills.

Slowly she started changing her wrong behaviour, her attitude and gained self confidence and became a responsible mother to her children and wife to her husband. She apologized for her mistakes and started a new life with our guidance.

Now she is faithful to her husband and took the responsibility of a mother and wife and she is serious about her carrier. She took health assistant course and at present she is doing her internship.

6. Bannerghatta Community College, Bangalore

Name: Ms. Jesna Jose

Course: Desk Top Publishing Operator (DTP)

I am so glad to share my success story with you. I am coming from Kerala. I have done my PUC. I was the past student of this Bannerghatta Community College. I did DTP Course from 2006- 2007. The subjects which I learned were Photoshop, Page Maker, CorelDraw, English and Life Coping Skills, etc. and they are very good. Because of this course, I got a good job IN Sara Soule Pvt. Ltd. with good salary. In the beginning, I was getting Rs. 4500 now I am getting Rs. 5000.

There is some improvement in my salary. I am also trying to get a better job. I learnt many new things from here. Now also I am learning from my company. I got good knowledge from this course. Sisters and teachers helped me a lot. I am really grateful to God for giving me a chance to study here.

7. Mysore Mines Community College, KGF

Name: Mr. V. Sathish Kumar

Course: Desk Top Publishing Operator (DTP)

My name is Sathish Kumar. I am a 1st batch student of Mysore Mines Community College. Before coming to this community college, I was studying in 1st grade college and my combination was PCMB Physics, Chemistry, Maths. and Biology. During my college days, I was not good in English; I was very poor in reading and writing. I never used to attend the classes and I was always playing with my friends and roaming aimlessly in my life.

Then I failed in mu PUC and I was at home since the past 10 months. My family members were very much worried about me. I then lost all hope. Suddenly one day, through my friend, I came to know a new college in St. Paul's Church Campus named Mysore Mines Community College and I joined this college. After coming to the community college I was very happy.

In this college they first taught me how to develop my personality and made me feel good and many things changed in me. I got hope for my future.

After finishing my DTP course I was sent for Training to Accent Technology by Fr. Ruben & Fr. Xavier. In Accent Technology I worked for the past 6 months as trainee and my income was Rs. 7,000 per month. My family members were very happy and I got hope in my life and then I got an other chance in a company named Scan Café Digital Solution. Here I am getting Rs. 5,000/- per month and the job was related to what I was studying in community college and now I am feeling free, my job is very easy and I have hope in my life that I have achieved something in my life. My praises go to Fr. Ruben, Fr. Xavier and Madam Geetha and I want to say a few words to my community college friends, "you have a bright future"

8. Archbishop Powathil Assumption Community College, Changanacherry

Name: Ms. P.G. Mini

Course: Fashion Designing

Mini. P.G. belongs to the Hindu S.C. in Palghat Dt. She has passed her SSLC with only 41% of marks making it impossible for her to join any regular college though technically she is eligible. With her inherent aptitude at designing, she wanted to join a Fashion Designing Course, but found the fee unaffordable. Then she came to know about a course from the advertisement in the newspaper and joined us at APACC since we charge only minimum fees. The classes in Life Skills and Communication Skills gave her more confidence. She on the job Training in Thirupur made her realize that she can communicate well in English and follow spoken Tamil. Today she is employed as a merchandiser in Kalian Silks, a famous chain of retail textiles drawing a salary of Rs. 4500.

9. Cluny Community College, Karaikal

Name: Ms. Arokia Selvi

Course: Fashion Designing and Garment Making

Arokia Selvi is from Tsunami affected area. She is a school dropout and had no father. Her mother is alive. She has two brothers. Her mother sells milk and looks after the family. She was not interested in studies. After knowing the concept of Community College she joined Diploma in Fashion Designing and Garment Making course.

She used to get angry very fast and the teachers found it difficult to help her. She had low self image. She tried many times to commit suicide before joining the college. She was talented but due to lack of self knowledge she had no self confidence. She did not have any knowledge of English.

Surprisingly she showed interest in learning and worked hard to get good marks. She showed interest in life coping skills and learnt about herself. She improved her self image and positive thinking and now she does not think of committing suicide.

She wants to have a better future. She says that she is not getting angry as before and tries to establish good relationship with everyone. She also says that she takes decision only after reflection. As she has developed her self confidence and is good at garment making.

She has bought a sewing machine. She stitches garments in her own house and earns well. Our industrial partners tried their best to appoint her in their shops. As she is getting many orders and earns more money she prefers to have her own shop.

10. Teresina Community College, Kalamasserry

Name: Ms. Jophila Treasa

Course: Office Management

Jophila joined the Teresian Community College, Kalamasserry in the 2007-2008 for one year Office Management Course. This institution helped me to be empowered and get motivated to work hard. It is actually from here that I realized my goal in life and what I have to do to attain that goal.

I also understood the role of women in the family and the society. Before joining this college I did not know to lead a prayer session or to say a spontaneous prayer. With the training I got here, now I can lead even prayer groups having more than 100 people.

Now I can interact with people of different categories without any difficulty. Not even once I felt that the one year I spent here was a waste of time. I am proud of my college. Many desirable changes were brought about in us through the curricular and co-curricular activities conducted here. We learned to cope with many adverse situations of life.

I am grateful to Sr. Vivian, all our teachers and all those people from different walks of life who have helped to make this community college a reality. At present I am working as an Office Assistant in M.B.D. Alchemic Private Company and drawing a salary of Rs. 3000/- per month.

I am also studying B.Com privately. Now I am able to stand on my own legs and can meet most of the expenses for my travel, clothing and education without depending on my family members. I also help others in need and also save a small amount every day. "May God Bless all those who helped me".

11. Vidhyadeep Community College, Bharuch, Gujarat

Name: Ms. Gamit Kalavati Ishwarbhai

Course: Health Assistant

Kalavati is from a poor family. She has one sister and one brother. She is the eldest in the family. Parents are so poor that her aunty paid her fees. She did one year Nursing Assistant course in Vidhyadeep and she was absorbed by one of the hospitals in Bharuch where they go for their internship. Now she is working for the last two and a half years. She is very confident in her work. The doctor finds her too good as she assists doctor in the operation. Her younger sister also studied in Vidhyadeep for two years. She too is working as an office assistant in Vyara. Their family condition has improved and both the sisters are able to support their parents today.

12. Vivekananda Prathisthan Community College, Jalgoan, Maharashtra

Name: Ms. Vanita Ramesh Dalai

Course: Pre-School Teacher Training

Montessory is a field of my interest. The reason being the children are innocent but not aware of their surrounding world. My liking is to correct the children by improving them physically and mentally.

According to one psychologist "Child is a *tabbularasa*" - a blank sheet of paper and one can write anything on. So we can give physically and mentally fit personality to society.

Therefore I have selected this course. Apart from this I want to become a self-sufficient woman and independent women. So after seeking a job I have joined this institution. Though I am physically handicapped, this course will help me to overcome it.

13. Ursuline Community College, Noatoli, Jharkhand

Name: Ms. Ursula Purti

Course: Tailoring and Embroidery

I am Ursula Purti from Keluga Bhandartoli. I have failed matriculation examination. Because of poverty I could not write my exam again. I was at home without any work. I was thinking that I was helpless. After some days I heard about Community College. And I got the opportunity to come to learn all kinds of stitching.

Besides this Sr. Jyoti takes different classes, but mostly I was touched by "Life Coping Skills". Through this class, I am increasing my knowledge.

Sr. Jyoti is teaching us to live a good life in the society. Before coming here I was self centered, without any botheration. But now by living together I am free with every one. For my future mission I want that I'll also stitch and get money instead of going out to earn money. Now I am not in the dark but I see that my future is bright. After joining the Community College I am very happy.

14. Bethany Community College, Punjab

Name: Ms. Chanda

Course: Health Assistant

Chandajoined our Nursing course with lot of apprehensions. An active, intelligent and hard working girl. She was very regular during the session.

Always prompt in her answers, she got selected by the Bharti Academy of Retail at a monthly pay of Rs. 5,000 she instead preferred to study further and is now studying for the second year of B.A.

15. Name: Mr. Binesh

Course: Hotel Management

Binesh is a talented, enthusiastic young boy. He joined our institute after finishing his +2. He learnt about the nuances of Hotel Management very willingly. Later he got job opportunities wherever he applied. A positive attitude and humble approach was the secret to his success. At present he is working at Vodafone Chandigarh for Rs. 10,000 per month.

16. Upaya Community College, Orissa

Name: Ms. Jinict Xaxa

Course: Health Assistant

I am Miss. Jinict Xaxa, daughter of Mr. Bijay Xaxa, resident of Cess Colony, Post, Kaplas, Dist-Sundargarh. I am a student of community college, Ramabahal. My qualification is intermediate pass. After finishing my intermediate, I joined the community college. Community College is a different college. I learned so many things which are now useful for me. Now I am working in JMJ Hospital. Every day different kinds of patients are coming for treatment. I learned in the Community College, how to cope with the problem and correct our problem. Before joining the community college I was very fearful and timid. Communication Skill, Life Coping Skill, Developmental English, Computer are very useful to my life. So I am very happy. I am working in hospital and earn some money. I have stood on my own strength. So my parents are also happy. So I thank the Community College and the staff members.

17. Name: MS. Anita Minz

Course: Health Assistant

At the outset I would like to extend my heartfelt thanks to the teachers of UPAYA Community College. I am going to write what I have benefited from this Community College.

When I was at home I felt very small, stupid and weak, unable to do anything and life was dark. But after joining the Community College and learning about the six subjects, namely Life Coping Skills, Communication Skills, Developmental English, Social Engineering and Nursing, I feel they were very important.

In all these subjects life coping and communication skills have helped me very much. After completing the Nursing training I joined in JMJ Grace Vision Netralaya, I could deal with the patients with politeness and understanding through my communication skills.

My feeling of worthlessness has changed into feeling of worth. Now I am able to help the doctor in the operation theater and manage other works.

There are certain times I felt very bad when I had to listen to the scolding of doctor, administrator, staff and other people. But after studying of Life Coping skills overcame all these feelings. Today I feel proud because I can stand on my own.

Along with helping my family, I am able to meet my expenses, take my responsibilities and trying to make the future bright. Now I am very happy. My parents are also happy.

Before coming to this Community College, the feeling that I had of small, weak and stupid has now changed. Now I feel that I am not less than anybody, I can do, anything if I will.

18. St. Aloysius Community College, Jabalpur, Madhya Pradesh

Name: Mrs. Geeta Varma

Course: Health Assistant

Mrs. Geeta Varma was born on 13th May 1975. She failed her 10th Std in 1999. She has her parents and two brothers. She was married off in the same year and has two children. Her husband holds a good job but squanders the money. He began ill-treating her. She endured all the ill treatment and she did not get any support from her in-laws family. Her husband did not bother to look after her or her children and he left them. She picked up courage and returned to her parents' home with the children. They being good and understanding, gave her shelter and tried to mend the relationship with her husband and in-laws but all in vain. They came to know of our Community College through a neighbour and approached us. On talking to her, we realized that she was very keen on standing on her own feet and to give the best education to her children. At that time, admissions were over and there was no vacancy, but for her luck, one girl dropped and we gave her admission. She belonged to the 2007-08 batch. Nursing Assistant study was not very easy for her as she had already discontinued her studies long ago. Her old and sick parents took the responsibility of taking care of her children as ours is a residential course. She finished the course with B+ grade and she was given placement in one of the hospitals. While studying here, she met the principal of St. Aloysius School and she managed to get admission for her son in the English medium school. Today, she is not only an earning member but also trying to solve her problem legally because she wants to live a dignified life. She is very grateful to us for the information we have given her.[22]

19. Name: Ms. Manju Minj

Course: Health Assistant

Ms. Manju hails from Andaman and Nicobar Islands. She was born 6th April 1979. She has her parents and three brothers.

She left Andaman and Nicobar Islands when she was 15, looking for greener pastures and stayed with an aunt in Jabalpur. She did her B.A. but couldn't find a job.

Her aunt came to know of the Community College and brought Manju to our institution. She joined our 2005-06 batch and worked hard in her studies and got through with A Grade.

She was given placement in a family to look after a bed-ridden woman, whose children are settled in America. They were so pleased with Manju's treatment of their mother that they decided to help her. When the patient passed away, she felt very sad because she had looked after her as her own mother. Later, she was able to find another job in Jabalpur hospital.

Right now, the relatives of that patient are helping her economically to do her GNM Course in the same hospital, where just one seat is available for an arts subject student and she was lucky enough to get that seat. She has finished her 1st year successfully and is doing her 2nd year. Once she completes her course, that family is willing to take her to the States. Manju is a woman of dreams and goals and she is looking forward to that day.

According to Manju, though she left her parents at a very young age and didn't meet them since then, yet she has met many good people, who gave her a lot of love, care, concern and all that she requires in life. She is extremely grateful to the Community College and to the generous family of whom she feels she is part.

References

1. Alphonse, Xavier, *Mismatch: Establishing and Developing Community Colleges in India*, MCRDCE Publications, Chennai, June 2002, pp. 28-29.
2. Alphonse, Xavier, *Mismatch: Establishing and Developing Community Colleges in India,* MCRDCE Publications, Chennai, June 2002, pp. 90-94.
3. Alphonse, Xavier, *Mismatch: Establishing and Developing Community Colleges in India,* MCRDCE Publications, Chennai, June 2002, pp. 112-117.
4. Alphonse, Xavier, *Mismatch: Establishing and Developing Community Colleges in India,* MCRDCE Publications, Chennai, June 2002, pp. 112-117.
5. Alphonse, Xavier, *Miracles of Hope,* March 2005, p. 28.
6. *Ibid*, p. 56.
7. Alphonse, Xavier, ***Change is Certain,*** ICRDCE Publication, March 2009 p. 61.
8. *Ibid.*, p. 147.
9. *Ibid.*, p. 29.
10. *Ibid.*, p. 56.
11. *Ibid.*, p. 145.
12. *Ibid.*, p. 181.
13. *Ibid.*, p. 182.
14. *Ibid.*, p. 221.
15. *Ibid.*, p. 21.
16. *Ibid.*, p. 113.
17. Alphonse, Xavier, *Miracles of Hope,* ICRDCE Publication, March 2005 p.190.
18. Alphonse, Xavier, *Change is Certain,* ICRDCE Publication, March 2009 p. 46.
19. *Ibid.*, p. 263.
20. *Ibid.*, p. 47.
21. *Ibid.*, p. 49.
22. *Ibid.*, p. 21.
23. *Ibid.*, p. 25.

PART II
COMMUNITY COLLEGES OTHER PARTS OF THE WORLD

20

Community Colleges in USA

1. American Community College – An Inspiration and a Model

Community Colleges are centers of educational opportunity. They are an American invention that put publicly funded higher education at close-to-home facilities, beginning more than 100 years ago with Joliet Junior College. Since then, they have been inclusive institutions that welcome all who desire to learn, regardless of wealth, heritage, or previous academic experience. The process of making higher education available to the maximum number of people continues to evolve at 1,130 public and independent Community Colleges. When the branch campuses of community colleges are included, the number totals about 1,600.

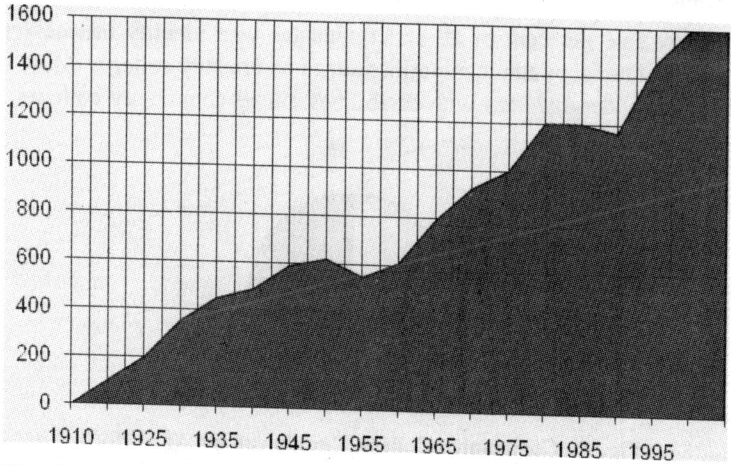

Fig. 1: Number of Community Colleges Including Branch Campuses: 1900-1998.

Source: National Centre for Education Statistics 1997 and AACC 1998.

About 46 per cent of all first time college freshmen attend community colleges. In fall 1997, more than 5.4 million students took credit courses at community colleges, and approximately 5 million more participated in noncredit classes. During the full 1996-97 academic year, more than 9 million students took credit courses at community colleges.

Community colleges' commitment to accessibility is facilitated by open admissions policies and low tuitions. Consequently, community college enrollment reflect the rich diversity of the nation. Community college campuses are populated with people of all ages, ethnic and cultural heritages, and socio-economic backgrounds.

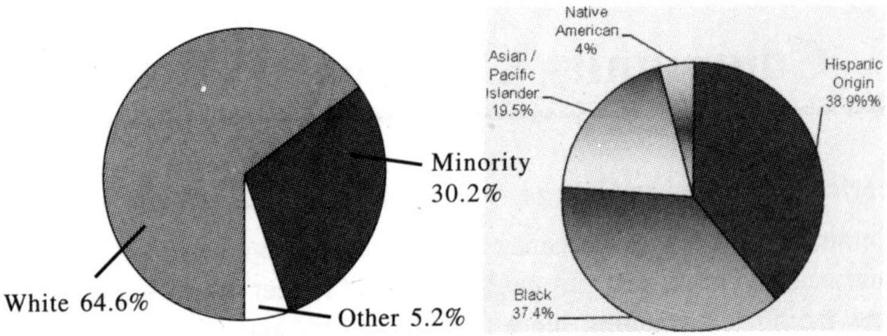

Fig. 2: Minority Student Enrollment in Community Colleges: 1997.

Source: National Center for Education Statistics 1998.

During the 1990's, minority enrollment at community colleges has risen. Minority students account for about 30 per cent of community college enrollment, as shown in Fig. 2.

Forty-nine per cent of all undergraduates who identify themselves as members of racial or ethnic minorities attend community colleges. More than half of all undergraduates with disabilities attend community colleges.

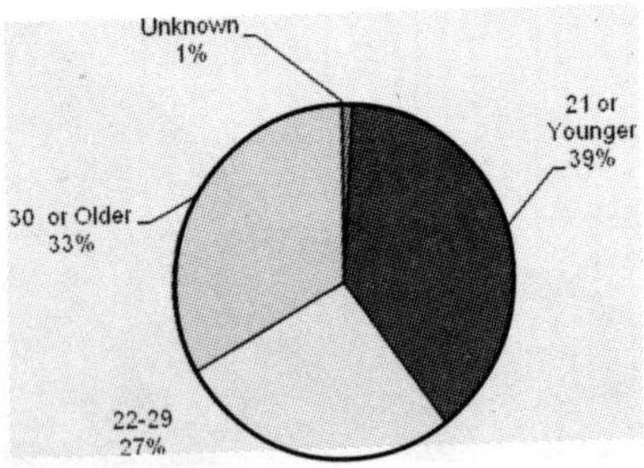

Fig. 3: Community College Enrollment by Age: 1997

Source: National Center for Education Statistics 1998.

Sixty per cent of community college students are older than 21. The number of students older than 40 is expected to increase significantly in the future. Because so many of those who attend community colleges are adults with work and family responsibilities, nearly two-thirds of community college students are part-times students.

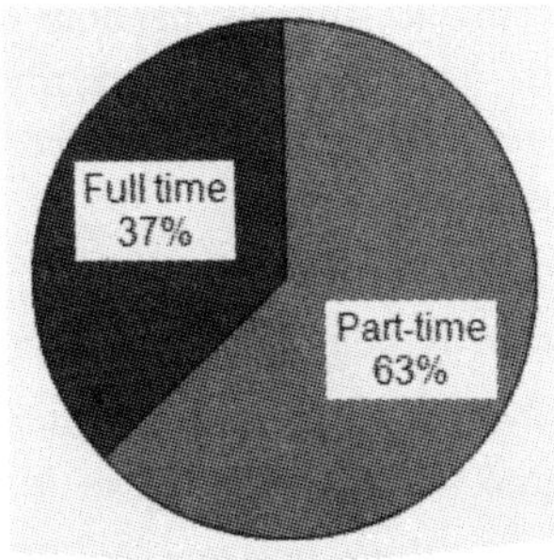

Fig. 4: Enrollment Status of Community College Students: 1997.

Source: National Center for Education Statistics 1998

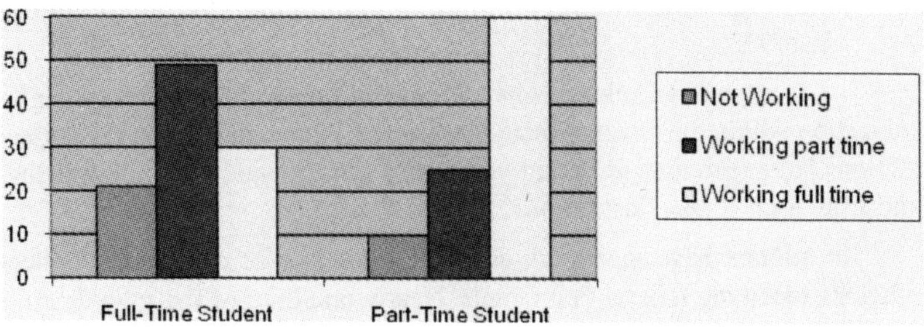

Fig. 5: Employment Status of Community College Students: 1995-96.

Source: National Center for Education Statistics 1997.

Thus, we see the following pattern in community Colleges:

- 30 per cent of community college students are members of minorities.
- 16 per cent of community college students are older than 40.
- 63 per cent of community college students attend part time.
- Nearly 50 per cent of all community college students work full time.
- 30 per cent of full-time community college students also work full time

Responding to local needs is an integral goal of community colleges. This commitment to local service, coupled with the promotion of lifelong learning has resulted in multifaceted curricula. Not only are community colleges training the future workforce, they are also instructing employed workers in new technologies. It is no longer uncommon for a person with a college degree to attend a community college for computer course or to otherwise update work skill.

While occupational and technical programs are the focus for many students, attaining credits that transfer for a baccalaureate degree continues to be a goal for a large segment of the Community College population. The number of community college students needing developmental education programs in basic skills has increased markedly in recent years. Adult education courses that respond to social and recreation interests are also popular at many colleges.

- More than 450,000 associate degrees and 200,000 certificates are conferred each year by community colleges.
- 37 per cent of all community college students receive an associate degree or certificate within five years of first enrolling.
- Another 15 per cent of these students are still pursuing post secondary education five years after their initial enrollment.
- The percentage of the U.S.population with an associate degree as their highest degree has risen from 5.9 per cent in 1992 to 7.2 per cent in 1997.

Community Colleges' low tuitions and financial aid have kept higher education within the reach of many Americans. Although community college tuitions have increased in recent years, they remain significantly lower than those at four – year institutions.

As tuitions have increased, so has the number of community college students receiving federal Pell Grants. Nearly one-third of these funds go to students enrolled at community colleges. Overall, the number and amount of financial aid awards at community colleges continue to be less than at four-year institutions because costs are lower and most students attend part time.

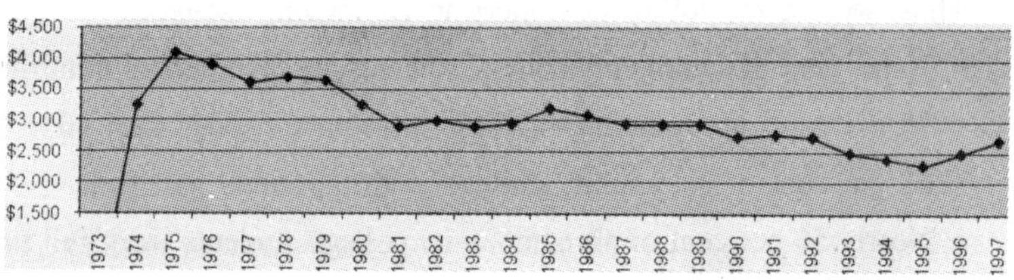

Fig. 6: Maximum Pell Grant value Adjusted for Inflation (Constant 1997 Dollars).

Source : Gladieux and Swail 1998.

- 33 per cent of public community college students received some type of financial aid in 1995-96.
- When controlled for inflation, the value of Pell Grants has decreased since 1974 (Fig. 6).

- Public community colleges' share of Pell Grants has increased relative to other higher education sectors.

Community colleges focus primarily on teaching and student learning. Throughout their history, community colleges have hired part-time instructors for the occupational expertise they bring to the classroom. As funding has tightened, community colleges have begun to rely more on adjunct faculty as a way to keep salary costs down.

- Nearly two-thirds of community college faculty are part-time employees
- State funds have dropped to about 40 per cent of community college revenue; they accounted for 50 per cent of community college revenues in 1980.
- Community college endowments amount to $1.2 billion.

The democratic principles upon which community colleges were founded are evident in their governing structure as well as in their admissions policies. Public community colleges are governed by trustees who are either elected or appointed by elected officials. Most trustees receive little or no financial compensation.

2. The Mission of the Community College

The Community College mission is the fountain from which all of its activities flow. In a few words, this mission is to provide access to post-secondary educational programs and services that lead to stronger, more vital communities. The way individual community colleges achieve this mission may differ considerably. Some colleges emphasize college transfer programs; others emphasize technical education. The mission of offering courses, programs, training and other educational services, however, is essentially the same for all community colleges. The mission of most community colleges is shaped by these commitments:

- Serving all segments of society through an open-access admissions policy that offers equal and fair treatment to all students.
- Providing a comprehensive educational programme.
- Serving the community as a community-based institution of higher education.
- Teaching and learning
- Fostering lifelong learning.

Open Access and Equity

Access has been a major theme in higher education since the end of World War II and community colleges have been at the center of the promotion of universal higher education. These two-year colleges have not always been open-access institutions, however. Three events contributed to making them so. Community Colleges commitment to open access in their admissions policies is perhaps the most misunderstood concept associated with these colleges.

First, the children born to returning veterans of World War II–the baby boomers reached college age during the 1960s. Along with their parents, many of whom attended college with the help of the GI Bill, the baby boomers came to realize that their future opportunities would be closely linked to a college education.

Second, the civil rights movement and the push for women's right broke down some of the barriers to disadvantaged groups. Eliminating poverty and ignorance became important national goals of the Great Society envisioned by President Lyndon B.Johnson and other national leaders, who promoted education, including higher education, as the most important means for achieving these goals.

Third, the demands for political and social action during the 1960s and early 1970s resulted in a federal commitment to increase financial aid for higher education. The Higher Education Act of 1965 and subsequent legislation at the national level made it possible for virtually anyone who could establish the need to receive financial assistance to attend college. The Higher Education Act, along with other federal and state programs, continues to provide financial assistance to students who need it.

Open access to higher education, as practiced by the community college, is a manifestation of the belief that a democracy can thrive, indeed survive, only if its people are educated to their fullest potential. Basic to the community college mission, then, is a commitment to open access in its admission policies and to fair and equal treatment of all students. Access is achieved by maintaining a low tuition rate and offering program choices; equity by removing artificial barriers to access for those traditionally unserved by higher education.

Access and equity mean more than just open admissions. They mean having a college within commuting distance of most residents and giving students choices in what they study. Open access and equity mean that once a student is enrolled, the college provides support services, including counseling, academic advising, and financial aid, helping to ensure that every student has the opportunity to succeed academically. Many colleges offer childcare, flexible scheduling, and distance education as part of their efforts to serve a population with diverse needs. Open access and equity mean that men and women from all ethnic and economic backgrounds can afford to attend the community college and no one is discriminated against in any academic program or service offered by the college.

Community Colleges commitment to open access in their admissions policies is perhaps the most misunderstood concept associated with these colleges. Open access does not mean that anyone can enter any program without the competencies required for effective learning. The pre-requisites for entering the college transfer programme at a community college are no different than they are at most four-year colleges and universities. The same is true of students entering any number of professional programs, such as nursing. Nevertheless, the community college differs from many institutions in the nation and in the world in the following way: Rather than turn away people who do not have the pre-requisites for college-level work, the community college offers avenues for students to obtain the necessary pre-requisites.

Comprehensiveness

The second commitment on which the community college mission rests, and one that relates to open access and equity, is the commitment to comprehensives in the college's program offerings. In addition to fulfilling the traditional university parallel function of offering the first two years of the bachelor's program, community colleges offer much more. Although it is impossible and unnecessary for all community colleges to offer all programs, students must have choices in what they study for a community college to accomplish its mission. Without choice in program and course offerings, open access and equity lose much of their meaning. For example, if the college transfer program is the only program offered, the college is not an open-access institution because students have no choice in programs. Many students who come to the community college do not meet the academic requirements for the transfer program; thus, if that program is their only choice, the door to the college is closed to them, and open access is little more than a hollow promise.

To understand why comprehensiveness is so important to the community college, one has only to consider student goals and community needs. By broadening program offerings, community colleges have extended educational opportunities to millions of students ignored by other higher educational institutions. Some students want and need programmes that lead quickly to employment. Others have the desire and the opportunity to pursue careers that require lengthier periods of schooling.

Community Based

It is no accident that the word community is part of the community college's name. Community-based means that a college is committed to serving the needs of a designated geographic area, often called the college's service area or service region. Although the definition of what it means for a community college to serve its community has changed over the years–

-including an expansion of the definition of service area as a result of computer-based distance learning – to be effective, the community college will see its mission as primarily one of providing education to its local community. By broadening programme offerings, community colleges have extended educational opportunities to millions of students ignored by other higher educational institutions.

Although the needs are as diverse as the communities served by the colleges, and may change over time, most communities have many needs in common and expect their college to meet those needs. Most communities want programs that permit students to transfer into a bachelor's degree program. Most want vocational and technical training, often including training that meets the specific needs of a local industry. They expect a choice of credit and noncredit courses that lead to certificates, degrees and diplomas. Most want the college to offer remedial or developmental courses that will assist students to qualify for college-level work. Most communities want courses and activities that meet the recreational, social and cultural needs of the community. Not every community college can meet all the needs of its service area, but within sometimes serious resource constraints, community colleges strive to meet community needs and maintain standards of excellence. Many community colleges, working closely with local employers, design and offer programs that provide a quick avenue to employment in fields for which there is a well-documented need.

Although cultural and social activities such as activities that enhance education and community life may not be part of the college's formal educational programme. Most observers agree that it is important for community colleges to sponsor art exhibits, sports events, concerts, drama productions, health fairs, community forums and other activities that enrich the lives of the people served by the college. The decision to sponsor one event rather than another may be the result of a broad need in the community (a health fair, for example), or may be the result of an individual or group's desire to sponsor an activity. Whatever the reason, it is important that the college respond to the community's professed needs, thereby enhancing the college's educational mission.

Programs and activities overlap, and sometimes there is a fine line between an activity that is part of a formal educational mission or simply a community service. Colleges seek to remain flexible enough to respond to diverse community needs while maintaining integrity as institutions of higher education.

Teaching and Learning

The Community College is devoted first and foremost to teaching and learning. Publishing in academic periodicals is not a mandatory aspect of the faculty's role, although this does not preclude community college faculty from publishing or presenting at conferences. Outstanding teachers may be devoted scholars, keeping up with their fields and sharing new developments with colleagues and students. The most important challenge of community college instructors is to develop the ability to adjust styles of teaching to the diverse learning styles of students and community college faculty and administrators take great pride in their commitment to teaching and learning.

Fostering Lifelong Learning

In the past, people may have assumed that education was an activity a person engaged in for a certain number of years, and when the student graduated, he or she would never return to the classroom. Now, however, more people see learning as a lifelong pursuit. Many find they must continue to engage in formal learning activities, such as those offered at the community college, to keep up with the skills and knowledge required for their jobs, and to be responsible and productive citizens. The U.S. Department of Education reports that enrollment of adults aged 40 or older increased from 17 per cent in 1993 to 21 per cent in 1997.

The community college's commitment to lifelong learning encompasses an almost limitless number of credit and noncredit courses, activities and programs designed to enhance the lives of the people in the college's service region for as long as they have the desire to learn. Students, many of whom are older adults, returns to the classroom to learn new job skills and improve existing ones. A recent trend is the growing number of students returning to community college after completing a master's or other advanced degree.

One of the strengths of the community college is that it makes little distinction between the lifelong learner and the full-time student in terms of the programs and courses in which students may enroll. Many of the courses and programs lifelong learners choose are the same as those designed for degree-seeking students. As older adults return to the community college to upgrade their skills or learn new ones, the distinction between the adult learner and the full-timer younger student diminishes.[2]

3. Milestones in Community College History

1862 : Passage of the Morrill Act

With its emphasis on agriculture and the mechanical arts, the Morrill Act of 1862, often referred to as the Land Grant Act, expanded access to public higher education, introduced the teaching of new types of courses, and included types of students previously excluded from higher education.

1870: The Kalamazoo Decision

The Michigan Supreme Court ruled that local school districts could construct and operate comprehensive high schools from public school funds. This precedent – setting decision opened the way to the development of the modern, comprehensive high school, which would, by the opening of the 20th century, provide many public community colleges with their initial home.

1901: Founding of Joliet Junior College

One of the earliest beneficiaries of the construction of large, modern high schools was Joliet Junior College. Founded under the influence of William Rainey Harper, president of the University of Chicago, Joliet Junior College is the oldest continuously existing public two-year college in the nation. While the junior college's courses were initially mixed in with those of the Joliet High School, by 1915 the junior college's enrollment had grown to such an extent that it necessitated the addition of a "junior college wing". This was the nation's first major facility constructed specifically for use by a public junior college.

1904: The Wisconsin Idea

The University of Wisconsin emphasized that its mission was to assist the general public through extension services and to provide support to the State government. The university declared that the entire State was its campus. Today, most community colleges view individual service regions as their campuses.

1917: Adoption of Junior College Accreditation Standards

The North Central Association of Schools and Colleges established specific standards for the accreditation of public and private junior colleges. These standards, governing such areas as admissions policies, faculty qualifications, and minimum funding levels, not only brought a degree of uniformity to the young junior college movement but demonstrated the willingness of and capacity for junior colleges to participate in America's unique system of institutional self-regulation.

1918: Founding of Phi Theta Kappa (PTK) Honor Society

PTK was founded to recognize and encourage academic achievement by two-year college students and provide them with opportunities for individual growth and development in academics, leadership, and service.

1920 : Founding of the American Association of Junior Colleges

Called together by Philander Claxton, U.S. Commissioner of education, and his higher education specialist, George Zook, more than 25 public and private junior college leaders met in St. Louis to organize the American Association of Junior Colleges. The association, proposed by the U.S. Bureau of Education to function as an accrediting body for the rapidly growing number of junior colleges, became a forum for community college issues and a source of mutual support for its members at a time when the potential of the junior college was not widely understood or appreciated.

1921: California Legislation Fostering Independent Community College District

Using proceeds from the Federal Oil and Mineral Act, the California Legislature created a Junior College Fund, the nation's first, to support the operation of locally governed junior college districts operating independently of the public high schools. California's Junior College Act of 1921 came to serve as a model for other states as they sought to put junior colleges on a sound fiscal and policy footing.

1928: The First State Junior College Board

Mississippi was the first state in the nation to organize a statewide governing board with specific oversight responsibility for the public junior colleges within its boundaries. The state's governing board worked closely with elected local boards in developing a strong network of public junior colleges that effectively balanced transfer and vocational programs.

1930: The Asheville Decision

Even as late as 1930, many state legislatures had yet to adopt specific legislation permitting communities to organize public junior colleges. This legal oversight did not deter communities, which organized junior colleges without explicit legal authority, much as they had organized high schools in the preceding century. The right of a community to take such a step was challenged in Asheville, North Carolina, with the North Carolina Supreme Court eventually ruling in favour of the community and its right to meet the educational needs of its citizens as it best saw fit. This decision did much to secure the legal standing of those public junior colleges that were still being operated without the benefit of state legislation.

1944: Passage of GI Bill of Rights

U.S. Congress passed the Servicemen's Readjustment Act, popularly known as the GI Bill, to provide financial assistance for veterans of World War II who wished to pursue higher education. Building on smaller federal student aid programs developed at the end of the Great Depression, the GI Bill represented the federal government's first attempt to provide student aid on a large scale, helping to break down the economic and social barriers to attending college.

1947: Higher Education for American Democracy

Published by the President's Commission on Higher Education, this report, popularly known as the Truman Commission Report, called for several things, including the establishment of a network of public community colleges that would charge little or no tuition fee; serve as cultural centers; be comprehensive in their program offerings with an emphasis on civic responsibilities; and serve the area in which they were located. The commission helped popularize the term community college.

1958: Introduction of A.D.N. Programs

With funding support from the W.K. Kellogg Foundation and Rockefeller family, community colleges in New York, California, Florida, and other states introduced two – year programs leading to an associated degree in nursing that entitled degree holders to sit for licensure as professional nurses.

1960: W.K. Kellogg Foundation Support of Community College Leadership Development

The W.K. Kellogg Foundation announced a series of grants to be used to establish University centers preparing a new generation of two-year college leaders. In all, 12 universities established junior college leadership programs. Hundreds of future deans and presidents would eventually graduate from the Kellogg Junior College Leadership Programmes.

1960 : California Master Plan for Higher Education

The three segment of California public higher education — the community colleges, comprehensive colleges and universities, and the University of California — agreed to a voluntary plan to divide responsibility for the State's rapidly growing number of undergraduates and provide the State's residents with the broadest possible range of educational opportunity without wasteful competition among the sectors.

1963: Federal Aid to Higher Education

1965 With the adoption of the Higher Education Facilities Act of 1963 and the first Higher Education Act of 1965, the federal government dramatically expanded its direct aid to community colleges and their students. Through the Facilities Act of 1963, communities were given the means to construct new campuses and enlarge existing facilities. Through the Higher Education Act of 1965, and its subsequent reauthorizations, the federal government provided a range of direct grants and loans to students based on need as a means of lessening the barrier of cost to higher education access.

1968: Creation of the league for Innovation in the Community College

B. Lamar Johnson founded the League for Innovation to promote experimentation and innovation in community colleges. The League limits its membership to 20 colleges, which are expected to demonstrate outstanding commitment to cutting edge thinking in leadership and direction of community colleges. Results and information are shared with community colleges across the nation.

1970 : Open Admissions at City University of New York

Breaking with a long established tradition of selective admissions, the City University of New York ended its policy of granting admission to only the most academically gifted graduates of New York's Public High Schools, and guaranteed admission to all high school graduates. This Policy change led to a rapid increase in enrollment, the introduction of large-scale developmental programs, and the organization of innovative community colleges in communities with the greatest economic need.

1971-Federal Aid for Strengthening Tribal Colleges

1978: Beginning with Navajo Community College in 1971, AACC assisted in winning federal aid for the construction and maintenance of community colleges operating under the jurisdiction of Native American tribes. These efforts culminated in 1978, with the adoption of the Tribally Controlled Community College Assistance Act and the expansion of the Community College to previously underserved communities throughout the West.

1972 : Name Change for Association

The American Association of Junior Colleges changed its name to the American Association of Community and Junior Colleges in 1972 to reflect the broadening terminology used by the institutions.

1972: Creation of Affiliated Councils

Councils are organizations whose purposes are consistent with the associations and whose programmes contribute to and significantly benefit the association and its members. Beginning in 1972, Councils that meet certain criteria may be eligible for affiliate council membership, which brings with it an added measure of recognition and benefits.

1972 : Establishment of Association of Community College Trustees (ACCT)

ACCT is the national organisation for the nation's Community College trustees. More than 6,000 trustees govern the nation's community colleges. ACCT places major emphasis on providing trustees with the knowledge, skills, and avenues for influencing public policy at the national and state levels. ACCT works closely with AACC in shaping, achieving, and promoting the community college mission.

1975: Creation of Presidents Academy

Composed of chief executives of AACC member colleges, the Presidents Academy provides opportunities for career development through workshops and meetings. Workshops vary in focus but are designed to enhance leadership skills, technology awareness, and public policy awareness in top college officials.

1978 : Proposition 13 in California

The passage of Proposition 13 in California signaled the beginning of an increased demand by the public for greater accountability from its public institutions. Community Colleges have been in the forefront in adopting strategies for ensuring the most effective use of public funds in an era of fiscal constraint.

1988: Commission on the Future of Community Colleges Report

The Commission's report, Building Communities: A Vision for a New Century, defined community "not only as a region to be served, but also as a climate to be created." Community Colleges were challenged to assume a leadership role in creating a renewed climate of community in their service regions.

1992: Second Name Change for Association

The Association changed its name to the American Association of Community Colleges in an effort to unify its diverse membership of technical, junior, and community colleges.

1998 : Hope Scholarship and Lifetime Learning tax Credits Established

The Hope "Scholarship" is a tax credit available to eligible students during their first two years of postsecondary education. The tax credit is available for two tax years to those students who have not completed the first two years of post-secondary education. The Lifetime Learning Credit is available for education beyond the first two years of college.

1998: Workforce Investment Act

This law substantially alters the federal government's role in job training, adult education, and vocational rehabilitation. Community Colleges will still have a major role in the delivery of training services, but there will be a new order in the system. Training will be delivered primarily through Individual Training Accounts (or vouchers) and one–stop career center systems.

1998: Carl D. Perkins Vocational – Technical Education Act, Reauthorization

The Perkins Act represents the major federal commitment to vocational education activities. The reauthorization removes, set-asides historically included in the laws for special populations and provides states flexibility in determining how best to spend Perkins dollars. Community colleges are considered important providers of post secondary vocational education.

2007 COMMUNITY COLLEGE FACTS AT A GLANCE

Total	1,195
Public	987
Independent	177
Tribal	31
Enrollment	
Total	11.5 million
Credit	6.5 million
Noncredit	5 million
Enrolled full time	41%
Enrolled part time	59%
Demographics	
Average Age	29
21 or younger	43%
22-39	42%
40 or older	16%
Women	60%
Men	40%
Minorities	35%
Black	13%
Hispanic	15%
Asian/Pacific Islander	6%
Native American	1%
First Generation to attend College	39%
Single parents	17%
Non-U.S. citizens	8%

Community College students constitute the following percentages of undergraduates:

All U.S. undergraduates	46%
First Time Freshmen	41%
Native American	55%
Asian/Pacific Islander	46%
Black	46%
Hispanic	55%
Employment Status	
Full Time Students employed full time	27%
Full Time Students employed Part time	50%
Part Time Students employed full time	50%

Percentage of Students Applying For / Receiving Financial Aid	
Any Aid	47%
Federal Grants	21%
Federal loans	11%
State aid	12%
Percentage of Federal Aid Received by Community Colleges	
Pell Grants	34%
Campus based aid	9%
Average Annual Tuition and Fees	
Community Colleges (Public)	$2,361
4-Year College(public)	$6,185
Degrees and Certificates Awarded Annually	
Associate Degrees	550,000
Certificates	295,000
Bachelor's Degrees - awarded by 29 public and 66 independent Colleges.	
Revenue Sources (Public Colleges)	
State funds	37%
Tuition and fees	17%
Local funds	21%
Federal funds	11%
Others	14%

On Campus Housing

Available at 233 public and 70 independent colleges.

Community Colleges at the Forefront

Health Care: 59% of new nurses and the majority of other new health-care workers are educated at Community Colleges.

International Programmes: Close to 100,000 international students attend community colleges-about 39% of all international undergraduate students in the United States.

Workforce training: 95% of businesses and organizations that employ community college workforce education and training programmes.

Homeland security: Close to 80% of firefighters, law enforcement officers, and EMTs are credentialed at community colleges.

Online education: Students at 41% of public community colleges can earn a degree entirely online and 92% of all institutions offer at least one internet based course.

Earnings: The average expected lifetime earnings for a graduate with an associate degree are $1.6 million - about $0.4 million more than a high school graduates earns.

American Association of Community Colleges One Dupont Circle NW, Suite 410, Washington, DC 20036.202-728-0200.www.nche.edu

2010 COMMUNITY COLLEGE FACTS AT A GLANCE

Number and Type of Colleges	
Total	1,173
Public	987
Independent	155
Tribal	31
Headcount Enrollment	
Fall 2007 Total	11.8 million
Credit	6.8 million*
Noncredit	5 million
Enrolled full time	40%
Enrolled part time	60%

Estimated enrollment increase fall 2007 - fall 2009: 6.8 million to 8 million (16.9%) **

Demographics	
Average Age	28
21 or younger	46%
22-39	40%
40 or older	16%
Women	56%
Men	44%
Minorities	40%
Black	14%
Hispanic	15%
Asian/Pacific Islander	7%
Native American	1%
More than one race	2%
First Generation to attend College	42%
Single parents	16%
Non-U.S. citizens	7%

Community College students constitute the following percentages of undergraduates:

All U.S. undergraduates	43%*
First Time Freshmen	40%
Native American	52%
Asian/Pacific Islander	45%
Black	45%
Hispanic	53%
Employment Status	
Full Time Students employed Full time	21%
Full Time Students employed Part time	59%
Part Time Students employed Full time	40%
Part Time Students employed Part time	47%

Percentage of Students Applying For / Receiving Financial Aid

Applied:	
Any Aid	59%
Federal Aid	43%
Received:	
Any aid	46%
Federal Grants	21%
Federal loans	10%
State aid	13%
Institutional aid	11%

Percentage of Federal Aid Received by Community Colleges

Pell Grants	30%
Campus based aid	9%
Academic Competitiveness Grants	14%

Average Annual Tuition and Fees

Community Colleges (Public)	$2,544
4-Year College(public)	$7,020

Degrees and Certificates Awarded

Associate Degrees	605,267
Certificates	325,452

Bachelor's Degrees - awarded by 31 public and 52 independent Colleges.

Revenue Sources (Public Colleges)

State funds	37%
Tuition and fees	17%
Local funds	21%
Federal funds	11%
Others	14%

On Campus Housing

Available at 258 public and 63 independent colleges.

FACT: The average expected lifetime earning for a graduate with an associate degree are $1.6 million - about $0.4 million more than a high school graduate earns.

FACT: Students at 41% of Public Community Colleges can earn a degree entirely online, and 92% of al intuitions offer at least one Internet-based course.

Data are a derived from the most current information available as a December 2009.

* Most Current IPEDS data (fall 2007)

** Estimate based on 2009 AACC Survey.

2011 COMMUNITY COLLEGE FACTS AT A GLANCE

Number and Type of Colleges[1]	
Total	1,167
Public	993
Independent	143
Tribal	31
Headcount Enrolment	
Fall 2007 Total	12.4 million[2,3]
Credit	7.4 million[2]
Noncredit	5 million[3]
Enrolled full time	40%[2]
Enrolled part time	60%[2]
Estimated enrollment increase fall 2008 - fall 2010: 15%[4]	
Student Demographics	
2007-2008[5]	
Average Age	28
Median Age	23
21 or younger	39%
22-39	45%
40 or Older	15%
First Generation to attend college	42%
Single Parents	13%
Non-U.S. Citizens	6%
Veterans	3%
Students with disabilities	12%
Fall 2008[2]	
Women	58%
Men	42%
Minorities	45%
Black	13%
Hispanic	16%
Asian/Pacific Islander	6%
Native American	1%

Community College Students Constitute the following Percentages of Undergraduates (fall 2008):[2]

All U.S. undergraduates	44%
First Time Freshmen	43%
Native American	55%
Asian/Pacific Islander	45%
Black	44%
Hispanic	52%

Employment Status (2007-2008)[5]

Full Time Students employed full time	21%
Full Time Students employed Part time	59%
Part Time Students employed full time	40%
Part Time Students employed Part time	47%

Percentage of Students Applying For / Receiving Financial Aid (2007-2008)[5]

Applied:

Any Aid	59%
Federal Aid	42%

Received:

Any aid	46%
Federal Grants	21%
Federal loans	10%
State aid	13%
Institutional aid	11%

Percentage of Federal Aid Received by Community Colleges (2008-2009)[6]

Pell Grants	31%
Campus based aid	10%
Academic Competitiveness Grants	15%

Average Annual Tuition and Fees (2010-2011)7

Community Colleges (Public)	$2,713
4-Year College (public)	$7,605

Degrees and Certificates Awarded (2007-2008)8

Associate Degrees	609,016
Certificates	323,649

Bachelor's Degrees - awarded by 48 public and 82 independent Colleges.

Revenue Sources (2007-2008)[9]

State funds	36%
Tuition and fees	16%
Local funds	19%
Federal funds	14%
Others	15%

On Campus Housing

Available at 254 public and 62 independent colleges.

Sources

1 AACC membership database, January 2011. 2 NCES. (2008). IPEDS Fall Enrollment Survey. [AACC analysis] 3 AACC membership database, 2006. [AACC analysis] 4 AACC 2009 and 2010 AACC fall enrollment surveys. [AACC analysis] 5 NCES. (2009). 2007-08 National Postsecondary Student Aid Study (NPSAS:08) [AACC analysis] 6 College Board. (2010). Trends in

Student Aid: 2010. [AACC analysis] 7 College Board. (2010). Trends in College Pricing: 2010. 8 NCES. (2008). IPEDS 2008 Completions Survey. [AACC analysis] 9 Knapp, Kelly-Reid, & Ginder. (2010). Enrollment in postsecondary institutions, fall 2008; graduation rates, 2002 and 2005 cohorts; and financial statistics, fiscal year 2008 (NCES 2010-152). 10 NCES. (2009). IPEDS 2009 Institutional Characteristics Survey. [AACC analysis]

Note: Sources are presented in abbreviated format. Go to www.aacc.nche.edu/fastfacts for full citations.

References

1. Alphonse, Xavier, *"Changing Track" – Community Colleges in India*, AIACHE Publications, New Delhi – December 1996.
2. B.Vaughan, George, *"The Community College Story"* Second Edition, Community College Press, 2000. (USA).
3. Catalog 03/04, *"North Harris Montogomery Community College District (USA)"*
4. B.Brawer, Florence and M.Cohen, Arthur *"The American Community College"* Jossey- Bass Publishers, Second Edition, 1991.
5. Latiner Raby, Rosalind and J. Valeau, Edward, *"Community College Models – Globalization and Higher Education Reform"* Springer, 2009.
6. Latiner Raby, Rosalind and J. Valeau, Edward, *"International Reform Efforts and Challenges in Community Colleges"* Summer 2007.
7. Catalgue, *"Hartnell College"* 2003 – 2004, Your Best Choice –Past, Present and Future.
8. Catalog, *"American Association of Community Colleges"*.
9. *"Northern Virginia Community College"* Fact Book 1999 – 2003.
10. *"Northern Virginia Community College"* Catalog 2004-2005.
11. News letter of the *International Community Education Association.*
12. J. Kemple, James and J.Willner, Cynthia *"Career Academies"* mdrc, June 2008

Websites:

13. http://www.art-search.com.au/information_education/community_colleges/
14. http://english.moe.gov.tw/ct.asp?xItem=9318&ctNode=506&mp=11
15. http://www.qualityresearchinternational.com/glossary/communitycollege.htm
16. http://en.wikipedia.org/wiki/Community_colleges_in_the_United_States

21

Community Colleges in United Kingdom

In the United Kingdom, 'community' college usually refers to a Sixth Form college or post compulsory education institution and is where students can achieve the A-levels, Scottish Higher, or other vocational qualifications (such as a GNVQ or an HND for example) needed for University. In other cases Community Colleges can also provide GCSEs to students of Compulsory School ages.

Education in England is overseen by the Department for Education and the Department for Business, Innovation and Skills. At local level, local authorities take responsibility for implementing policy for public education and state schools.

Further Education (often abbreviated "FE", called continuing education in U.S. English) is a term mainly used in connection with education in the United Kingdom and the Republic of Ireland. It is post-compulsory education (in addition to that received at secondary school), that is distinct from the Further Education offered in universities (higher education). It may be at any level above compulsory Further Education, from basic training to Higher National Diploma or Foundation Degree.

A distinction is usually made between FE and Higher Education ("HE") which is Further Education at a higher level than secondary school, usually provided in distinct institutions such as universities. FE in the United Kingdom therefore includes Further Education for people over 16, usually excluding universities. It is primarily taught in FE colleges (which are similar in concept to United States community colleges, and sometimes use "Community College" in their title), work-based learning, and adult and community learning institutions. This includes post-16 courses similar to those taught at schools and sub-degree courses similar to those taught at higher education (HE) colleges (which also teach degree-level courses) and at some universities.

In the United Kingdom, community college usually refers to Sixth Form in Secondary School, College or post compulsory education institution and is where students can achieve the A-levels, Scottish Higher, or other vocational qualifications (such as a GNVQ or an HND for example) needed for University. In other cases Community Colleges can also provide GCSEs to students of Compulsory School ages.

Further education is different from school or Higher education in many ways. Most FE courses are one year long or less and many courses are part time, so that students only attend a college for a short time. Also most colleges are not residential. Many FE courses involve practical skills, and are work related. Courses attract a wide range of students, both in age, background and experience.

These factors mean that there is potential to develop the links between the college and the community and businesses with which it works.

The reasons for further education colleges embarking on strategies are to regenerate the economy. The reasons and strategies are diverse and colleges may involve themselves in the process to a greater or lesser degree. At the one end of the spectrum is the college that responds to the demand for industrial training by providing courses on campus to the employees of local companies – at the other, the college that actively participate with employers and community organizations in schemes aimed at creating jobs with training and career opportunities, to the extent that the college itself, alone or in partnership, develops its own business ventures.

One purpose of this: Is to argue and illustrate the case for the direct involvement of a college in business activity, so that the college itself is transformed from a mere provider of education and training to a multi faceted enterprise, at the service of the community, locally, nationally and internationally, and engaged in productive economic activity, job creation, high quality industrially relevant training and the provision of work experience. One very important aspect of this transformation is the support it gives to the development of a new technical curriculum directly relevant to the needs and interests of the mass of the population. The new curriculum, made possible by the submersion of the further education college in business and community activity, may lead to a unity of theory and practice (praxis) which could eventually replace existing anachronistic forms of academic knowledge. It might also provide the conditions for mass life time participation in education.

Entrepreneurial endeavour is creative, active and transformatory. These properties and values must be manifested in the new vocational or technical curriculum. Everyone will participate in entrepreneurship for the collective improvement of their lives, for the good of humanity and for the preservation of the planet.

The structure adopted for this book is intended to reflect the interactive or dialectical nature of embarking upon a programme of economic regeneration. In setting out to transform the community, the college succeeds also in transforming itself. In seeking to provide a relevant education for unemployed people, the need for a comprehensive new technical curriculum becomes apparent. And in the production of this multi authored book, the essential methodology of developing theory in the course of reflecting on practice (praxis) is demonstrated.

Since 2001, FE in England has been managed by the Learning and Skills Council (LSC), the largest government agency funding education provision. The LSC has a budget of some £13 billion and is organised on a regional basis through around 47 local councils. The LSC has a particular mission to improve and expand further education provision, driven by the UK government's desire to increase standards in post-16 student retention and achievement, particularly in skills-based vocational provision in FE colleges. Recent government-driven LSC and Department for Children, Schools and Families policies, such as Success for All and the Skills Strategy, articulate this vision.

The Learning and Skills Improvement Service (LSIS - formerly the Quality Improvement Agency and Centre for Excellence in Leadership) is the sector owned body supporting the development of excellent and sustainable FE provision across the learning and skills sector. Its aim is to accelerate the drive for excellence and, working in partnership with all parts of the sector, builds on the sector's own capacity to design, commission and deliver improvement and strategic change.

The Learning and Skills Network LSN offers training and consultancy.

Colleges in England that are regarded as part of the FE sector include:

- General FE and tertiary colleges
- Sixth form colleges (Community Colleges)
- Specialist colleges (mainly colleges of agriculture and horticulture and colleges of drama and dance)
- Adult education institutes

In addition, FE courses may be offered in the school sector, both in sixth form (16-19) schools, or, more commonly, sixth forms within secondary schools.

From September 2007, teachers working in FE in England are required to gain professional status, known as Qualified Teacher Learning and Skills (QTLS). The first stage of QTLS is an initial 'passport to teaching' module. The second stage is full teacher training, which would typically take up to five years to complete. The qualification covers both taught and practical skills, and also requires teachers to undertake 30 hours of continuous professional development per year.

Good quality teaching is indicated by the award of the Training Quality Standard, an initiative to improve the quality of provision for vocational education, while all colleges and FE providers are subject to regular inspections.

Lifelong Learning UK is the independent sector skills council responsible for the qualifications and standards for teachers working in FE. The trade unions for FE staff are the University and College Union and the Association of Teachers and Lecturers. Teachers working in the sixth form colleges, sixth form schools and sixth forms of secondary schools are eligible to join the teaching unions which recruit in the secondary school sector.

In England, further education is often seen as forming one part of a wider learning and skills sector, alongside workplace education, prison education, and other types of non-school, non-university education and training. Since June 2009, the sector is overseen by the new Department for Business, Innovation and Skills, although some parts (such as education and training for 14-19 year olds) fall within the Department for Children, Schools and Families.

While they might differ in how it should be undertaken, both conservative and labour governments have prioritized action aimed at regenerating the economy. With government funding of over £3 billion, the further education sector in England and Wales, through the work of its colleges, is expected to play a major role in equipping the country's workforce with the work skills to meet the changing needs of industry. But it is only one of a whole range of initiatives aimed at encouraging national, regional and local economic development.

To deal with the previously separate interventions of government departments (22 different programmes in 1994 including Urban Development Corporations, City Challenge, Urban Programme and Section 11), Government Officers of the Regions (GORs) have been created to co-ordinate the work and funding of five departments; Environment, Trade and Industry, Home Office, and Treasury. The GORs administer a new Single Regeneration Budget (SRB) allocated for the purpose of economic regeneration through a process of competitive bidding by partnerships of local or regional organizations.

The European Union has also contributed substantially to regional policies aimed at addressing unemployment and helping industry and the workforce adapt to change. Two funds, the European Social Fund (ESF) and the European Regional Development Fund (ERDF), are particular relevant to urban economic regeneration, and these are spent according to a set of priorities known as objectives.

Specific programmes relevant to college economic regeneration initiatives are adapt for retraining those whose jobs are at risk from industrial change, horizonfor assisting disadvantaged groups enter the labour market, NOW for planning equal opportunity, and youthstart for dealing with youth unemployment. leonardo is a programme for vocational training, and TEMPUS is a university student mobility and exchange programme with Eastern Europe.

These sources of regionally-directed funding have provided vital support for college and community economic regeneration initiatives, and could, if properly planned and coordinated, make a substantial contribution to reviving the local economy and reducing unemployment.

The government set colleges the task of serving company training needs by providing employers with the range of courses they required. Individual students had to be given opportunities to acquire skills and qualifications of direct relevance to employment, while people displaced by economic or technological change wishing to change career or re enter the labour market would be offered a chance to retrain. Colleges were seen as playing an important role in this respect in local economic development. The government's belief in the role of education and training in economic development led it to establish a national framework of occupational qualifications and to use the framework as a device for setting attainment targets for training and education. Instituted in 1986, the National Council for Vocational Qualifications saw vocational qualifications, directly related to a person's competence in employment, as essential to improving the country's economic performance.

Paradoxically, while the development of National Vocational Qualifications (NVQs), based on competence in the work place may have increased the relevance of vocational qualifications to the needs of employers, it has made it more difficult for those who are not employed to gain the industrial experience necessary to become competent and gain qualifications. The onus is placed on colleges to devise occupation specific work experience for their unemployed students. The creation of realistic work placements brings colleges one step nearer to engaging directly in industrial and commercial activity.

Successful, well qualified professionals, valuing education for education's sake, often fail to recognize the courage of those who are forced to choose study as their only possible escape route from poverty and long term unemployment. These students experience of school was frequently cruel and unpleasant and the prospect of further study is not attractive. Even in a supportive college environment, immense strength of mind in the face of the drudgery and humiliation frequently experienced is required to achieve competence in the basic skills literacy and numbers. Students need to be convinced that the effort is worthwhile.

Large numbers of college students are initially motivated to study solely in order to gain qualifications to improve job or promotion opportunities. They believe implicitly that the acquisition of qualifications improves their prospects of employment. The worth of a college is assessed on the relevance of the curriculum on offer in providing access to jobs, promotion or more advanced study. College staff understandably invest considerable effort in ensuring that passing out students gain employment or places in higher education.

A-level now consists of six modules studied over two years. Normally, three modules are assessed at the end of the first year, and make up a stand-alone qualification called the "AS-level" (or Advanced Subsidiary level, not to be confused with an older AS-level, the Advanced Supplementary level). Another three modules are assessed at the end of the second year, which make up the "A2". A2 modules do not form a qualification in their own right; the satisfactory completion of the AS and A2 modules in the same subject is required to constitute a complete A-level. Modules are assessed by exam papers marked by national organisations and internally-assessed.

The introduction of the new GCE Applied A-level suite, taken from the old VCE A-levels, generally has a more vocational twist. For example, the new GCE A-level in Applied Business combines the traditional theory based subject 'Business Studies' (which can be studied as an A-level itself) and adds a more practical and hands-on approach to it. In this case, for the mandatory modules in the AS year, the candidate is expected to create a simulated Marketing Proposal (module 1) and Recruitment and motivational package (module 2) as opposed to just studying the processes. This essentially asks the candidate to show a more thorough insight by actually applying the theory. Given that many universities have shown a dislike of vocational subjects as opposed to the traditional ones, their reaction to the new applied suite remains to be seen. However, considering the subject is now much broader and more "student-friendly" it is hoped that universities will see that this subject is no less than the traditional Business Studies given that the traditional aspect of the subject is not fully lost. The new GCE Applied A-levels are available in: Art and Design, ICT, Business, and Science.

Full-time education is compulsory for all children aged between 5 and 16 (inclusive). Students may then continue their secondary studies for a further two years (sixth form), leading most typically to an A level qualification, although other qualifications and courses exist, including Business and Technology Education Council (BTEC) qualifications and the International Baccalaureate. The leaving age for compulsory education was raised to 18 by the Education and Skills Act 2008. The change will take effect in 2013 for 17-year-olds and 2015 for 18-year-olds. State-provided schools are free of charge to students, and there is also a tradition of independent schooling, but parents may choose to educate their children by any suitable means.

Higher education typically begins with a 3-year Bachelor's Degree. Postgraduate degrees include Master's Degrees, either taught or by research, and Doctor of Philosophy, a research degree that usually takes at least three years.

A-level examinations are administered through a series of examination boards. These were originally based on the major UK universities but have over the last 50 years merged into six very large organisations, AQA, OCR, Edexcel, WJEC and CCEA. Some of these boards also offer A-levels to international students, specifically Edexcel. Another large organization which offers GCE qualifications for international students only is CIE. OCR and CIE are both branches of the parent organization, Cambridge Assessment. In the UK it is customary for schools to register with multiple examination boards and to "mix and match" A-levels to get a combined curriculum that fits the school profile.

The passing grades for A-levels are A*, A, B, C, D and E. The A* grade was introduced in September 2008 for higher education entry in 2010, and is awarded to candidates who achieve an A in their overall A-level, with a score of at least 90% at A2. There is no A* grade at AS or unit level. There was formerly an O grade, awarded to candidates who did not pass the advanced level exam, but were deemed to have attained a standard equivalent to ordinary level.

References

1. Frankel, Anna and Reeves, Frank, *"The Further Education Curriculum, In England – An Introduction"*, Bilston College Publications, 1996 (UK).
2. Reeves, Frank, *Further Education as Economic Regeneration*, Bilston College Publications (UK).
3. Reeves, Frank "*Community Need and Further Education*" British Cataloging in Publication Data, 1993.
4. Reeves, Frank "*The Modernity of Further Education*" British Cataloging in Publication Data, 1995.
5. *Education and Training in Britain*, Foreign and Commonwealth Office, London.
6. *A Guide to the National Curriculum*, Teacher Training Agency, London.
7. *Vocational Qualifications in England*, Wales and Northern Ireland.

22

Community Colleges in Australia

Australia has had a System of Technical and Further Education (TAFE) and Community College for many years. Training is conducted under the National Training System, the Australian System for Vocational Education and Training (VET) under the Australian Quality Training Framework (AQTF), in which employers, the States of Australia, and the Commonwealth Government, formalise a curriculum available for Registered Training Organisations (RTOs) to teach and assess the competency of students. Courses are part of the Australian Qualifications Framework.

Technical and Further Education (TAFE): Features

- The Australian Technical and Further Education (TAFE) system is the largest provider of tertiary education and training in the Asia- Pacific region. TAFE is a government owned and nationally operated system of institutions. TAFE qualifications are recognized and transferable internationally. With well over one million students, TAFE's contribution to Australian Society is highly significant.
- TAFE specializes in training for the work force and is the largest supplier of training to industry in Australia. TAFE graduates are in demand by business and industry for their wide range of practical and technical skills.
- With more than 100 years of experience in providing quality programs, TAFE institutions represent a first-class standard of international education. Students from more than 30 countries around the world study at TAFE institutions in Australia. These students chose to study at TAFE because they know that a TAFE education will increase their career prospects and future study opportunities.
- TAFE courses are also offered by Queensland University of Technology, RMIT University, Swinburne University of Technology

and Victoria University of Technology, all listed in the Universities section of this guide.

- TAFEs or their outlying schools are in most large towns, and cities.
- Community College Australia provides affordable education, training and lifestyle courses to their local communities. There are over 50 Community Colleges across New South Wales and Victoria. SGSCC - St George and Sutherland Community College is one of the largest colleges with a 30 year history, the college specializes in Disability, Leisure, Work Skills, School Age and English programmes.

Australia's Education system is divided into Five Sectors. They are:

1. The Universities.
2. A Vocational Training System through its Technical and Further Education (TAFE) Colleges.
3. The ELICOS institutions which offer English Language Intensive Courses for Overseas Students.
4. A number of Private Colleges and Schools giving courses in subjects such as business studies, hotel management and aviation.
5. Primary and Secondary Schools.

When university education was introduced into Australia during the 1850's, the University of Sydney and the University of Melbourne were modeled after Oxford and Cambridge in Great Britain. By 1911, a university had been established in each of the six major metropolitan centres to keep up with the rapidly developing country.

There was a rapid growth in population and the economy after World War Two, which led to the creation of several new universities to meet the public demand for higher education. Like the older universities, the new institutions followed the British system for tertiary education and included characteristics such as public status, government funding, institutional autonomy, academic specialization, as well as central accreditation, and a three - or four year academic degree as the basic degree.

English Language Intensive Courses for Overseas Students are offered by a number of private, semi private and public institutions.

You can follow an English language course:

- To prepare for University entrance.
- To sit for one of the international English language examinations such as IELTS, TOEFL or the Cambridge Certificate of Proficiency.
- Or simply to improve your general knowledge of English.

Many universities have ELICOS centres attached to their campuses. Private ELICOS centres are in all of the capital cities and in some rural areas. Most TAFE system also have an ELICOS centre and offer a wide variety of English Language courses.

Semesters are usually more flexible than the universities and the student has greater freedom to choose the starting date and the duration of the selected courses.

Unlike the universities and TAFE College, the ELICOS centres do not usually have any entrance requirements. A test of the students' English Language proficiency is normally given on arrival at an ELICOS centre.

Private institutions also offer a range of awards such as diplomas and certificates for vocational purposes. The individual institutions decide on admission requirements, courses and the duration of courses. Business colleges have both certificate and diploma courses. Diploma courses are usually over 40 weeks and certificate courses range from 12 to 30 weeks.

Australian schools provide a standard and quality of education equal to the best in the world. Each state Government has responsibility for its own schools but the Australian Government takes a strong interest in ensuring comparable standards and maintaining the quality of teaching. The qualifications awards in each state are regarded as being the same standard as far as tertiary entry is concerned.

A wide range of courses is given in vocational education and training. The TAFE College (similar to British polytechnics) provide most of the skills needed for the Australian workforce. TAFE provides training at professional, para-professional, post trade, trade and operative levels. TAFE courses are developed in collaboration with industry to ensure that the most up-to-date training is given.

(i) Box Hill College of TAFE - Course Information

Diploma (three years), associate diploma (two years), advanced certificate (one year), and certificate (one year or six months) courses are offered in the following areas: Accounting, Marketing, Hotel and Restaurant Management, Travel and Tourism, Office Administration, Computing, Electronics, Computer Technician, Art and Design, Child Care, Dance Instruction, Graphic Art, Horse Studies, Laboratory Technology, Music, Textiles, Professional Writing and Editing, Architectural Drafting, Automotive, Building Survey and Mapping, Mechanical Design Drafting, Floristry, Hairdressing.

Studies in Matriculation and Foundation Programs are also available, as are English Language Programs for beginners to advanced and IELTS preparation courses.

(ii) Holmesglen College of TAFE - Course Information

Degree programs are offered in Computing Technology (in association with Monash University), Manufacturing Technology (in association with Monash University), and Accounting (in association with Deakin University).

Associate Diploma/Advanced Certificate courses are offered in Accounting, Marketing, Sales Management, Computer Programming / Microcomputing, /Information Technology, Secretarial Studies/Office Administration, International Trade, Public Relations, Travel and Tourism, Banking and Finance, Human Resources/Personnel Management, Media, Professional Writing and Editing, Theatre Technology/Stage Management, Computer Technology, Materials Technology, Resource Management, Architectural Drafting, Interior Design, Building Construction, Building Inspection, Ceramics, Horticulture and Plumbing. Matriculation/Foundation programmes are offered in Business Studies, Science and Humanities.

(iii) TAFE New South Wales - Courses Information

There are over 60 courses currently on offer to international students. Subject areas include: applied Science, Aviation, Art and Ceramics, Building Studies, Business and Secretarial, Computer Studies, Engineering Studies, Design (Fashion, Graphic), English Language Courses, Fashion Production, Hotel and Tourism, Maritime Studies, Marine Engineering, Matriculation (Foundation Studies) and Rural Studies.

(iv) TAFE Queensland - Course Information

Courses offered include English Language (ELICOS), Hotel Management, Travel and Tourism, Computing Studies, Business Studies (including management, accountancy and marketing), Engineering, Secretarial Studies Hair and Beauty, Fashion Studies, Child Care, Aviation, Art and Design.

(v) Advanced Standing

Generally, completion of a TAFE Associate Diploma would allow students to apply for and be granted advanced standing of up to one year in a relevant bachelor degree. Credit for diploma courses is usually more, depending on the subjects' studies and results achieved.

There are 37 Australian Universities maintaining a high level of excellence and located in every state and territory of the country.

While the majority of Australian campuses are urban, coastal locations, most states also offer study in a rural setting. Australian university vary in size between 3,000 and 27,000 or more students.

The college has a large English Language Centre and English language programs are offered at all levels from beginners to advance. At the advanced level, specific courses are available in academic and occupational languages

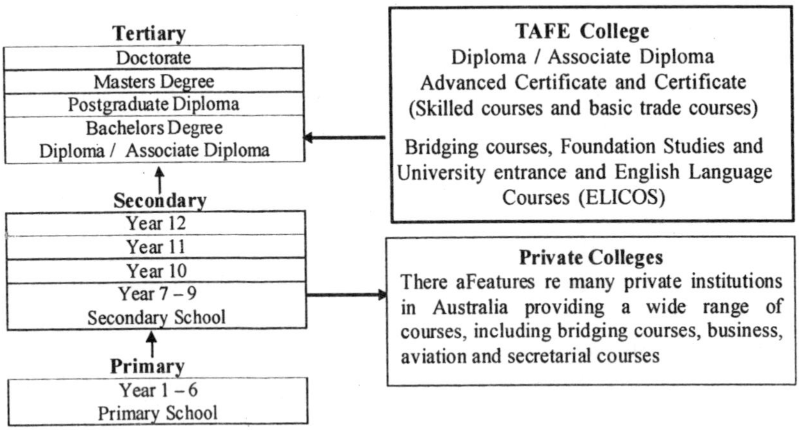

skills. All courses focus on preparing students for studies in Australia and include components in a variety of subjects' areas. All courses prepare students for the IETS test and/or the TOEFL test.

Individual TAFE institutions (usually with many campuses) are known as either colleges or institutes, depending on the state or territory. TAFE colleges are owned, operated and financed by the various state and territory governments. This is in contrast to the higher education sector, whose funding is predominantly the domain of the Commonwealth government and whose universities are predominantly owned by the State governments. Higher Education in Australia is not free. Australian university has to charge tuition fees to meet the high costs of running a university, although some scholarships are available.

In Australia, technical and further education or TAFE institutions provide a wide range of predominantly vocational tertiary education courses, mostly qualifying courses under the National Training System/Australian Qualifications Framework/Australian Quality Training Framework. Fields covered include hospitality, tourism, construction, engineering, secretarial skills, visual arts, information technology and community work.

At the completion of each program an extensive evaluation and rating system was used to determine content relevance and workplace suitability of the programme. A rating of 90% plus was the benchmark for a successful training outcome. This evaluation then formed the basis for a materials and program delivery review and analysis. As each program was delivered over two or three days a subsequent day was required to allow both the Australian trainer and Malaysian counterpart/trainer to thoroughly analyze the programme. The process was monitored by the project managers and problems and major changes were mediated through reference groups and the project managers.

For quality assurance and maintenance of standards a sample number of assessments were marked and validated by the Management Studies trainers over the period of the program. This progressively led to the ownership and independent delivery of the programme by CLC. Qualifications range from certificate, advanced certificate, diploma and associate diploma. The courses extend from six months to two years and credit transfer universities. Diploma and associate diploma courses transfer directly into degree programmes, with advanced study at Australian Universities. An associate diploma allows for up to one year advanced study towards a three year bachelor degree. All courses are fully accredited by the Australian Government. Advanced Certificate courses take one year. Associate Diploma courses take two years and lead directly into degrees, with advanced standing at Australian universities. Where students transfer to degree courses in the same field, they can complete the degree in two years.

Students enrolled in degree programmes have the choice at the end of the first year either to complete the Associate Diploma at the college or to transfer directly into the second year of the Bachelor degree courses at the associated university. TAFE colleges generally award qualifications up to the level of advanced diploma, which is below that of Bachelor degree within the Australian Qualifications Framework. In many instances TAFE study can be used as partial credit towards Bachelor degree-level university programmes.

From 2002 the TAFE education sector has been able to offer Bachelor degrees and post-graduate diploma courses to fill niche areas, particularly vocationally focused areas of study based on industry needs. As at June 2009 10 TAFE colleges (mainly in Victoria, but also Western Australia, ACT, and Queensland) now confer their own degree-level awards and post graduate diplomas, though not beyond the level of Bachelor degree; this practice is somewhat controversial due to the blurring of once clearly defined boundaries between sectors. Students who enroll in these undergraduate degree courses at TAFE are required to pay full fees and are not entitled to Commonwealth Government supported student fee loans. While Universities have the ability and power to design and offer their own degree courses and each TAFE degree course must be assessed and approved by the Higher Education Accreditation Committee (HEAC).

TAFEs in some states can also teach senior high school qualifications, like the VCE and the Higher School Certificate. Some universities, e.g. Charles Darwin University and Royal Melbourne Institute of Technology, offer TAFE courses; these are funded by the local state and territory governments. Some High Schools also deliver courses developed and accredited by TAFEs. Some private institutions also offer courses from TAFEs, however they more commonly offer other vocational education and training courses.

Note that many Australians refer to all sub-degree courses as 'TAFE' courses, no matter what institution creates or delivers the course. Before the 1990s, the TAFEs had a near monopoly in the sector. TAFE courses provide students an opportunity for getting certificate, diploma, and advanced diploma qualifications in a wide range of areas.

References

1. Pinto. E., "*Technical and Vocational Education in Australia*", January 1999.
2. Australian Education, "A Guide for International Students" 1995.
3. S P Maj, D Veal, L Yassa "*A Preliminary Evaluation of the New Cisco Network Security Course*" Edith Cowan University, Perth, Western Australia, September 2010.

23

Community Colleges in Germany

In contrast to Australia, both universities and community colleges clearly display a sequentially differentiated system. The possibility of entering the labor market at any stage during higher education or continuing with one's studies implies flexibility in the planning of educational careers. The decision for or against participation in tertiary education is broken down into several smaller decisions at different stages in the life course.

The Dual System can also be defined as a combination of learning in the "serious" world of a company career and learning in the "protected" world of the vocational school, where the companies concentrate on imparting practical knowledge, while the vocational schools concentrate on imparting theory. It is also becoming more and more difficult to strictly separate the functions of the company and the vocational school due to the new information and control technologies which have been integrated in the training regulations and have led to a trend towards an increasing amount of theory in vocational training. The term "dual" also denotes a specific

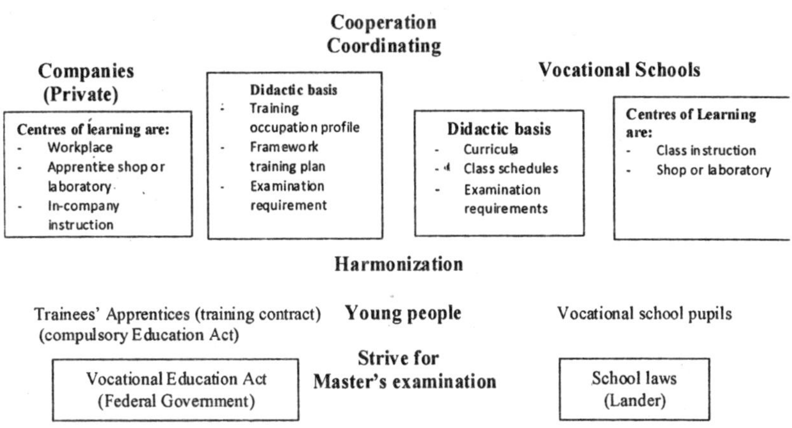

constitutional situation in Germany, in that the Federal Government is responsible for vocational education in the companies and the Lander for the vocational schools. The following figure clarifies the legal organization and teaching structure of the Dual System of vocational training.

The Origins of the Dual System: An important step on the way to today's Dual System of Vocational Training was undoubetedly the Industrial Code of the North Germany Federation issued in the year 1869. According to this code, "...assistants, journeymen and apprentices, or individual classes of the same," could be "obliged by town statutes to attend a further training school of the town, as long as they had not reached eighteen years of age, and the employers and master craftsmen are obliged to allow the time required for attendance."[1]

The Vocational Education Act in 1969 play in the Development of the Dual System: While, up to this time, vocational training in the Dual System was only regulated in some sectors, or as a self-administration task in those branches of the economy involved in training, the Vocational Education Act now represents an extensive and detailed regulatory work which emphasizes, promotes and safeguards public responsibility in vocational training. At the same time, this act granted those social groups which are particularly interested in vocational training, namely employers and employees, a decisive influence and organizational capacities. This concept is characterized by the appointment of employer, employee and vocational school representatives to the committees and bodies which organize vocational training in a developing, advising or implementing capacity, this being regulated by the Vocational Education Act. The adoption of the Vocation Education Act – which was supported by the overwhelming majority despite individual points of criticism – also legally sanctioned the Dual System of vocational training as the predominant qualification system in Germany.

The Dual System of vocational training practiced in Germany is characterized by, among other things, the fact that it includes all sectors of the economy, as well as the liberal professions, and that all sectors are basically regulated in the same manner.

In detail, this means that:

- The regulations of the Vocational Education Act apply equally to all sectors,
- Acceptance and contract conditions are the same for all sectors,
- The formal structure of the training regulations does not differ,
- The participation of employers and unions is regulated in the same manner for all sectors.
- The chambers are, with a few exceptions (e.g. housekeeping, urban households), the competent bodies for all sectors.

- Final examinations based on the same regulations and framework conditions are taken in all sectors.
- Compulsory vocational school education and vocational school attendance are basically regulated in the same manner for trainees in all sectors.
- In our discussion of the core dimensions of labor-market structures we assume that flexibility plays an important role, as it influences the possibilities for labor-market entrants to get a suitable job. Flexibility both offers incentives to re-enter education in the case of an unsuccessful or unsatisfactory first job and lowers the risks involved in giving up a job.
- We argue that there are three reasons why transitions from higher education to work are less ordered in flexible labor markets. First, a higher turnover-rate of workers in the labor market facilitates early exits from the educational system due quite simply to the number of vacancies. Attractive jobs will divert students away from education more often than in labor markets where entrants face high disadvantages in comparison to insiders. As previous research has shown, flexible labor markets do indeed manage to integrate school leavers faster than more regulated systems (Wolbers 2007). Second, once a position is reached in a flexible labor market, the value of holding this position is smaller than in regulated labor markets. As job safety is lower in flexible labor markets, the chance of losing it is higher. Moreover, it is then easier to find a new job, which further reduces the value of holding a position. Third, re-entry into the labor market after a second period in the education system is easier. Lock-in effects in the educational system can be expected to be shorter, which reduces the costs and the risk of re-entering the education system.

There are various reasons for the reticence of the government in the statutory regulation and the financing of vocational training. However, it must first be pointed out that it is in no way the case that the government is not involved in vocational training at all. On the one hand, the vocational schools, as one of the two pillars of the Dual System, are state-operated and, on the other hand, the government controls in-company vocational training via the Vocational Education Act and other laws. However, the government has no intention of replacing the Dual System of vocational training with a scholastic system of vocational training.

Thus, there are various reasons for the fact that the government plays a largely secondary role and limits itself to important controlling instruments for vocational training:

1. The decisive involvement of the companies in vocational training has a long tradition in Germany.
2. The Dual System has proven effective: in particular:
   - It reaches the great majority of young people with its training activities.
   - It secures practice-related and (also with the help of the vocational schools) theory-based qualifications.
   - It considers the concrete qualification demands of the companies and the economy.
   - It is capable of reacting flexibly to demographic fluctuations, and
   - It relieves the government budget because the companies themselves bear the costs they incur for vocational training.
3. There is a consensus that, due to the associated tendency towards bureaucracy and a lack of practical; content, the general nationalization of vocational training would not be able to adequately meet the interests of young people or those of the companies and unions.

Although the government demonstrates general reticence, it does train its own apprentices in its authorities and institutions.

For the purpose of our inquiry, we draw upon the following distinction between dimensions of educational structures that we assume strongly influence the transition patterns between school and work: First, the mode and type of stratification displayed by the education system have to be considered. The mode of stratification has an impact on the allocation process in the labor market, usually by a corresponding hierarchy of entry positions, while the type of stratification (i.e. either via several parallel tracks leading to the same educational level or else via sequential courses each offering a full degree) has an influence on the feasibility of interrupting one's educational career. In the latter case, students can enter the labor market earlier without giving up their educational goals, or they can re-enter education easily to gain a higher degree.

Second, the evolution of different tertiary educational systems depends on the mechanisms of coordination predominant in higher education. These are either largely state-controlled or market-based. They differ in the extent to which centralized control is operative with regard to curricular and institutional issues on the one hand, and in the degree to which institutions are free to develop their own profile by catering for consumer demands with specific educational programmes, on the other. In line with Arum et al. (2007), we argue that the pattern of labor-market entry will differ depending on the degree of state control. We extend their argument that deregulated systems will lead to more institutionally diversified systems and assume that certain institutions within those systems will offer more flexibility for educational career patterns. In a market-based system, second-tier institutions and institutions with low prestige are especially likely to offer greater flexibility with a view to acquiring a comparative advantage in attracting (non-traditional) students. In the case of state-controlled systems there is less need for flexibility as a competitive asset, and it will depend on policy-makers whether the educational system offers more or less flexible pathways to graduation.

The third characteristic of higher education that we consider to be relevant for transition patterns relates to the labor market. Both standardization of educational provisions and occupational specificity provide information on the abilities and competencies of school-leavers. This reduces uncertainty for both students and prospective employers as to whether is according to the occupation trained to a student's own interests and preferences or the respective job demands.

However, degrees in sequentially stratified systems are not only designed as terminal degrees but also function as an entry qualification for the next stage in an educational career. This ambiguity reduces their value as signals about the skills of labor market entrants. Degrees from lower cycles in sequentially stratified systems may still be good signals about the general ability of an applicant that can be drawn upon in subsequent educational cycles, but they may also be less useful in detecting occupational skills. This in its turn may result in more mismatches on the labor market and more time spent looking for a job at the outset of a young person's career. By contrast, education systems offering standardized courses and comparable quality between its institutions accompanied by a degree of occupational specificity can be expected to stabilize labor-market entry, as the match between applicants and jobs should be better.

There is a certain difference in that the business and administrative professions and the liberal professions involve further training examinations instead of master's examinations. The master's examination in the skilled trades also differs from the master's examinations in the other sectors in that it not only authorizes a person to train apprentices, but is also associated with the right to establish and manage a skilled – trade business.

The closer the training is to company practice, the more realistic it is. This increases the opportunities of young people on the job market. Consequently, the training company bears most of the legal responsibility for training. Academic vocational education supplements in-company training. Due to the fact that they lack a company training partner, full-time vocational schools must ensure practical experience through internships, which is considered to be very difficult. The social partners and also the government offices continue to strive to train most young people in the Dual System.

In accordance with Art. 45 Para 1 of the Vocational Education Act, the competent bodies monitor "the implementation of vocational training and provide support by advising the trainee recruiters and the trainees. They are required to appoint training counselors for this purpose. The trainee recruiters are obliged to provide the information and documents required for monitoring and to permit the inspection of the training centers."

For example, the monitoring of the proper implementation of training covers the observance of the:

- In-company training schedule
- Ban on employment for non-training-related work
- Release to attend vocational school and inter-firm training programmes
- Obligation to provide training materials at no charge
- Obligation to appoint and employ trainers
- Observance and application of the pertinent legal regulations (Vocational Education Act, Law on the Protection of Minors at work, Maternity Protection Act, Industrial Safety Law and other labour and welfare regulations).

In accordance with the responsibility of the Federal Lander, for the schools, the vocational schools are subject to the supervision of the Ministers of Education and Cultural Affairs of the Lander. In some Federal Lander, School supervision is handled on the district level by so-called middle-level authorities.[2]

References

1. Munch, Joachim and Arnold, Rolf, "*Questions and Answers on the dual system of Vocational Training in German*" bmb+f, Federal Ministry of Education, Science, Research and Technology (Germany)
2. "Vocational Training – An investment in the future", *CIMI: Vocational Training in Germany Dual System*, December 1998.

24

Community Colleges in Taiwan (Republic of China)

Taiwan's first community college was opened in 1998, over 80 more such schools have popped up across Taiwan. You can now find them everywhere from up in the mountains, to the outlying islands, and Aboriginal tribal lands. Student numbers at the colleges are up to nearly 100,000 a semester. The speed and sheer energy with which these colleges have taken off really is another string in Taiwan's bow.

Given that they are called "community colleges," you could probably guess that their main objective is to take knowledge and fundamental concepts from ordinary colleges and universities and make them more accessible to the community as a whole. This focus is the most obvious difference between community colleges and the "continuing education" classes at universities, art classes, and community education groups. The stated goal of Taiwan's community colleges is the "training of a modern citizenry" and-by establishing socially-minded courses-giving the citizenry the knowledge and ability to serve society.

One might wonder, how could one hope to achieve such lofty ideals in today's materialistic, busy society? After six years of experiment and adjustment, how far have community colleges come in making these ideals reality? And what kind of reactions have they been the catalyst for?

Civil society refers to the arena that allows collective action to take place without bureaucratic and institutional coercions over public interests, values and issues. In order to create such an arena, efforts have been made, based on various perspectives and disciplines such as sociology, political science, and education. The questions of how a civil society, in which people function for common interests and public good, can be sustained, and how and why people are able and willing to act as capable citizens committed to public affairs and values.

The most effective answers to these questions: Quigley (2000) argues that adult education, given its long history in promoting people's ability to have their say, plays a critical role in taking radical actions to engage in the social movement of constructing a more democratic and inclusive society, in which marginalized voices are heard and are taken into account seriously. Such a grassroots approach appeared inspirational in the early nineties to some social reformers who were conscientiously concerned with promoting local and community awareness when Taiwan was undergoing some major societal transformations. These people combined the vision of building a civil society through social development with efforts at educational reform, and they proposed the idea of establishing community colleges as a means to provide learning opportunities for people to become effective and capable citizens to promote and practice democracy (Gu, 2001; Huang, 1997). As a result, the first Taiwanese Community College was established in 1998, and the model is continuously evolving into a visible social force to foster the building of a civil society.

Overview of the Taiwanese Community College

In the educational context in Taiwan, "Community Colleges" refer to another developing model focusing primarily on the long-standing track of vocational schools and junior polytechnic colleges that confer vocational degrees. Therefore, to facilitate discussion and minimize rhetorical confusion, and in parallel to their international counterparts, "Community College" used in here to refer to the Taiwanese "community universities".

Origin and Mission

Several social movements, such as farmer movements, labor union protests, and judicial reforms, prevailed over the authoritarian government; in less than two decades, the Taiwan government has implemented many political and social reforms and the country has been peacefully transformed into a more mature democracy. This transformation has been known internationally as the silent revolution in Taiwan.

Governance

Pioneering community colleges in Taiwan were established without comprehensive legal directions or foundations, as efforts to institutionalise grassroots educational reform progressed faster than government regulations (F. Huang, 2002). As a result, community college advocates and administrators had a rough start identifying and ensuring government support from finances and infrastructure, and promoting the recognition of community college certificates and degrees. They sought assistance from local governments and formed partnerships that highlighted the fundamental visions and values which were similar to those of charter schools in the United States.

Linkage with Community Colleges and Formal System

The National Association for the Promotion of Community Universities (NAPCU) and some members of the wider education community are in a dispute with the Ministry of Education (MOE) over whether or not community colleges should be able to grant formal academic degrees. The disagreement centers on different perceptions of the fundamental role that community colleges should play.

In some other countries, students at community colleges are able to earn academic degrees or apply a percentage of the credits they earn towards a degree at a formal university. In these countries, community colleges can act as a gateway to higher learning for students who possess a limited academic background or those who do not have the financial means to attend a larger university. In Taiwan, currently nearly 50 per cent of the students at community colleges have earned a bachelor's degree or graduate degree, indicating that the colleges are playing a limited role in reaching those with less education.

In November 2006, the government made a move to address the concerns of educators who would like to see community colleges play more of a gateway role. A new policy stipulated that students who earn 40 credits in specific community college courses—including natural science, the humanities, social science and art—certified by the MOE would be eligible for a high-school equivalency certificate. The MOE also specified that these students would earn the right to compete with other high school graduates for a chance to enter formal universities. This marks a significant change, but is still far from establishing community colleges as a gateway to mainstream university education. Chou believes that building the reputation of community colleges will help their development and could lead to eventual changes in government policy.

A student Pan's total of 150 credits exceeds the 128 credits required to earn a bachelor's degree at many formal universities, while her husband Chen has 125 credits. However, they both agree that while the prospect of earning a college degree is tempting, it is not important enough for them to regret their decision to study at a community college. "Putting classroom knowledge into practice is often neglected by mainstream education institutions, but it's heavily emphasized by community colleges," Chen says. "As more people get a clearer picture of the nature of education provided by community colleges, he believes that the "informal" knowledge gained from classes such as those at YCU "may even prove to be more useful than any formal college diploma could be."

Curriculum, Programmes, Funding, Evaluation and Certification

Three categories of programs are offered: academic, life skills programs and community involvement programs (Huang, n.d.). Academic programs are basically general education in the areas of liberal arts, social sciences, and natural sciences. Life skills programs provide a large array of courses to enrich personal interests and life skills. The last but not the least, community involvement programmes, lead students to become actively involved in community affairs and provide them opportunities to develop a sense of citizenship. A certificate is granted after the completion of each course, and learners who attain 128 credits receive an associate degree. Certificates and degrees are granted by community colleges as rewards for the time and effort students devoted to learning and a visible recognition of what they have accomplished. In terms of grading, a pass/fail system is used in community college contexts, indicating that grades or GPA are not significant to student success as they are in formal education. All the same, there has not been much discussion in Taiwan regarding issues related to student success.

Credits in Taiwan refer to the phenomenon by which people acquire education and participate in schooling, receiving credits as if they were admission tickets for refining their social roles, such as finding jobs, getting promotions, and so on.

Although the community college system in Taiwan has pedagogy similar to most of its international counterparts, such as valuing personal enrichment and knowledge acquisition for individual and collective purposes, its uniqueness depends on its curriculum.

As mentioned earlier, three types of programmes are offered by Taiwan's Community College system : academic, life skills and community involvement programs, of which the last is unique and has obtained a growing visibility. Different from academic and life skills programs that are mainly designed by administrators or instructors, community involvement programmes enable learners to become active participants by standing up for their interests and needs, and in shaping their learning experiences.

From this perspective, such programs present a hidden spirit of empowering underserving people to initiate what is good for them, to solve personal and community problems. Some community involvement programmes in Taiwan are operated in community theaters, by environmental cultural reservations, etc. These programmes show strong links with events where the Community College sense as a site for nurturing the study of the locality. For instance, Chia-yi-City Community University has positioned itself as an agent to rediscover and revive local history and collective memories through the efforts of mapping the Chia-yi ecological system and establishing a mini exhibition hall of traditional and cultural artifacts on the campus.

Specifically, community involvement programmes share the philosophy of community education, which is a program that "focuses on college-community interaction, utilizes the community as a learning laboratory and resource, helps to create an environment in which the community educates itself, and evaluates its success by citizen successes that are recognized as significant by the community itself" (McGuire, 1988, p. 9).

Adult education (educational programmes designed for people who regard learning as a means of developing their competency or resolving personal problems), lifelong learning (intermittent education, whether or not undertaken in school settings), community services (efforts undertaken through institution cooperation and community groups or agencies in order to directly serve individual and community educational needs not met by formal schooling or certificate programs), continuing education and community-based education (programs designed by the citizens for the good of the community) are common formats discussed in the community college literature (Baker III, 1994; Cohen and Brawer 2003; Fields, 1962; Gleazer Jr., 1974; McGuire, 1988).

These five formats present some common characteristics, including: access to all with a multitude of entry points in time and place, continuous service to the learner throughout life, values and priorities set on the basis of needs of the people, flexibility to respond quickly to community needs, and performance orientation and criteria (McGuire, 1988), among the five, continuing education is the least seen format since such a program institution in Taiwan is mainly administrated by industries and government sectors. However, the other four are equally popular in Taiwan. Literacy courses for foreigners and immigrants, seminars on safe usage of drugs, environmental protection and reservation workshops are some of the most prevalent content areas.

In sum, community involvement programmes represent a unique trend and orientation of the Taiwanese Community Colleges. Through these programmes, Community Colleges provide a platform for their students to hold diverse community-based activities and extend the participation opportunity to those community citizens who even do not enroll. As a result, learning does not just occur in the classroom and limit to people enrolled, participation as an audience can also receive updated information and knowledge to replace old assumptions. The community, on the other hand, would be transformed into a dynamic learning system that is able to educate itself.

Examples of Current Practice

Ching-shui Theater run by Taichung Coastal Community University was the awardee of the Best Community Involvement Program of the Year Award in 2006. Members of the Theater compose their scripts based on the history and happenings in the community. They especially enjoy looking for stories of regular community members; as a result, they visit the community frequently and interview people for inspirations. Through conversations and community participation, the actors and actress come up with screenplays that are extremely close to the lives of people living in the area, and present their work as a means of public services to the community. Their efforts have been seen and the Theater has been recognized as a valuable local cultural entity by the community as a whole.

Collaborating with local and regional non-governmental organizations (NGOs) to establish a community learning network is deeply infused in the Community College practices in Taiwan. Not only are they advocates and think tanks, Community Colleges also play a coordinating role among other NGOs involved in the network to integrate community resources. Yi-lan Community University invited a dozen of regional mountaineering associations, wilderness protection groups, and community organizations to form a task force to come up with a loop trail system in the Yi-lan area.

Since the beginning, these organizations had a shared resolution that the trail system would be community–oriented, meaning local history, ecology, and assets would be infused. Therefore, how the college coordinated the project was to involve experts from participating NGOs in decision making, and cooperate their respective professional knowledge into the plan. As a result, the loop trail system became not just a collection of hiking trails; it is a system in which landscaping, community development, and local business are all tightly connected to community values. In terms of operation, community residents assist the maintenance and serve as rangers and guides telling visitors stories about Yi-lan (National Association for the Promotion of Community University, 2004).

American Community College has been regarded as a "most effective democratizing agent in higher education" (Dougherty, 1994, p. 6) because of their grass roots origin of standing for open admissions, geographic proximity and financial affordability to the potential students from the community they served. Given the introduction of the Taiwanese Community Colleges, there is no doubt that they share similar characteristics with their American counterparts. Taiwanese Community Colleges are grassroots lifelong learning institutions offering various programmes to those who have had no access to further education opportunities. Through community involvement programs, these colleges themselves are also gradually solidifying their unique positionality as praxis to build a deliberative democracy and civil society since learners and community members not only have the access to learn but actually experience and practice modern knowledge and skills that are critical for participating in a democratic society. In others words,

Community Colleges in Taiwan became the community's catalyst of collaboration by means of providing programs to meet diverse educational needs and of creating public space (Boyte and Kari, 1996) to vitalize community members' willingness for community participation.

In conclusion, we believe that community colleges in Taiwan have played a critical role, liberalizing subjectivity and power of citizens through lifelong learning opportunities to embrace multidimensional worldviews and take actions for common good. These community colleges are outcomes of the Taiwanese democratization efforts in the 1990s, and have matured into an active participating entity in the social network of signifying indigenous spirits and culture from a learning perspective. Learning institutions must respond to social movements, and globalization has been one crucial trend of social changes since the end of the twentieth century. In association with concepts of civil society, knowledge emancipation, and service learning, community colleges in Taiwan were initially established in the light of global trends of adult education and lifelong learning. After nearly 10 years of practice, community college advocates and petitioners have strengthened their grassroots commitments to appreciate and respond to local voices, since those localized assets are valuable components to complement globalization.

References

1. Latiner Raby, Rosalind and J. Valeau, Edward, *Community College Models – Globalization and Higher Education Reform,* Springer, 2009.
2. *Taiwan's Community Colleges— Making the Community a Classroom* by Geof Aberhart.
3. Wn, Rober, PhD, "Moving Towards Community College: A New Alternative in Postsecondary Technical Education in Taiwan": *Republic of China*, December 12-15, 1999.
4. http://www.sinorama.com.tw/en/show_issue.php?id=200489308090e.txt and table=2 and h1=Education and h2=Universities.
5. http://english.moe.gov.tw/ct.asp?xItem=9318 and ctNode=506 and mp=11.

25

Community Colleges in Papua New Guinea

Pursuing and Promoting Excellence in Technical Vocational Education and Training (TVET) for a Healthy, Wealthy and United Papua New Guinea-Community College Education System.

The Education System in Papua New Guinea (PNG) has gone through rigorous changes as per the National Education Reforms in 1993. There have been top-ups to Elementary Schools, High Schools, and curriculum reforms. These changes are yet to address certain issues, which still affect the majority of Papua New Guineans who miss out on the formal education and or skills training; including those who leave school (push – outs) because they are unable to meet the requirements for high level studies.

Community College will be an alternative system of education to provide the youth of the Nation a viable option for them to integrate into the community to make a living. Community College System will empower the youth of today for their adulthood for tomorrow. It reinforces moral, ethical norms for a better society.

The Community College is an alternate system of education, aimed at empowering the disadvantaged and the under privileged sections of the population. It will promote job oriented, work related, skills-based and life coping education. It envisages access, flexibility in curriculum and teaching methodology, cost effectiveness and equal opportunity to all Papua New Guineans. The Community College System aims to achieve the liberation and empowerment of the exploited and deprived groups of society by releasing and developing the sources within, through middle level skills development and facilitating self-actualization.

Community College is a Multi-Campus Realty (an integration of existing programs and Indian Community College Concept), and it is a skills-based education going to the people instead of the community moving towards education institution as is currently practiced in Papua New Guinea (PNG).

It visualizes and attempts to be part of the community, for the community and by the community, and to produce responsible citizens, candidates eligible for employment, valuable family and community members, and self sufficient individuals, communities and societies.

It is envisaged that the Community College will respond to the deficiencies of the Vocational System through community and industry-institutional linkage, competency based training and assessment, appropriate qualification within the existing "qualification framework", training on site (locally), life skills education and training, and job oriented programs consequently decided on the basis of the provincial and community economic and social needs and demands.

The objectives are to make provisions conducive for the application of programmes, mechanisms and management of the community college system.

Curriculum

Community College will rely on curriculum developed by TVET and ICRDCE in respect to the immediate need of the community and the surrounding industries. It might be involved in curriculum development where there are no existing curriculum materials to meet community and industry demands. The use of the industry occupational standards (by the NATTB) will be required for the nationally recognized trade and certificate courses.

Community College Curriculum will be coordinated by the Deputy Director (Secretariat) and will be accountable for the content, quality and relevance in ensuring that the course content and standards meet the needs of industry, commerce, government and the community.

Community College will adopt and adapt curriculum for courses offered by the respective colleges or universities, and liaise with TVET curriculum for the Higher or Certificate level courses (National Certificate). Community College curriculum section will work closely with the National Training Council (NTC) to meet material training priorities, and the National Apprenticeship and Trade Testing Board (NATTB) for trade testing.

National Curriculum

NATTB has developed National Occupational Competency Standards (NOCS) in partnership with industry, and TVET has developed Modules that are adequate for all levels of training for community colleges. National Occupational Competency Standards (NOCS) are driven by input from business, industry and community. Curriculum is written to national occupancy standards. Short courses or part-time courses (modules) attended will be given credit towards courses studied.

Therefore:

- National occupational competency based standards are driven by input from business, industry and community.
- Curriculum is written to National Occupational Standards.
- Credit will be made available for those who have gone through certain training stages (modules) from other learning institutions or training providers.
- Awards for Community College graduates will be in line with the awards by TVET Division participating training providers and National Apprenticeship and Trade Testing Board (NATTB).

PNG National Qualification Framework (PNGNQF)

Community Colleges offering higher level courses (accredited trades) will be guided by the PNGNQF to enable formal assessment, certification and recognition of skills (including prior learning). The PNGNQF will also recognize and support the need for specialized curriculum oriented to rural and village (community) development. These curricula will be underpinned by short courses in areas such as electrical, mechanical, building, forestry, agriculture, fishery, nursing, tourism, hospitality, etc.

Competency Based Training and Assessment

All courses for Community Colleges shall be delivered, using Competency Based Training and Assessment (CBTA) mode of delivery. TVET has developed series of courses in CBTA format; and STRU has developed short courses (community based) in CBTA format that will be ideal for community colleges. Special courses requiring new curriculum will be coordinated by the Secretariat with the Board of Studies (BOS) to be written in consultation with the industry and community. The Community College staff will be required to be involved in the development of the new curriculum.

Curriculum Structures and Standards

Course structure: Courses shall be structured to provide appropriate and relevant education and training for the community and by the community and based on community and industry and economic and social demands of villages, communities, Districts, Provinces and the nation. Courses shall be designed and developed for:

- Community based education and training programmes.
- Industry based education and training programmes.

- Post Primary based education and training programmes.
- Post Secondary based education and training programmes.
- Full pledged degree programmes.

Programme Structure

There shall be horizontal and vertical programme structure established to provide for:

- Community based education and training programmes.
- Industry based education and training programmes.
- Post Primary based education and training programmes.
- Post Secondary based education and training programmes and
- Full pledged degree programmes.

Qualifications

There shall be standard qualifications, subject to Papua New Guinea National TVET Qualifications framework for different programmes offered in Community Colleges. Qualification is awarded for programmes from post grade 8 one-year programmes to post grade 12 two-year programmes by:

- The Department of Education
- For undergraduate programmes by the participating universities
- By the Community College and Community College Education Secretariat respectively for approved Community and Industry based short term programmes as specified by the respective Community Board of Government.

Recognition of Prior Learning

Those who had experience with recognized qualification will be exempted from some units or modules and will be awarded "credits" towards their program of study. In this case, prior learning would be taken into consideration while completing other required units or modules to qualify for certification after completing all academic requirements.

The NATTB

The NATTB is responsible for compliance with national occupational standards. It also monitors and assesses compliance as well as approving guidelines and programmes. Community Colleges will register with and be approved by NATTB as Trade Testing centers.

Accreditation

Accreditation is the process by which a course is officially recognized by another learning institution from an institution offering similar course of the same program. In order to meet this requirement an institution offering such courses must be officially registered to meet NTC requirement. In respect to this, Community Colleges have to be registered within the NTC guidelines and the courses offered are recognized by the PNGNQF. It is anticipated that Community College Secretariat will seek accreditation from NATTB, TVET and participating universities to issue qualifications and accredit students for student vertical articulation and or horizontal mobility where appropriate.

Modeling PNG Community College Curriculum and Programmes

The Four Parts of the Community College Curriculum are Strand One-Life Skills, Strand Two-Work Skills, Strand Three-Internship and Hands on Experience and Strand Four-Preparation for Employment and Evaluation. The outline of the courses given in Table 5.1 below is an example for the National Community College at Marienberg. It follows the similar curriculum structure as seen in Indian Community Colleges except work skills.

Community College Curriculum

Strand One – Life Skills

Course No.	*Courses Name*	*Duration (weeks)*	*Hours*	*Credit Points*
1.	Students Orientation	1	30	1
2.	Life Coping Skills	6	180	6
3.	Interpersonal Relationship and Communication Skills	4	120	4
4.	Development English	6	180	6
5.	Basic Computer Applications	4	120	4
	Total	21	630	21
	Strand Two – Work Skills			
1.	Career Guidance and Counseling	1	30	1
2.	Work Skills	20	600	20
	Total	21	60	2
	Strand Three – Internship and Hands on Experience			
1.	Internship and Hands on Experience	8	390	13
	Total	8	390	13
	Strand Four – Preparation for Employment and Evaluation			
1.	Preparation for Employment and Evaluation	2	60	2
	Total	2	60	2

Each of the courses offered is credited with hours of work and are given points. Thus, 30 hours of work is one (1) credit point. Therefore, to qualify for a diploma award a student should complete four strand courses for the duration of 52 weeks and clocking a total of 1710 hours to qualify for 57 credit points.

Curriculum Structure

The Curriculum Structure for the National Community College consists of Four Parts and is referred to as Strand. The term "Strand" is used because it is commonly used in higher training institutions of the National Department of Education and Universities.

Strand One: Life Skills

Life Skills program is compulsory for all students. The courses offered are Student Orientation, Life Coping Skills, Interpersonal Relationship and Communication Skills, Developing English, and Basic Computer Applications. This program is offered for a duration of 21 weeks, clocking 630 hours in total and earning 21 Credit Points.

The content of each course will be offered or written in units and strictly follow the time frame. Each course units will have clear time for theory and practical in order to achieve a required credit point, which is equivalent to number of hours, spent. For instance, in Life Coping Skills, students are required to complete 28 units in total and spend a total of 6 weeks, clocking 180 hours in order to earn 6 credit points.

Strand Two: Work Skills

Work Skills program is driven by employer needs or community needs. For instance, Work Skills programs that will be offered at Marienberg are Diploma in Agriculture Technology, Diploma in Rural Health Nursing, Diploma in Desk Top Publishing, Diploma in Office Management, Diploma in Building Technology, and Diploma in Tourism and Hospitality.

Students are selected into these programs based on their choice and interest.

Source of Funding

The establishment of Community College in PNG requires a good standard and uniform policy guide to effectively implement Community College Concept. The following are extracts from the general Community College Policy Guidelines in establishing Community Colleges in PNG. These guidelines are developed by PNG Community Education Secretariat.

The Operational Policy Guidelines Governing the Functions, administration, organization and operative systems of the Community College Systems

The Community College Education System will be non-commercial, non-profit making. Social and service-minded agencies involved in establishing Community Colleges. The colleges will be run by the Department of Education, International Education Agency or Private Permitted Agencies rooted in Community Based Activities, that have public interest and are service minded at heart.

The agency responsible for each college must carry out need analysis of the employment opportunities in Industrial, commercial, rural agricultural sectors and social needs of the area. Based on the Need Analysis made periodically by the Community College, the College should submit to the relevant Board of Studies the curriculum incorporating the job-oriented courses in consultation with the industry and community. This should be a continuous exercise done once every three years.

Any agency permitted to start a Community College must submit to the Department of Education and the Office of Higher Education and at the time of application itself evidence of partnership with industries and other organizations with the employment potential where on the job training and hands on experience will be provided. Based on the competence of individuals trained at Community Colleges an assessment for job placement can be made.

No Community College shall be given approval without industrial partnership because it cannot fulfill the intent of the alternative and inclusive education and training. Collaboration with the industries, community governments and administrations, agricultural, commercial and services organizations of the local area and the involvement by the society and the National, Provincial and Local level Governments is paramount.

Community College Establishment

There shall be Providers of Community College Programmes. There shall be Government established Community Colleges, funded and maintained by the Government through its agencies. Agencies, refers to;

- National Department of Education,
- Provincial Divisions of Education, and
- Affiliated agency colleges.

Private providers shall establish Community Colleges and run approved programmes. The private providers, refers to;

- Industries
- Self-help Community based organizations,

- Churches and
- International Education Agencies.

Quality Assurance

There shall be a system of monitoring and evaluation executed by the Community College:

Education secretariat through the;

- Head of Institutions.
- Head of Provincial Education Divisions.
- Inspectoral system of Technical Vocational Education for.
- Community based education and training programs.
- Post Primary based education and training programs.
- Post Secondary based education and training programs[1].

Reference

1. Baidoo Hanson, Benjamin, "Community Colleges: Hope for the Under Privileged of Papua New Guinea (PNG) - *A Paper on the Introduction of Community College Education System*" October 2009.

26

Community Colleges in Vietnam

The "Vietnamese Factor" Tran (1998) researched the French and Soviet influences on HE in Vietnam, and her conceptual framework is called the "Vietnamese Factor" (p. iii). She argues that the emergence of the emergence of modern HELs was a result of French colonial interests and the "Vietnamese factor": "With their inherent education aspirations, the Vietnamese were not passive recipients of foreign inventions' (p. iii) she further asserts that the "Vietnamese factor" was equally apparent when the country was closely allied with the Soviet Union. Contrary to common assumptions, the evolution of Vietnamese universities during the past several decades was not determined by the Soviet Union.

It was first of all guided by Vietnamese pragmatism. The use of [the] Soviet higher education model by the Vietnamese is characterized by Vietnam's judicious adaptation of the model to serve the country's needs. ... It is the combination of foreign ideas and Vietnamese higher education. (Tran, 1998, pp. iii-iv)

This "Vietnamese factor" is important to understanding the international collaboration that has occurred in the development of Vietnam's Community Colleges. When Vietnamese Community Colleges seek advice and training from an international partner, this should not be interpreted as adoption of the international source as it may influence the adoptions and adaptations. This dynamic is understandable because without funding, the opportunity to develop a diversified HE system is severely constrained, and absent prior experience with community colleges, seeking models to draw from seems prudent.

Early International Collaboration and University Support Can Tho University, in the Mekong Delta. Has long been a proponent of establishing Community Colleges (Oliver, 2002), and this University is well known for its skill in developing productive international partnerships (Tran and Sloper,

1995). Also, the Netherlands has been giving support to HE in Vietnam, including Can Tho University, for the past 30 years, and today's projects are valued at $24 million (US$35 million) (Royal Netherlands Embassy Hanoi representative, December 12, 2007, personal communication). The Netherlands initially provided funding to MOET for technical programs that could seed the development of Community Colleges, and although Can Tho University would have assisted with the establishment of all these HELs in the Mekong Delta, the National Assembly decided that sis Community Colleges would be established, two in the North, one in the Central region, and three in the South (Oliver, 2002). Thus, the funding was used to begin the development of one core programme, either in food processing or mechanical engineering, at each of six Community Colleges.

The Local Context of Vietnam's Community Colleges

Having discussed globalization in relation to Vietnam's Community Colleges, this section will look at some of their local features and challenges. Although it is difficult to specifically describe Community Colleges in Vietnam because they are still a work in progress, some general characteristics can be provided. The challenges described are at the systemic level and generally represent the views of the Community Colleges.

Different Kinds of Programmes, Evaluation and Certification

In an addition to college (3-year) degree programs, the community colleges offer continuing education with the goals of helping learners to find jobs, enhancing their knowledge and effectiveness, increasing their job security, and raising their earnings. Kien Giang Community College offers short courses for working adults to gain supervisory skills in a number of specializations, such as construction projects, computer installation, IT, and foreign languages. Also, Can Tho University has consistently advocated for transfer programs, but it was not until 2006 that MOET gave permission to transfer graduates in eight fields of study from community college to universities in the Mekong Delta region. Currently, Dong Thap, Kien Giang and Vinh Long Community Colleges can transfer students to Can Tho University and Tra Vinh University. Hay Tay and Ba Ria-Vung Tau Community Colleges also have recently established transfer and submit their proposals to MOET for approval. Among the approved fields of study are Animal Husbandry, IT, Fiancé, General Accounting, Aquaculture, Business Administration, Electrical and Civil Engineering, and Food Processing and Technology. In the future, it is anticipated that articulation will be introduced for more fields and universities.

Faculty: One of the difficult challenges facing the Community Colleges is the scarcity of qualified faculty; particularly in Vietnam's rural areas (ten of the 12 Community Colleges are rural). But this is a problem across

Vietnam's HE system; even many of the university faculty does not have graduate degrees because the "pipeline" is small and the pay is low in HE. In the rural areas, the number of people having bachelor's degrees as well as career field experience is limited. Hoang (2007), the general secretary of the VACC, reported that there are 1,466 administrators and faculty at 11 Community Colleges (Tra Vinh University was included). Of these, 242 (16.5%) have postgraduate degrees, 891 (60.7 %) have a bachelor's degree, and the rest are at 'different levels" (Hoang, 2007. p. 4). For a more specific example, Hau Giang Community College, in the Mekong Delta, began operating in December 2005 and has a total of 2,318 students (Ha, 2007). Its personnel structure includes three senior administrators, 35 lecturers, 16 adjuncts and 29 administrative departmental staff. Five have master's degrees, 46 have bachelor's degrees, and eight are college (normally a 3-year degree) or secondary school graduates (Ha, 2007). Because many of Vietnam's Community Colleges lack a sufficient number of trained faculties, they often invite administrators or specialists from other organizations to give lectures. Students obtain more practical knowledge through the practitioner's and shared "stories" that link course content to the work content; however, inviting (adjunct) faculty also presents some problems. Some adjunct faculty lack teaching experience and scheduling their classes can be difficult because their primary job responsibilities have a much higher priority: therefore, the quality of teaching can be adversely affected.

The Community Colleges face some challenges that need to be addressed within the structures of their "local" context, particularly in governance at the national level. Based on the meanings of internationalization used in the chapter, it is important for those outside Vietnam who are interested in pursuing collaboration with Vietnamese community college to be aware of, and sensitive to, these challenges.

Of great concern to the Community College leaders is that their intuitions continue to operate under a provisional regulation that was promulgated by MOET Decision Number 37/2000/QD-BGC and DT, dated August 29, 2000. Many provisions in this regulation are no longer suitable to the current situation. Thus, the community colleges urgently need new regulations that will give them a legal basis for operating more effectively. A draft of the permanent operating regulations written by the rectors was introduced at the March 2007 US-Vietnameses Community College Conference held in Kien Giang, and international participants were asked to provide comments: the feedback was considered while finalizing the document. The final version of the regulations was submitted to MOET and currently is going through the approval process. In Vietnam, it is imperative that HEIs have official government regulations under which they can operate. Without theses regulations, the community colleges' functions are complicated, their efficacy could be questionable, and their future existence could be jeopardized.

Another concern of Community College leader is the way in which these institutions are represented in the Educational Law. Because Community Colleges do not have a long history in Vietnam and they are not clearly conceptualized, the regulations specifically authorize, this troublesome. Additionally, in the view of these leaders, Vietnam's participation in the WTO will accelerate the processes, changing economic policies, and creating new approaches to human resource development. The Community College leaders think that in formulating a strategy to advance education and training, the community college model becomes a very important part of the rules and operations of the community college model. In brief, community college features need emphasis and clarity within the Educational Law.

The Community College leaders also have been discussing the need to clarify the role of community colleges and to increase their autonomy. Many of these leaders think the regulations should specify that community college fulfill two primary purposes: (a) teaching students the basic curriculum for the first two years and enabling them to continue the following two years at a university, and (b) training the community's workforce with knowledge and skills that serve local socio-economic development. The absence of discussion concerning a 2-year associate degree, as is found in North American community colleges, may exemplify the important role played by the "local" when working with international partners.

According to one of Tra Vint Community College (TVCC) project members, the Canadian partners discussed the value of the 2-year degree with MOET in 2002, but this concept was not interesting. With regard to autonomy, the community college leaders think their institutions should be able to operate in a flexible manner, allowing for responsiveness to the evolving needs of their local communities. In summary, Vietnam HEIs and community colleges need regulation that enhance increased responsibility for management and operations at the institutional level.

From a more holistic perspective, Vietnamese community college leaders think their is a great deal of redundancy, or overlap, in the responsibilities and functions of HEIs in Vietnam, thus creating inefficiencies in the distributions and use of limited financial and human resources. Vietnam has been diversifying the HE sector for approximately 20 years, and it may be time to review the system in the light of restructuring through some consolidation.

The analysis required to do this also could lead to clarification of the community college model and other institutions in the 3 year sector to strength their sustainability and operational effectiveness. Additionally, cooperation and communication among the community college and between the universities and colleges have not been developed. Explanations for this may be both cultural and economic; some societies are more open than others, and competition for very limited resources can create barriers to sharing information.

The community college leaders are interested in developing ways to assess the effectiveness of the community college model now and into the future; however, the concepts of strategies planning and institutional effectiveness for quality improvement are relatively new in Vietnam. Additionally, the community colleges soon will be required to go through Vietnam's new quality accreditation process, including a self study.

Thus, as mentioned previously, the VACC has decided to address this concern by developing a center for quality accreditation that could assist all the Community Colleges in the country. There is a need to develop assessment measures that go beyond the traditional audits, which primarily deal with use or resources. The Community College leaders will look in international assessment models, as did MOET over a several year time frame when they were deciding on a accreditation process for Vietnam, but undoubtedly the final form will ultimately reflect local accountability requirements and the socio-culture context.

When responding to the forces of globalization, Vietnam's Community College leaders understand that they need to make careful choices (the "Vietnamese factors"). Diverse international experiences can influence practical operations, and adaptations can contribute to the country's socio-economic development locally and nationally. They also know that in the age of globalization, it is necessary for community colleges to be sensitive, proactive, and effective in addressing national and local needs.

Community colleges recruit first-year students using the students' scores on the National Entrance Examination that is controlled by MOET and administrated by public universities, or the Community College may administer its own entrance examination. In the case of Kien Giang Community College, it's Directorial Board (rector and vice rector) decides which entrance examination will be used.

Based on the "cut score" (the minimum score for a student to be admitted to a university or college), as determined by MOET for the National Entrance Examination, and the quota (number of students to be admitted per year) approved by the Provincial People's Committee, the Directorial Board decides the final cut score to admit new students and reports this information to MOET. Students' high school grades also are factored into the admission decision. Because the demand for HE in Vietnam is greater than the capacity to provide it, open admissions as found in North American Community Colleges are not feasible, and although most students would prefer to attend a university, the opportunities are limited.

At Kien Giang Community College a relatively high percentage of the students have gained admission. In 2006, nearly 86% of the students who took the entrance examination were admitted, and approximately 70% of the Province's postsecondary students attend the community college. Many of these students are from lower-income groups and thus must work, and some of the students are from minority groups (e.g., Khmer and Chinese). Non-traditional-aged students are accommodated through short courses for workforce development.

Source of Funding

Provincial government funding comprises a portion of the Community College's budget but the largest part comes from other funding sources. For example, Kien Giang Community College currently receives 20% of its operating budget from the Provincial People's Committee (to pay for the administrative and teaching staff) and 80% from other sources, such as student tuition, training contract with businesses, income from scientific research and services (Science and Technology), and financial support from governmental and nongovernmental organizations inside and outside of Vietnam[1].

References

1. Latiner Raby, Rosalind and J. Valeau, Edward, *Community College Models – Globalization and Higher Education Reform*, Springer, 2009.
2. Harvey. J. David, *Policy Recommendations for Community Colleges in Vietnam*, University of Sanskachewan, Saskatoon, April 2005.
3. http://www.uniterra.ca/who-are-we/partners-profiles/vacc/
4. http://daihoc.tripod.com/
5. http://www.usatoday.com/news/education/2009-09-23-vietnam-community-college_N.htm

27

Community Colleges in Hong Kong

There is an increasing global recognition of the importance of widening the access to higher education for accommodating students from all strata of the society for an equal educational opportunity as well as fostering the idea of life long learning and learning society (OECD, 1999a, 1999b, 2001; UNESCO, 1998). Responding to this global education reform, the SAR Education Commission proposed to encourage the establishment of various types of post-secondary colleges, while accommodating the existing institution (Education Commission, 1999, p. 22). The immediate result of the proposal was the establishment of several community colleges in early 2000, offering mainly Associate Degree programmes. From the public, there are voices raising queries over the role of Community College in the higher education system as well as whether Community College can serve the similar function of traditional university in the provision of undergraduate education.

Community College: A New Born Baby of Hong Kong Education System: Community college emerged as a new type of post-secondary institution in Hong Kong as the last millennium came to a close. In less than five months after the publication of the "*Education Blueprint for the 21st Century*" by Education Commission which proposed to encourage the establishment of various types of post-secondary colleges (Education Commission, 1999, p. 22), several community colleges were established by the University of Hong Kong (HKU School of Professional and Continuing Education — Community College), the Hong Kong Baptist University (HKBU International College), the Chinese University of Hong Kong respectively to offer Associate Degree programmes.

Following the announcement in his Annual Policy Address (Tung, 2000, p. 22) by the Chief Executive of the Hong Kong Special Administrative Region Government that within ten years, 60% of the Senior Secondary

School leavers will receive tertiary education, more community colleges began to mushroom. The College of Higher Vocational Studies of the City University of Hong Kong (established since 1996), the School of Professional Education of the Hong Kong Polytechnic University, the University of Science and Technology, Lingnan University, the Hong Kong Open University, the Hong Kong Institute of Education and various other private higher education institutions announced that Associate Degree (AD) programs will be launched in the school year of 2002.

Associate Degree programme is only one form of post-secondary qualification. The SAR government envisages the emergence of a wide range of self-financing sub-degree programmes leading to Associate Degree, higher diploma and professional diploma (EMB, 2001, pp. 2-10). The current and planned intake is full-time, self-financing post-secondary places (Associate Degree and Higher Diploma) in 2000/01 and 2001/02.

The SAR government also takes active initiative to support the development of many of these providers into community colleges.

Community college is surely a new born baby in the education system in Hong Kong. It is certainly the main focus of development in the coming decade. In May 2001, the SAR Government, in explaining the fulfillment of the target of providing 60% of the relevant age group with tertiary education, announced that the Associate Degree places will be expanded to around 30,000 in number in the next 10 years. Community college will be developed as one of the main providers of these places. To date, these newly founded Community Colleges in Hong Kong are modeled after the community or regional colleges in North America, since they have much resemblance on their counterparts in North America in terms of programs offered.

They mainly launch associate or sub-degree programmes. Upon completion of the associate degree, students can transfer to other universities to complete their degree programs, based on a credit unit transfer system. For instance, over 10 overseas universities have agreed to accept graduates of Hong Kong Baptist University's Associate Degree programmes for direct admission to their degree programmes. Similarly, 28 local and overseas universities (including the University of Hong Kong) have agreed to accept Associate Degree graduates of HKU SPACE's Community College (EMB, 2001, pp. 1-3). This new arrangement indeed has widened access for those students who possess the ability and the will to pursue for a degree but have failed to enroll in degree programs at local universities because of the highly selective admission conditions.

The highly selective nature of Hong Kong education system has created many barriers for those who aspire for a degree. Public examination (Hong Kong Certificate of Education Examination and Hong Kong Advanced Level

Examination respectively) has always been the sole device for screening students for sixth form education and admission to higher education in Hong Kong. Despite higher education expansion since the 90s, keen competition for undergraduate education remains.

Data in 1996 indicated only 38% of students entered sixth form courses after secondary five (UGC, 1996, p. 1), while only half of the students who sat for the Hong Kong Advanced Level Examination were admitted to degree programmes funded by the University Grants Committee (UGC). This bottle neck phenomenon is expected to remain for some time as degree places have been strictly restricted to 14,500 (in number) by UGC since 1996.

With the introduction of Community College, students are given more options to consider and the higher education progression path becomes highly flexible. Students will no longer be restricted to a narrow choice of programmes and institutions simply because of the availability of places or due to performance of a single public examination.

Community college also provides flexibility to those students who do not wish to enter higher education immediately after senior secondary education but would like to work or travel for a few years upon completion of senior secondary education. Community College allows students to enter higher education at their most desirable time.

It is very crucial that local community colleges resolve this issue in the near future as the flexibility of community college lies in the credit unit transfer system. Based on this system, courses taken at community colleges will be recognized by universities, as long as the result achieved are above average level. This may mean a grade C or above, or it depends on the negotiated arrangement between institutions.

This flexible arrangement enables students to enter programme and to transfer to another one when the risk is lowest. During the first two years at college, students may choose between courses of generic or interdisciplinary nature which enables them to discover more deeply about the nature and content of the subject discipline before deciding on the final and most desirable subject discipline that matches one's own career goal, personal interests and needs in the subsequent degree programmes.

After all, one of the goals of the current education reform in higher education is how to encourage universities to adopt a genuine system for fully transferable credit units (Butler and Hope, 2000; Education Commission, 1999, p. 22). Should this goal be realized, it will have tremendous implications on the future development in higher education in Hong Kong. Briefly speaking, it would reduce unnecessary competition between institutions and widen up individual choices of programs and institutions. The success of credit unit transfer system in community college is an important advancement leading to a comprehensive introduction of credit unit transfer system in all the degree granting institutions.

For Associate Degree programmes to be recognized by universities as well as by the public as a whole, quality assurance is of utmost significance. One important step to ensure quality before a course is conducted is accreditation.

At present, Associate Degree programmes offered by the UGC-funded institutions and the Open University of Hong Kong, which are self-accrediting institutions (except Hong Kong Institute of Education), have their own internal accreditation mechanisms. Associate Degree programmes offered by other institutions are to be accredited by the Hong Kong Council for Academic Accreditation (HKCAA) to ensure consistency and comparability.

Apart from providing more tertiary learning opportunities, the SAR Government must also encourage student participation by support measures by expanding financial assistance to qualified needy students. The SAR Government propose to introduce a means-tested grant scheme for most needy students, offer means-tested low-interest loan for other needy students and extend non-means-tested loan to all students.

Critics of the policy of expanding Associate Degree places opine that this is only a government measure to alleviate the general sense of frustration of those who are not admitted to tertiary education under the existing higher education structure.

They claim that the government in so doing only postpones the time for the senior secondary school leavers to face the problem of employment, especially at this period of economic downturn. What the government should do in counteracting such opposition is to convince the public of the importance of economic and social benefits, both to the individual and to society as a whole, of a raise in education standard of a large proportion of the population.

Secondly, the government should also start educating the public to readjust their expectation for economic benefits of education. While the notion that education is an investment that pays still holds true, the expectation for the "pay" should be realistic. The reality of mass higher education is that as more students receive it, the economic and social benefits will no longer be confined to a small group, as in the days of elite higher education.

Hence while everybody in the higher education sector still gains, the gain (such as life long income) will probably not be comparable to their counterparts in an elite higher education system. The general uplifting of education standard of a majority of the relevant age group, rather than a minority, is nevertheless a healthy feature that should be supported. It is indeed an important step in human and social capital investment in Hong Kong in the new millennium.

Further expansion in first degree places among UGC institutions is still under careful consideration. Most likely, it will be pending on the results and findings of the new round of higher education review conducted by the University Grants Committee from 2001-02 under the Chairmanship of Lord Sutherland and the planning of the next triennium budget of the UGC. Before any new plan is made, the new learning opportunity opened up by community colleges would certainly help lessen the pressure of the demand for undergraduate education, which is inevitably rising owing to the rapid population growth and economic and social development in the past decades.

Developing along this trend, Hong Kong has joined many developing and developed nations in accommodating a wider participation in higher education as an important strategy for enhancing economic, social, and cultural development in a fast changing global knowledge based economy.

According to the Education and Manpower Bureau, the SAR government will offer loans to assist non-profit-making providers with their start up expenses to establish new community colleges. This policy on establishing more community colleges aims to develop a diversified higher education system, widen students' choice and encourage healthy competition (EMB, 2000, p. 10). By the end of 2001, a number of school sponsoring bodies such as, Vocational Training Council, Hang Seng School of Commerce, Po Leung Kuk, Caritas Adult and Higher Education Services, Tung Wah Group of Hospitals etc., has shown interest in establishing community colleges and offering Associate Degree programmes.

To the public of Hong Kong, the establishment of Community College is a rather new concept. During the British administration, undergraduate education in Hong Kong was strictly controlled by the University Grants Committee funded degree granting institutions and the Open University. Students who wished to pursue for a degree locally must enroll into one of the degree granting institutions. The policy strictly adhered to the tradition of the British higher education system prevalent in the 1950s. University was the only chartered institution for granting degrees and offering undergraduate education. This traditional concept of undergraduate education remains a popular and the mainstream thinking in Hong Kong.

It is not surprising, therefore, when the idea of Community College was introduced to the pubic, doubts on the role and the function of community college were raised. At the open consultation sessions organized by Education

Commission, responses were mixed.

There were different interpretations about the nature and the functions of community college. Some considered community college as a post-secondary institution which offers adult education and leisure courses for the community, as a means to promote life long learning; others regarded it as a new interface between senior secondary education and undergraduate education.

Similarly, there were queries on the feasibility and effectiveness of setting up community college based on geographic location of the community, since the proximity of communities, population density, and the well developed mass transportation system of Hong Kong reduce the heterogeneity of community college in different communities. Indeed, not many people realized that community college carries a diverse range of educational functions and missions as university performs. In fact, community college in many other nations performs just as well as a miniature university and many have eventually transformed into a full size university. Many such experiences can easily be found in the development of Community College in North America.

References

1. Man-Sing, Yung, *"Community College: A New Born Baby of the Hong Kong Education System for the New Millennium"* Hong Kong Teachers' Centre 2002
2. http://www.cityu.edu.hk/col/
3. http://www.e-architect.co.uk/hong_kong/hong_kong_community_college.htm

28

Community Colleges in Thailand

The Aim of Community College

To improve the quality of life of the local people to enhancing opportunities to higher education, providing both education and training.

Community College in Thailand was defined as an educational institution that provided two kinds of programmes: 2 year Associates Degree Programmes and Intensive Short Training or Short Term Programmes. These programmes are in areas relevant to local economic and social development. Education and training in the community college emphasize variety in terms of both management and courses offered in order to respond to the needs of people from various walks of life. The programmes are designed to ensure that graduates will have the knowledge and skills necessary for their careers, further education.

Focus: Life Long Education for all, Equality and Participatory development.

Features of Community College Administration

1. Openness and easy access for community people to education and training.
2. Variety in curriculum or programmes.
3. Contribution to community economic development.
4. Content and outcome focused teaching and instruction.
5. Low expense burden.
6. Collaboration with government as well as private sector.
7. Flexible administration and management with quick response to social change.
8. Ownership by community.

Programmes, Curriculum, Certification, Evaluation and Funding

Two large types of curricula: 2 year associate degree curricula and short term curricula.

Academic Overview

FGCC is based on the American model of community college, providing useful, vocational training in a learner-focused environment. Community College programmes serve two basic student populations: students planning to transfer to a university, and students looking for employment training. Students can expect their classes to enrich their English language through an integrated curriculum. The educational areas of study in FGCC focus on English language training, computer and IT (Information Technology), science, social sciences and humanities. English and Computer classes reflect the needs of the local community, providing up-to-date skills and certification for employment.

The teaching objective is to provide a broad base of educational experience on technical/practical/ vocational skills. Students who complete the general education requirements at FGCC will move towards a close cultural understanding, prepared for a lifetime of learning. Students who embrace their FGCC education will graduate with a certificate and a wider skill base to enable them to generate better opportunities, increasing prospects of entering university and finding more fulfilling employment.

Curriculum

The FGCC Curriculum offers 3 study focuses: Core courses (compulsory), Additional requirement courses (some compulsory) and Elective courses. First year curriculums are aimed towards building up the students' language modules, and complimented with additional courses and elective courses. Second year courses focus on more specialized subject learning with a strong language element. All students at the start of the academic year take English placement examinations. The students are given personal guidance on choosing a curriculum that suits their skills and motivations.

Students may choose to take additional elective courses outside of the 70 credits required for graduation. A full-time student is defined as a student carrying twelve to fifteen (12-15) units of work per semester in order to make normal progress towards the Certificate and/or transfer requirements. Students desiring to take an overload - more than 18 units but less than 22 - must have a counselor's approval.

General Course Requirement Structure	
(A) Core courses: Language Arts	
Basic Languages:	36 credits
(B) Additional Requirements	
Sciences, Computer and Maths	9 credits
Social Sciences	6 credits
Humanities	6 credits
(C) Other courses from any area of study	13 credits
Total Credits	**70 credits**
Year 1	
1st Semester	**Total: 11 Credits**
LAEN 100 Intensive English - Beginning	3 credits
LAEN 111 English Communication - Beginning	3 credits
NSCO 100 Using the Computer: PC (Windows)	3 credits
1 additional required course	2 credits
2nd Semester	**Total: 12 Credits**
LAEN 101 Intensive English - Intermediate	3 credits
LAEN 112 English Communication - Intermediate	3 credits
LAEN 121 Reading Comprehension I	3 credits
1 additional required course	3 credits
3rd Semester	**Total: 12 Credits**
LAEN 131 Business English I	3 credits
LAEN 141 Basic English Composition	3 credits
LAEN 151 English Grammar and Usage	3 credits
MAGM General Mathematics	3 credits
Year 2	
1st Semester	**Total: 9 Credits**
LAEN 152 Advanced English Grammar and Usage	3 credits
2 additional required courses	6 credits
2nd Semester	**Total: 12 credits**
LAEN 122 Reading Comprehension II	3 credits
LATH 121 Thai Literature, or LATH 101 Usage of Thai Language	3 credits
2 additional required courses	6 credits
3rd Semester	**14 Credits**
LAEN 142 Advanced English Composition	3 credits
4 additional required courses	11 credits

What is an Associate in Arts/Science Certificate? What does it mean for students?

The 2-year Associate in Arts/Science Certificate is a qualification unique to Thailand. Although not officially recognized by the Thai Education Authority, the Certification of Arts/Science is recognized as what it is - proof of a 2 year general secondary education, focusing on English language skills, uniquely taught by qualified native English speaking teachers. The Certificate exhibits dedication to general higher education and demonstrates advanced English language skills. FGCC students are to complete a minimum of 70 credits from required and elective courses during their two-year study.

Students who excel academically will be able to transfer credits to selected universities and/or use the extra skills they have learnt to progress faster through tertiary education system.

Transferability: Currently three universities will accept exceptionally prepared FGCC graduates as transfer students into limited departments: Mahasarakham University, Rakhamhaeng University and Sri Nakharinwirot University in Bangkok. In the future FGCC hopes to integrate its graduates to many other universities, not only in Thailand, but internationally. The FGCC certificate offers training favorably looked upon by universities.

FGCC also provides specialized training in English and specialized training for TOEFL examination preparation, which will allow students to pass university entrance examinations with much more ease.

References

1. Latiner Raby, Rosalind and J. Valeau, Edward, *"Community College Models – Globalization and Higher Education Reform"* Springer, 2009.
2. http://www.fgcc.ac.th/academic-en.html
3. http://www.kiasia.org/en/Group_Tier2.asp?GroupTierId=2and SubGroupTier_ID=175

29

Community Colleges in China

Introduction

Community Colleges have been emerging in China and have the potential to be the main candidate to address the nation's needs for the next rush of higher education expansion. As the concept of Community Colleges has been borrowed from the United States and applied to address local needs, there have been some innovative variations in developing the models of Community Colleges to adapt to China's environments. The majority of all of the Community Colleges in China that are in existence today were developed over the last ten year. Further more, China's Community Colleges often have evolved recently from vocational colleges, adult educational schools, district – work universities or teachers' colleges, etc., in general, the movement towards the establishment of a Community Colleges system in both the United States and China follows the same general multi-mission community college model.

Given that the history of establishing Community Colleges is barely a decade old in China, there is no one dominant model yet. This is the experimental phase of letting "One-Hundred Blossoms" bloom before selecting the hardiest and most attractive. What kind of Community Colleges may serve best the local needs? What kind of institutional framework is needed for establishing and sustaining Community Colleges in China? Who should be the active participants? What kind of sustainable financial scheme is needed to maintain such a community college system? Unlike in the United States where a Community College can serve an area with a diameter of more than 20 miles, a Community College campus in China must be close to the students' residential or working places due to the lack of private transportation means and other conditions that limit geographical access. We believe a learning centre must be established in close proximity to the location of concentrations of migrant workers so that education can be delivered in close proximity and overcome the physical accessibility problems. Some number of such learning centers linked by shuttle buses can serve as the connected campuses for a Community College.

There are quite a few different models that can be used to plan, build, and run such a learning center-based community college. The first one is the current township adult schools that may extend their reach to the migrant workers. The second one is a community institution that is established for mobilizing local financial resources and boosting local social development. The third one is a social-investment coalition with an existing university that may build and run the learning centre-based Community Colleges as university branches. The university strategy has advantages in bringing strong educational programs and technology for the migrant workers demand through their "financial ballots" in determining what education to provide and in what way to deliver it. In the process of Community College development, all four models may be pertinent where each is tailored to be communities fitting those conditions that are required for it to perform best.

The Role of China's Current Community College System in Higher Education

After China adopted Deng Xiaoping's "Open Door" policy in 1979, China has undertaken research on, and even tried to develop its own, Community College systems. Some of them are called Community Colleges, and many others use different names.

China's 3-year Vocational College System

Since the 1980s, China has developed a Vocational College system. Most of such colleges offer 3-year degree programs oriented to training skilled workers for the labor market. Such a 3-year degree in higher education allows the graduates to go to the labor market with some technical and professional preparation and also enables further studies at universities or access to independent-learning examinations either on a full-time or part-time basis for bachelors degrees. As such, the 3- year degree is quite similar to the associate degree by the American Community Colleges, a junior layer of higher education, is between high school education and the bachelor's degree.

As early as in October 1980, Jinling Vocational University was established in Nanjing. In the same year, the Minister of Education of China approved 13 such universities and 33 in 1984 and 22 in 1985. The Department of Vocational Education, Ministry of Education of China, oversaw the operation of these colleges. Some well-established comprehensive universities started to set up vocational schools and offer 3-year vocational degrees. In October 1989, the Minister of Education of China approved the founding of the college of vocation and technology, Tianjin University, and the College of Vocation and Technology, Zhejiang University. In 2005, there was a total of 1,091 vocational institutions, about 61% of the total institutions of higher learning in China. They admitted 2.86 million new students that year that comprised 53% of all the admitted new students of institutions of higher learning in China in 2005, and the total number of students enrolled was 7.13 million, about 46% of all the full-time enrollments. It can be seen that the vocational institutions have already reached the capacity to serve half of the full-time students for higher learning.

The vocational institutions of higher learning have so far been located in cities with large populations and served local needs for higher education drawing mostly on local educational resources. There are many Minban (private) vocational institutions and some of them are well-known such as Jianqiao College in Shanghai that has been granted the rights to offer bachelor's degrees since 2006 by the government. Although these institutions have covered many areas for serving the local needs for higher education, they do not cover much of the vast rural areas, large numbers of small towns, even small cities, where community college-type education is badly needed and yet to be developed.

Many Chinese Technical Vocational universities are switching their names to Community Colleges. Established Chinese universities have begun to change their names as China has gradually endorsed Community College-type education for serving the local needs for higher education. Chen Zhili, the then Minister of Education of China, said in 2001 that China should try to use Community Colleges for extending higher education to cities at the district level because the cost and tuition is lower and the students can go to school locally. Gradually institutions are following suit by changing their names to Community Colleges. But, none of theses institutions were designed as Community Colleges. In 1994, a then vocational school changed its name into Jinshan Community College located in Jinshan District, Shanghai. By 2000, there were six colleges with the name of Community College in China, they were Beijing Chaoyang Community Colleges, Nanjing Qinghuai River Community College, and four Community Colleges in Shanghai that no longer have the Community College name today. The development of Community Colleges got its momentum through the success of the Open University experiments of China's TV University.

China's Technical Vocational university system has had quite a long history, and it has undergone a significant reform since 1999 when it started to do Open University experiments. It now offers a degree at the same level as the 3-year vocational degree from the vocational institutions of higher learning. This degree is quite similar to the associate degree of the American Community College, and so for convenience we may just call it an associate degree. China's TV University covers almost all parts of China in terms of its administrative hierarchy, mirroring China's government administration hierarchy and its government bureaucracies at each level: central, provincial, district, county township and the village level where the administration is locally elected rather than appointment from the top.

Although the TV system is hierarchical from the top all the way to village, and in theory covering a service to all of China with its 1.3 billion people, each level of the TV University is actually financially independent, and has a dual governance. The government at each level has the jurisdiction over its TV University at the same level of government and nominates the head of the TV University and provides some public finance. Since the TV system spreads to the community and is mostly locally run, it is potentially a strong system to adopt the community college system. During the past few years, many local TV universities have changed their names to Community Colleges, or have many different names with community college a one of their names. Examples include Hangzhou Community College, Taizhou Community College, and many TV Universities at the district level in Shanghai. Unfortunately this system has missed the new target and failed to cover the newly developed manufacturing areas or factory parks where almost all the new residents are migrant workers.

A Community Participation Model – Cost Sharing

From our action research for 2 years we believe a cost-sharing system is financially feasible. The migrant workers are willing to pay a large proportion of the cost, and the employers and local governments have an interest in contributing to raising skills and educational levels. Some evidence of this is that the Central Government has increased its spending on the education and training of the migrant workers year-by-year.

Experiment of the Community Participation Model

We wanted to run an experiment with all the design features that we have proposed, yet it was obvious that we did not have the resources to do a full-fledged experiment. We finally decided to run a small learning centre to test many of the concepts to this community college-type model on the premise that a learning centre is the organic cell that will be used to comprise this proposed community college.

Partnership with the Local Government

Our experiment site was called YS Apartments that is a residential area for migrant workers. At the time we started the experiment, there were about 6,000 migrant workers living at YS Apartments. The Property Management Company does not just maintain the apartments but also serves as a government agent to assume some government responsibilities. As we were told, the Property Company is actually the representative of the township government at that site. So we started a partnership with the Property Company for running the educational experiment. The Property Company provided the experiment with many resources.

Partnership with a Local Multinational

FL is a Fortune 500 global company headquartered in the United States. FL is the biggest local company at our experimental site, and it hired more than 80% of those who lived at YS Apartments. We devoted considerable effort trying to motivate this company to participate in the experiment actively.

Our engagement with the company taught us it is crucial to motivate the local employers to participate, and such involvement requires patience and care, especially when dealing with large enterprises. Our reception was mixed.

"Help is needed for social responsibility efforts". FL's Local training center helped us start the English Corner at our experimental site. The partnership for the experiment was terminated due to the failure of the second round table meetings together.

What we Learned are the following:

(1) A local stakeholder's participation-model could provide resources for a community college-type solution for more education, and the local government can be a leading partner in such a partnership that can execute the government leadership and control;

(2) Alternatively, the township would have to bear a much higher financial burden for delivering the education;

(3) Community participation model for providing education to workers could confer local resources that are otherwise not available for the workers education, yet it is very time-consuming and complicated in convening all parties to reach a successful and consensual agreement;

(4) If successful, this model may enhance local participation for social development and local democracy.

A Model of Community College Founded by Social Investment

An alternative model, of stakeholder participation in building and running a Community College for the migrant workers could be to establish a not-for-profit organization, applying the legal format for a for-profit business to carry out the social investment business of the Community College.

Proprietorship Community College

How can a community college be a profit one? Is the source of public funding a necessary condition for a certain college to be categorized as a community college? Where are the necessary conditions for a college to be categorized as community college? We believe the following are the necessary conditions for a college to be considered as one community college.

The Mission

The mission of the Community is to provide affordable higher education and other types of education and training programmes for all. If publicly funded, the college will charge a very low tuitions as the American Community Colleges' in – state tuitions charge; if privately funded, the college enlists low – cost strategies. No entrance barriers. The colleges does not exclude any adult who wants to learn based on his / her pervious educational preparations.

Local needs. It serves local education and training needs.

Local Community Participation. It is run with the participation of local academics' employers and students. With our definition of community college, a profit college can function as a Community College as long as the tuition charge is low enough or there is a public financial aid system for students who need it.

A Community College system is aligned with social development in a society. Therefore, Community Colleges differ from country to country depending on their unique social and economic environments. It is difficult to find a good definition that may apply to all the Community Colleges in the United States and other countries. If a community college is different from other institutions of higher education, there must be some unique characteristics that allow it to be classified as a Community College. What are they? Broadly, defined they are Education institutions that: (1) provide post – compulsory education of various types including, but not necessarily limited to, associate degree programme that represent a middle layer between high school education and the bachelor's degree level; (2) mainly serve the community's educational needs; (3) Govern with an active community participation. Perhaps the future boundaries around the definition of a Community College can be easily broken. The online communities, for instance, may develop their own Community Colleges in the future and therefore the boundary of a community may lose its physically local characteristics. So there is no doubt we will have a rich set of community college practices and models in China due to its local diversifications and the complexities of local, social and economic dynamics that differ from place to place.

The reality is that the number of workers is large and their characteristics are different from one industrial park to another; with so many different communities, some may easily work together while others may not. With so many local government agents and their officials, there can be a complex of different perspectives and attitudes on goals and operations. Thus, one model may work best in some areas and the others may work better somewhere else. It is better than the community participation in terms of educational innovation and effectiveness of management. It is second to the community participation in terms of public financial burden and community models be encouraged. It is possible that one model works better in certain areas and the other better in others. However, the community partnership might be better because it has the least public financial burden.

The profit oriented one may not be the most effective one until a successful business model is developed and tested by the market. At an early stage, private investment will not be attractive because of the uncertainty of the market. After a period of growth of such educational business, the profit schools may be provided with public responsibilities and funding. The governments may provide subsidies or simply buy services from these schools. To meet a socially adequate consumption level, the cost supply could be higher than the price, and therefore, such goods would become public or quasi-public goods with government funding. In such a case, the public should provide resources to make sure the socially adequate consumption level is reached. There are many ways for the public to do so.

It is possible that educational services purchased with public funds would be produced most efficiently if subsidized by government- regulated for-profit schools. But this is not likely to happen in the near future because there are very few for-profit schools in the factory parks now due to the lack of successful for-profit business models. As a result, pilot testing of such a model will not just be important for private business, but also crucial to the public. Finally it is possible that a mixture of models may work better than just one. One initiative that we are pushing forward is a mixed one with both social and private involvement. The idea is that we break down the operation of a school system into different parts and whenever possible we encourage the business to run the parts of the school system that could be profitable.

The Luwan Community College in Shanghai

Luwan Community College is one of the six subprojects supported by the Community Colleges in China Project of the US and China Education Foundation (USCEF). Unlike some other subprojects that provided financial support to existing programs and institutions, Luwan Community College is a totally new product initiated by an action grant awarded to a large sponsoring institution, i.e., the Shanghai Teachers University (STU). STU selected Luwan District as its partner because of its longtime pioneer role in urban management and community work, particularly in social welfare and community service.

Luwan Community College was a good example of the particular Chinese context since:

1. It had the District Bureau of CAA, the department in charge of local communities and community-based undertakings, taking the initiative; and
2. It made the best sense of the "community" in China by clearly identifying with "community work." The College actually reflected the many faces of a community establishment serving the CAA's purpose of mobilizing community resources and addressing all kinds of community needs.
   - To serve directly the development of economic construction and various kinds of social life in Luwan District.
   - To train social workers particularly community social workers, for Civil Affairs Administration.
   - To offer vocational and continuing education.
   - To provide transfer opportunities.

Vision and Mission

Community College education is slowly being recognized as a strong element in the popularization of higher education as well as an important provider of life long education with emphasis placed on employment training, general higher education, and life long education including both credit and non credit courses.

The establishment of the community college system emphasizes the remedial function as a way to channel and provide more post secondary educational opportunities for high school graduates. The Associate degree is recognized as a formal post secondary degree that is a step below a full four year baccalaureate degree and is accorded certain status in employment. Financially the colleges are sustained primarily through student tuition. Vocational education in areas that reflect local labour needs are the major educational foci for Community Colleges that are coming into operation.

Community Colleges and Community Work

As part of a major restructuring of post-secondary education in China, Community colleges are emerging in its cities under various auspices and with general support from the government. In terms of overseas assistance, the US-China Education Foundation has been playing an instrumental role through its Community Colleges in China Project with funding from the Ford Foundation. Community colleges in China cannot be fully understood without adequate knowledge of the Community Service movement and keen awareness of the main problems of China's higher education system.

The key issue here is not which types of Chinese colleges should be included or how Community Colleges would fit into existing structure, but the Chinese educational system must be further reformed to meet the demands of rapid socio-economic development.

Community Support

Community support from Luwan District was also sound and strong. Under the auspices of the District CAA, the Community College initiative best matched the needs of the community and fitted in with the broad context of urban community work including community services. The educational opportunity it rendered was particularly welcomed by those "social workers" working in the communities who had long been driven by the need for professional development. The profile of the "community workers" had changed a lot during the past decade, with many young and educated personnel now working in the neighbourhoods. Compared to most inland provinces, Shanghai's communities were generally in a better position to support such a new undertaking. And Luwan had always been situated at the forefront of various community explorations (Zhang, Zhu, and Chen, 2000). For example, the District administration recently established a policy that anyone entering "social work" must first obtain professional training and certification, which represented an important step toward professionalization in the country. The positive response of the first classes and due to the increasing needs of the community, the College had to offer more training sessions in its inaugural year than the originally planned three. All these were self-supported with funding from the District itself. The cooperative educational model between an established university and the local authority may allow for sustainable development of the community college undertaking. Clearly, Luwan would have hardly made its case without its partnership with STU. However, the ambitious plan for Luwan Community College to be formally affiliated with STU has not been materialized, which has prevented the former from entering a new and higher phase of development.

A New Trend

It should be noted that a new trend is to focus on Community Colleges as a unique and advantageous layer in higher education. This is, however, the most problematic for China since there are major policy obstacles to the development of "true" Community Colleges in the country. Since the Luwan-style Community Colleges are not yet recognized as a formal part of higher education (thus can haldly attract the interest of regular students), now Chinese three-year vocational technical colleges are taking the central stage.

Nevertheless, the key issue is not which types of Chinese colleges should be included or how Community Colleges would fit into existing structure, but the Chinese higher education system must be further reformed. Community colleges in China as an undertaking should be committed to being a change agent or it will eventually result in failure despite a very successful and excellent start.

Opportunities and Challenges

1. The Luwan Community College is a meaningful exploration with manifold implications. As a community college it represents something new that may help with the reform of the Chinese educational system. As a college of social work it is an effort to fill in a gap by providing the most needed, although minimal, training to the frontline workers in social services and community organization. The College, however, began at an extremely low level, and its future development as a real college will require tremendous and constant input.
2. The most urgent and first issue is lack of qualified faculty. Even if all courses of the College will be taught by STU faculty, it is still a fundamental issue facing all social work programmes in China. Before the faculty with required credentials can be produced at home and abroad, a measure can be taken to support intensive summer faculty seminars conducted by overseas visiting professors to provide necessary quality assurance in professional education.
3. The second issue is the lack of suitable textbooks and other teaching materials. Purchase of a minimun collection from abroad is necessary, and this can be done if funding is provided. Purchase alone, however, will not resolve the issue since overseas textbooks may not meet the needs of Chinese practice. A plan should be made for Chinese educators and overseas consultants to work together to produce Chinese social work textbooks that are long overdue.
4. The third issue concerns specifics of organization, community connection, social work faculty and teaching assignment, governance and institutional budget, student development and admission procedures, articulation plan, social work education vs. community work research, and expansion vs. standardization of Community College projects (Alfred et al., 1999; CSWE Commission on Accreditation, 1994). It may be premature to discuss some of the topics at this early stage, though as the College evolves they will move up the agenda and it is better sooner than later to pay attention to the issues involved. To better understand the community context and monitor the fit of Community Colleges in China, for instance, we should not just rely on second-hand information but need some direct research

projects. In this regard, the possibility to create a long-term research base has been discussed with the leaders of a community within Luwan District.

5. Last but not least, an important issue is about curriculum design (e.g., general education vs. professional foundation courses) Because of the fundamental differences between Chinese and American social and educational systems, this issue cannot be resolved by merely playing with some course names and requirements. On one hand, it requires a thorough understanding of the American debates on general education as well as the CSWE curriculum policy on professional foundation content. On the other, it entails knowing the differences between China and the U.S. in educational philosophy, values, knowledge bases, resources, and needs. To resolve this issue, therefore, a substantial amount of time will be needed for consultation, research, and communication.

Combined with some general observations, the Luwan case renders several useful *suggestions* for developing Community Colleges in China.

- We need to be prepared for the difficulty and complication of setting up such a new educational model in China. Specific issues include: formal college education vs. community/continuing education, human services training vs. four-year and graduate social work education, and general education vs professional / specialist curriculum design. We may get lost if we only have a simple educational paradigm in mind.
- The Chinese way may well go against our intention if we do not put it in context. In initiating a new Community College, for instance, we may fail if we start by exclusively focusing on general education, which is an issue even for well-established institutions in China. Here a developmental point of view is crucial. We should be more flexible during the initial phases, allowing for such activities and programmes as vocational/practical training to go first.
- At the current stage, we should consider at least *three different faces of Community Colleges in China*:
    1. As a new sector/layer of higher education, public or private, for all academic and professional education and training.
    2. As a professional education and development center for community workers or community service providers.
    3. As a community/continuing education center. The American model may also accommodate these components, but the weights may be assigned quite differently.

4. It is also important to create transfer opportunities for its graduates. Although currently non-existent in China, such opportunities can be made to happen in the future. On the other hand, support from the community pivotal in the community college initiative.

5. Finally, all Community Colleges in China may not need to identify with education for social work, but they should try to fit in with the community, or in other words "community work" and the community service movement in China.

Main Problems Faced by Luwan Community College in China

- A gap between the Chinese Community college initiative and its overseas counterparts in terms of purposes, resources, curriculum design, etc.; and
- A gap between China and Western countries in higher and professional education in terms of values, knowledge base, applicable skills, resources, and needs. All such issues demand more comparative studies. For instance, instead of offering professional social work education at the Community college level, which may not be recognized in more developed countries, we may consider an associate curriculum in human services as is the case in many U.S Community Colleges.

Institutional Requirements

Luwan Community College has the responsibility and the authority to determine the requirements and course offerings of its programs in accordance with its institutional mission. These requirements and course offerings shall be published and communicated to students and the public. Colleges and universities shall treat transfer student and native students on an equitable basis. In particular, all students shall be expected to meet equivalent standards for regular admission to programs and to satisfy comparable program requirements.

Baccalaureate institutions shall notify Community Colleges of changes in lower division course requirements for baccalaureate degree two years prior to their implementation for transfer students, and shall consult with Community College academic officers when significant changes are under consideration. Once changes in lower division baccalaureate degree course requirements have been adopted and published, baccalaureate institutions shall allow a grace period of two years before the changes become effective for transfer students. This policy applies to lower division course requirements of all subdivisions of an institution.

Transfer Admission

Admission policies and specific program requirements shall be clearly stated in official documents. Transfer student admission will be determined following an assessment of academic performance and potential on the same basis as native student.

Transfer of Courses

College-level courses offered by regionally accredited colleges and universities shall normally be accepted in transfer by the receiving institution. In addition, some courses not normally transferable will be accepted as part of a Direct Transfer Agreement (DTA) Associate degree. Information about the transferability of college courses shall be provided by all institutions through regular advertising of prospective students and through college publications.

Transfer of Credits

The numerical value of credits shall be maintained in transfer. When a course is acceptable in transfer, the receiving institution shall grant to the student the same number of credits as originally assigned to the course. When translation is required between semester and quarter credits, the conversion to be used is 1.5 quarter credits for each semester credits.

Credit earned in transferable courses shall be granted without regard to the date at which the course was completed. In some degree programs, especially in scientific and professional subjects, students may be required to acquire current knowledge or to refresh their knowledge by repeating courses taken at a prior date. Credit will not be granted a second time for such repeated courses. This policy applies equally to home credit and to transfer credit.

Transfer of Grades

The grades assigned in transferable courses by the sending institution shall not be altered by the receiving institution. Courses completed with grades of 'D' or above shall normally be accepted in transfer (except at the Evergreen State College, where a minimum of 2.0 or 'C' is required for transfer). Non-traditional grading practices require special handing, depending on the nature and circumstances of the program from which and to which a student is transferring, but receiving institution's shall take steps to assure all students receive equitable treatment.

Transfer of Vocational / Technical Courses and Programmes

Vocational/technical courses offered by Community Colleges that are comparable to courses in baccalaureate programs or applicable to baccalaureate degrees as determined by the receiving institution shall be granted transfer credit. Up to 15 credits of course work at the 100 level or above, that are otherwise non-transferable vocational/technical courses, may transfer as part of a Direct Transfer Agreement (DTA) Associate degree meeting the Guidelines.

Conclusion

In Summary, Community Colleges in China are a promising undertaking with far-reaching significance, though they will need time to grow and be upgraded to be comparable with their counterparts in the United States. The Luwan Community College is an outstanding initiative, though its progress will need to be closely monitored and constantly supported not only with funding but also research, evaluation, and professional guidance. All these will require long-term commitment from its funding sources, its partner STU, and all parties involved.

References

1. Latiner Raby, Rosalind and J. Valeau, Edward, *Community College Models – Globalization and Higher Education Reform,* Springer, 2009.
2. *"International Higher Education",* the Boston College Centre for International Higher Education, Number 60, Summar 2010.
3. L. Tsang, Chui, *Community Colleges: Visions and Lessons,* Shanghai Association Community College, 2003-2004.
4. Chen, Sheying, "Community Colleges and Community Work in mainland China" – The case of Luwanin Shanghai.
5. http://www.shacc.net/

PART-III
BIBLIOGRPHY AND RESOURCE MATERIALS AVAILABLE AT ICRDCE

APPENDIX

Directory of Community Colleges in India

State-wise List of Community Colleges

Sl. No	*State Name*	*Number of Community Colleges*
1.	Tamil Nadu	208
2.	Puducherry	04
3.	Andhra Pradesh	11
4.	Karnataka	23
5.	Kerala	12
6.	Maharashtra	07
7.	Madhya Pradesh	06
8.	Gujarat	01
10.	Jharkhand	11
11.	Chhattisgarh	01
12.	Orissa	07
13.	Himachal Pradesh	01
14.	Haryana	02
15.	West Bengal	04
16.	Uttar Pradesh	04
17.	Punjab	01
18.	Assam	01
19.	Jammu & Kashmir	01
20.	Bihar	01
	Total	**307**

Directory

TNOU Community Colleges

TAMIL NADU

1. Madurai Community College, Madurai (July, 1997)
2. Melapudur St. Anne's Community College, Trichy (July, 1998)
3. Immaculate Community College, Cuddalore (September, 1998)
4. Palayamkottai Community College, Tirunelveli (September, 1998)
5. SCAD Community College, Cheranmahadevi, Tirunelveli Dt. (September, 1998)
6. St. Luke's Community College, Nazareth, Tuticorin (July, 1999)
7. Bishop Selwyn Community College, Palayamkottai (July, 1999)
8. Periyakulam St. Anne's Community College, Theni (January, 1999)
9. Amala Annai Rural Community College, Devakottai, Sivagangai (August, 1999)
10. Rural Community College, Nanguneri, Tirunelveli . (July, 1999)
11. St. Mary's Community College, North Kundal, Kanyakumari (July, 1999)
12. Grace Community College, Kaliakkailai (July, 2000)
13. Udhayam Rural Community College for Women, Thuraiyur (August, 2001)
14. Nirmala Community College, Chennai (August, 2001)
15. Ertram Community College, Siruganur, Trichy (April, 2002)
16. Kanchipuram Community College, Mamandur (June, 2002)
17. Adaikala Annai Community College, Pallavaram (July, 2002)
18. Dr. Chandran Devanesen Rural Community College, Karanai, Chennai (July, 2002)
19. Sahaya Annai Community College, Madurai (July, 2002)
20. YWCA Community College, Chennai (August, 2002)
21. Nano Nagle Community College, Chennai (August, 2002)
22. Sivagangai Community College, Sivagangai (August, 2002)
23. Notre Dame Community College, Colachel (June, 2003)
24. Loyola Community College, Ranipet (July, 2003)
25. Don Bosco Community College, Dindigul (July, 2003)
26. Smile Community College, Kalaiyarkovil (July, 2003)
27. IIDA Community College, Kellys (August, 2003)
28. IIDA Community College, Aminjikarai (August, 2003)
29. Sacred Heart Community College, Villupuram (October, 2003)
30. Stanisma Community College, Sivagangai (July, 2004)
31. Pravaham Community College, Venkatapuram, Vellore (February, 2004)
32. St. Anne's Community College, Aralvaimozhy (March, 2005)
33. Jeevan Rural Community College, Srivilliputtur (June, 2005)
34. St. Charles Community College, Jolarpet (July, 2005)
35. Coonoor Community College, Coonoor, Niligiri (July. 2005)
36. Karunakarya Community College, Chennai (July, 2005)

37. Joan of Arc Community College, Tirunelveli (July, 2005)
38. IIDA Community College, Mahabalipuram (July, 2005)
39. Tamil Nadu Community College, Trichy (July, 2005)
40. Veda Mari Community College, Villupuram (August, 2005)
41. Jasper Daniel Community College, Chennai (August, 2005)
42. St. Patrick's Rural Community College, Villupuram (September, 2005)
43. Kaaniyappa Community College, Arani, Thiruvallur (September, 2005)
44. St. Joseph's Community College, Nagapattinam (September, 2005)
45. Arcot Lutheran Church (ALC) Community College, Parangipettai (September, 2005)
46. Holy Cross Community College, Kulasekaram, K.K. (September, 2005)
47. Kovalam Community College, Kovalam, Kancheepuram (November, 2005)
48. KRUPA Community College, Paddappai (July, 2005)
49. Trust Community College, Vengadampatty (July, 2005)
50. Cluny Community College, Tindivanam (July, 2006)
51. Gangasaras Community College, Pattukottai (July, 2006)
52. Sharon Community College, Salem (July, 2006)
53. Servite Community College, Amibikapuram, Trichy (August, 2006)
54. Holy Cross Community College, Trichy (August, 2006)
55. Assisi Community College, Kulapakkam, Chennai (August, 2006)
56. CSI Coimbatore Diocese Community College, Coimbatore (August, 2006)
57. Dharapuram Rural Community College, Dharapuram (August, 2006)
58. IID Community College, Pallavaram (August, 2006)
59. SMSH Community College, Kadayanallur, Tirunelveli (August, 2006)
60. St. Paul's Community College, Lalgudi, Trichy (August, 2006)
61. Ravel Community College, Coimbatore (August, 2006)
62. BWDA Community College, Villupuram (August, 2006)
63. Ceyrac Community College, Kancheepuram (July, 2007)
64. New Life Community College, Medavakkam (July,2007)
65. Vivekananda Community College, Ramanathapuram (July,2007)
66. Mariyalaya Valaragam Community College, Tirupur (August, 2007)
67. New Life Development Community College, Saidapet, Chennai (August, 2007)
68. Marialaya Community College, Chennai (August, 2007)
69. New Hope Community College, Chennai (September, 2007)
70. Bethel Community College, Coimbatore (September 2007)
71. SMA Community College, Keeranur (September, 2007)
72. Antoniammal Community College, Thiruvarur (July, 2008)
73. ICCW Suder Community College, Srivilliputtur (July, 2008)
74. Thanthai Augustine Pereira Community College, Tuticorin (July, 2008)
75. Namakkal Community College, Namakkal (July, 2008)
76. Swami Vivekananda Rural Community College, Kanagacheetykulam (July, 2008)
77. Gandhi Community College, Thiruvalur (July, 2008)
78. Development Community College, Arni (August, 2008)

79. Development Community College, Medavakkam (August, 2008)
80. Arockia Annai Community College, Mannargudi (August, 2008)
81. Kodaikanal Community College, Kodaikanal (August, 2008)
82. Bethel Agricultural Fellowship (BAF) Community College, Tirunelveli (August, 2008)
83. Don Bosco Community College, Keela Eral (September, 2008)
84. Paul Antony Community College, Sivakasi (July, 2009)
85. Seva Rural Community College, Manali (July, 2009)
86. Pearl Rural Community College, Paramakudi (July, 2009)
87. Vetri Community College, Tuticorin (July, 2009)
88. Messiyah Mission (MM) Community College, Kanyakumari (July, 2009)
89. Thenkoodu SHG Agri Community College, Tirupattur (July, 2009)
90. SIGA Community College, Utheiramerur (July, 2009)
91. Thirumalai Community College, Vellore (July, 2009)
92. Horizon Academy Community College, Thanjavur (July, 2009)
93. Tmt. A.C. Krishna Rao Community College, Chennai (July, 2009)
94. St. Clements Community College, Madurai (August, 2009)
95. Karmuhil Rural Community College, Madurai (August, 2009)
96. BAF Community College, Marandahalli (Dharmapuri) (September, 2009)
97. Mount Carmel Community College, Eleyankanny (September, 2009)
98. Vasantham Community College, Tirupur (September, 2009
99. Hindustan Community College, Padur, Chennai (January, 2010)
100. Padma Rajam Community College, Madurai (February, 2010)
101. Meenakshi Community College, Madurai (February, 2010)
102. Annai Teresa's Community College, Lalgudi, Trichy (February, 2010)
103. Moderator Gnandason Community College, Nagercoil (February, 2010)
104. Hi-Tech Community College, Nagercoil (February, 2010)
105. Aravindar Community College, Villupuram (February, 2010)
106. Aameena Community Collegce (February, 2010)
107. Bhagvan Sri Ramana Educational Trust Community College, Tindivanam (February, 2010)
108. Satharasankottai Village Community Collegem Sivagangai (February, 2010)
109. AMD Foundation Community College, Thiruvarur (February, 2010)
110. Shevaroys Community College, Salem (February, 2010)
111. Cholai ACL Community College, Mangadu (February, 2010)
112. Chenagai Community College, Chengalpattu (February, 2010)
113. Nesam Community College, Old Washermentpet, Chennai (February, 2010)
114. CSI Polytechnic Community College, Salem (February, 2010)
115. Sethupathi Community College, Coimbatore (February, 2010)
116. Annai Industrial Training Community College, Perudurai (February, 2010)
117. Siva Community College, Pollachi (February, 2010)
118. Nachimuthu Polytechnic Community College, Pollachi (February, 2010)
119. Jothis Community College, Erode (February, 2010)
120. Reedmas Community College, Erode (February, 2010)

121. Sri Renugambal Community College, Polour (February, 2010)
122. Pope Community College, Thiruvannamalai (July, 2010)
123. IITT Community College, Tirupur (June, 2010)
124. Venus Community College, Tiruvellore (June, 2010)
125. Mark Community College, Chennai (June, 2010)
126. Thiran Community College, Trichy (June, 2010)
127. VJ Community College, Madurai (June, 2010)
128. Velammal Community College, Madurai (June, 2010)
129. Sugam Community College, Villupuram (June, 2010)

130. Fathima Community College, Ariyalur (June, 2010)
131. Wilpa Community College, Coimbatore (June, 2010)
132. Women's Indian Association Community College, Chennai (June, 2010)
133. Little Flower Community College, Nanguneri (June, 2010)

134. D.B. Jain Community College, Thoraipakkam (June, 2010)
135. Bethel Community College, Myladuthurai (June, 2010)
136. MET Community College, Arumpakkam (June, 2010)
137. Arulmigu Chandigeswarar Community College, Pollachi (June, 2010)
138. Sri Palavan Community College (June, 2010)
139. SRS Community College of MNTN, Pathirikuppam (June, 2010)
140. The Christian Institute for Technical Education Community College, Oddanchanchatram (June, 2010)
141. Vasantham Community College, Usalampatti (October, 2010)
142. Santhalingar Community College, Coimbatore (October, 2010)
143. Doss Community College, Arakkonam (October,2010)
144. Samaritan Community College, Yellagiri Hills (October, 2010)
145. Mahatma Gandhi Community College Department of Prison, Puzhal (December, 2010)

Puducherry

146. IID Tabor Community College, Karaikal (July, 2005)
147. Cluny Community College, Karaikal (September, 2007)
148. Karaikal Polytechnic Community College, Karaikal (June, 2010)

OTHER STATES

Andhra Pradesh

149. St. Joseph's Community College, Vishakapattinam (August, 2005)

Non-Governmental Organizations (Non-TNOU)

Tamil Nadu

150. Madras Community College, Chennai (August, 1996)
151. Chennai Corporation Community College, Chennai (February, 1999)
152. Barenbruck Community College, Surandai, Tirunelveli (July, 1999)
153. Sundaram Arul Raj (SAH) Community College, Tuticorin (July, 1999)
154. Vicarite Community College, Mulagumoodu (July, 2000)
155. Kotagiri Community College, Ooty (September, 2000)

156.	Ruhsa Community College, Vellore	(October, 2000)
157.	Devaki Community College, Karaikudi, Sivagangai	(July, 2001)
158.	Zen Community College, Karaikudi	(May, 2005)
159.	Nagle Community College, Theni	(August, 2005)
160.	Prasannakumari CWC Community College, Chennai	(February, 2008)
161.	Sudharsan Community College, Karaikudi	(August, 2008)
162.	Sree Ambikai Community College, Aruppukottai	(July,2009)
163.	Wellness Community College, Kottivakam	(September, 2010)
164.	Parkavan Community College, Trichy	(October, 2010)
165.	IID Community College, Perungudi, Chennai	(August, 2004)
166.	Vasantham Rural Community College, Vellore	(August, 2009)
167.	MAM Polytechnic Community College, Trichy	(February, 2010)
168.	We know Industrial Community College, Trichy	(February, 2010)
169.	Ammai Appa Polytechnic Community College	(February, 2010)
170.	Er. Sri Palavanam Memorial Community College	(February, 2010)
171.	Nellaiyappar College of Higher Education Community College	(February, 2010)
172.	K.R. Motors Institutions of Automobiles Studies Community College	(February, 2010)
173.	Seventh Day White High School Community College, Vikravandi	(February, 2010)
174.	Auxilium Educational Society Community College	(February, 2010)
175.	Annamalai Polytechnic Community College, Karaikudi	(February, 2010)
176.	Kovilur Madalayam Community College	(February, 2010)
177.	Madhar Nal Thondu Niruvanam Community College	(February, 2010)
178.	Sri Kamatchi Trust Community College	(February, 2010)
179.	Green Valley Community College, Sriperumandur	(February, 2010)
180.	Academy for Design and Technology Community College, Chennai	(February, 2010)
181.	SRM Info Tech Community College, Chennai	(February, 2010)
182.	Green Valley Community College, West Mugappair	(February, 2010)
183.	Rudhraveni Muthusamy Polytechnic Community College, Udumalpet	(February, 2010)
184.	Shree Dhevee Beauty Clinic Community College, Erode	(February, 2010)
185.	Sri Ragavendra Polytechnic Community College, Namakkal	(February, 2010)
186.	Jayam School of Nursing Community College	(February, 2010)
187.	Shivani Community College, Trichy	(June, 2010)
188.	Gateway Community College, Trichy	(June, 2010)
189.	Sivabackiam Industrial School Community College, Trichy	(June, 2010)
190.	Madras Institute of Technology Community College, Chennai	(June, 2010)
191.	Sri Rengeswarar Polytechnic Community College, Namakkal	(June, 2010)

MS University Communtity Colleges

192.	Athithya Community College, Tenkasi	(July, 2000)
193.	Spectrum Community College, Shencottai	(July, 2002)
194.	Lavini Community College, Ambasanudram	(July, 2009)
195.	Annai Velankanni Community College, Murugankurichi	(July, 2009)
196.	Sri Peththanakshi Amman Community College, Vilathikulam	(July, 2009)
197.	Great Foundation Community College, Tirunelveli	(July, 2009)
198.	Kayalpatnam Community College, Kaualpatnam	(July, 2009)
199.	Dove Community College, Mudalur	(July, 2009)
200.	Kanyakumari Community College, Mariagiri, Kulapura, K.K. Dist.	(July, 1999)
201.	Ramachandra Community College, Erachakulam, K.K. Dist	(July, 2000)
202.	Bensam Community College, Nagercoil	(July, 2000)
203.	Mary Jenkins Memorial Community College, Chungamkadai	(July, 2003)
204.	Rajendra Community College, Moolachel	(July, 2004)
205.	Dr. Jeyachandra Community College, Kanyakumari	(July, 2004)
206.	Zion Community College, Nagercoil	(July, 2004)
207.	Lekshmipuram Community College, Lekshmipuram, Neyyoor	(July, 2006)
208.	IMC Community College, Kanyakumari	(July, 2006)
209.	El-Bethel Educational Community College	(July, 2009)
210.	Anugraha Community College	(July, 2009)

University Community Colleges

211.	Avinashilingam University Community College, Coimbatore	(July, 1999)
212.	Bharathidasan University Community College, Trichy	(December, 1998)

OTHER STATES

Puducherry

213.	Pondicherry University Community College, Puducherry	(June, 1995)

Andhra Pradesh

214.	JMJ Community College, Tenali	(July, 1999)
215.	JMJ Community College, Hanuman Junction	(July, 1999)
216.	St. Theresa's Community College, Eluru	(January, 2003)
217.	St. Ann's Community College, Arilova	(August, 2005)
218.	St. Ann's Community College, Rajam, Srikakulam	(August, 2005)
219.	Maria Nivas Community College Nandigama	(July, 2006)
220.	JMJ Community College, Guntur	(July, 2007)
221.	IIDA Community College, Nellore	(September 2007)
222.	Holy Cross Community College, Thimmarajupalem	(August, 2009)
223.	University of Hyderabad Community College, Hyderabad	(September, 2005)

Karnataka

224.	Bannerghatta Community College, Bangalore	(August, 2001)
225.	K.G.F. Community College, Kolar Gold Fields, Bangalore	(August, 2001)
226.	Tarbes Community College, Bangalore	(March, 2003)

227. St. Xavier's Community College, Khanapur (July, 2003)
228. St. Teresa's Community College, Mysore (August, 2003)
229. St. Joseph's Community College, Bangalore (July, 2005)
230. Bangalore Community College, Bangalore (July, 2005)
231. Gulbarga Community College, Gulbarga (July, 2005)
232. Our Lady of Victories Community College, KGF (July, 2005)
233. Rosa Mystica Community College, Mangalore (January, 2006)
234. Mysore Mines Community College, KGF (March, 2006)
235. Carmel Community College, Bidar (June, 2006)
236. Bethany Community College, Kulashekar, Mangalore (August, 2006)
237. Vijayamari Community College, Mangalore (August, 2006)
238. Shanthi Kiran Community College, Humnabad (August, 2006)
239. Bethany Community College, Shimoga (August, 2006)
240. Auxilium Community College, Madanthyar P.O. (August, 2006)
241. Concerns Community College, Bangalore (August, 2007)
242. St. Paul's Community College, Belgaum (August, 2007)
243. Shishumandir Community College, Bangalore (January, 2008)
244. Satvidya Rural Community College, Chamraynagar Dt. (July, 2009)
245. Our Lady of Mercy Community College, Indiranagar (July, 2009)
246. Advantage Elder Care Trust Community College, Bangalore (October, 2010)

Kerala

247. Auxilium Community College, Kottiyam (September, 2001)
248. Auxilium Community College, Kattappana (July, 2002)
249. Auxilium Community College, Palluruthy (July, 2002)
250. Kitex Community College, Aluva, Cochin (December, 2002)
251. Auxilium Community College, Trivandrum (July, 2003)
252. Teresian Community College, Kalamassery, Cochin (November, 2003)
253. Archbishop Powathil Assumption Community College, Kottayam (July, 2005)
254. Mount Carmel Community College, Kottayam (July, 2006)
255. St. Xavier's Community College, Trivandrum (September 2006)
256. Marian Community College, Kuttikkanam (September 2007)
257. Christu Raj Community College, Kottayam (August, 2008)
258. Sanjo Community College, Marottichal (October, 2009)

Maharashtra

259. Vivekananda Prastishthan Community College, Jalgaon (July, 2001)
260. Auxilium Community College, Ahmednagar (June, 2004)
261. SVD Community College, Andheri (July, 2006)
262. Gnanajyothi Community College, Thane (August, 2006)
263. Eusebia Community College, Pune (July, 2008)
264. Symbiosis Community College, Pune (July, 2009)
265. Vishwkarma Community College, Amravati (August, 2009)

Madhya Pradesh

266. B.S.S.S (Bhopal School of Social Sciences) (July, 2004)

Community College, Bhopal

267. St. Aloysius Community College, Jabalpur (St. Aloysius College Campus) (July, 2004)
268. St. Aloysius Community College, Jabalpur (JOGNI Campus) (July, 2004)
269. St. Aloysius Community College, Jabalpur (Satyalayam Campus) (July, 2004)
270. Samaritan Community College, Pateri, Satna (August, 2006)
271. NICT Community College, Jhabua (August, 2009)

Gujarat

272. Vidhyadeep Community College, Bharuch (July, 1999)

Goa

273. Don Bosco Community College, Goa (August, 2003)

Jharkhand

274. Montfort Rural Community College, Lachragarh, Simdega (December, 2003)
275. Ursuline Community College, Noatoli, Gumla (February, 2004)
276. St. Joseph's Community College, Simdega (December, 2004)
277. Montfort Community College, Hazaribagh (March, 2005)
278. Deepanjali Community College, Gumla (November, 2005)
279. Kolhan Community College, Chaibasa (September, 2006)
280. St. Joseph's Rural Community College, Bhusar (September, 2006)
281. Livens Community College, Dighia (October, 2006
282. Preriton Ki Rani Community College, Chanho, Ranchi (January, 2007)
283. St. Joseph's Community College, Namkum, Ranchi (August, 2008)
284. St. Joseph's Community College, Jamshedpur (August, 2009)

Chhatisgarh

285. Kerakacchar Community College, Pathalgaon (September, 2002)

Orissa

286. UPAYA Science and Technology Community College, Rajgangpur (May, 2005)
287. St. Joseph's Sevasadan Community College, Bhubaneswar (July, 2007)
288. Sevalaya Community College, Jharsuguda (August, 2007)
289. New Life Development Community College, Rourkela (August, 2009)
290. VYK Rural Community College, Angul (August, 2009)
291. IIYD Community College, Kandhamal (August, 2009)
292. Sahavikas Community College, Kandhamal (August, 2010)

Himachal Pradesh

293. M.S. Panwar Community College, Solan (May, 2005)

Haryana

294. Pratyasha (CSST) Community College, Faridabad (August, 2005)
295. Government Polytechnic Community College, Manesar (September, 2007)

West Bengal

296. Cluny Community College, Kalimpong (August, 2005)
297. North Bengal St. Xavier's Community College, Rajganj (November, 2008)
298. Nekimuddin Community College, Medinapur (January, 2010)
299. Maria Gorothi Community College, Jalpaiguri Dt. (June, 2010)

Uttar Pradesh

300. St. John's Community College, Varanasi (July, 2005)
301. Bethany Community College, Noida (July, 2006)
302. Aligarh Community College, Aligarh (September, 2009)
303. JMVS Community College, Lucknow (October, 2010)

Punjab

304. Bethany Community College, Ludhiana (August, 2006)

Assam

305. Bethany Community College, Guwahati (September, 2008)

Jammu & Kashmir

306. New Life Development Community College, Srinagar (August, 2008)

BIHAR

307. Arunodaya Social Education Centre, Patna (June, 2010)

Bibliography

Books:

Alphonse, Xavier, *Ons Sal Oorwin, Vaardighede om die lewe te hanteer*, D.O.U Die Orantorium Uitgewery Publication, January 2007. (Africans Language)

Alphonse, Xavier, *Safaltha – Jeevan Samannya Ki Kalayai* (We Shall Over Come), SKIP Publication, April 2007.

Alphonse, Xavier, *Tears into Cheers: The extraordinary Stories of Miracles of Hope of Tsunami affected young Men and Women through the Community Colleges*, ICRDCE Publication, Chennai, September 2006.

Alphonse, Xavier, and Sekar, Rajini, *Health is Wealth – A Text Book on Health Assistant for Community Colleges in India*, (Volume I and II), ICRDCE Publication, Chennai, December 2007.

Alphonse, Xavier, *An Introduction to the Community College System (Tamil)*, MS University Publications, Tirunelveli – September 1998.

Alphonse, Xavier, *Best to the Least – Profile of Community Colleges in India*, MCRDCE Publication, Chennai, November 2004.

Alphonse, Xavier, *Changing Track – Community Colleges in India*, AIACHE Publications, New Delhi – December 1996.

Alphonse, Xavier, *Including the Excluded: History of the Community Colleges in India*, MCRDCE Publications, Chennai – January 1999.

Alphonse, Xavier, *Reaching Out: Community College Movement in India – An Update*, MCRDCE Publications, Chennai, July 2001.

Alphonse, Xavier, and Peter Xavier, *Aiming Small is a Crime*, MCRDCE Publication, Chennai, January 2003.

Alphonse, Xavier, *Back to the Villages: Towards the Profile of a Rural Community College*, ICRDCE Publication, Chennai, September 2006.

Alphonse, Xavier, *Believing in Miracles – Profile of Community Colleges in India* (Vols. I and II), ICRDCE Publication, Chennai, March 2009.

Alphonse, Xavier, *Best for the Community: The Proceedings of the Fifth National Consultation and the Launching of ICRDCE*, Chennai, 2006. ICRDCE Publication, Chennai, February 2007.

Alphonse, Xavier, *Bloom and Blossom : A source book on eco-friendly sustainable agriculture for integrated rural development*, co-authored by Mr. S.A. Kader Ibrahim, MCRDCE Publication, Chennai, December 2005.

Alphonse, Xavier, *Change is Certain – Success Stories of Community Colleges Students in India*, ICRDCE Publication, Chennai, March 2009.

Alphonse, Xavier, *Change or Be Changed – A Text Book on Life Coping Skills for Undergraduate Students*, ICRDCE Publication, Chennai, June 2008.

Alphonse, Xavier, *Community College Empowerment Endorsed : The History of Recognition and Accreditation of Community Colleges in India*, MCRDCE Publication, Chennai, December 2005.

Alphonse, Xavier, *Community Colleges in India Education for Livelihood: The Concept and Implementation of Community College System in India*, Gyan Publishing House, New Delhi, October 2006.

Alphonse, Xavier, *Computer Made Easy: A Textbook on Basic Computing Skills*, MCRDCE Publication, Chennai, March 2005.

Alphonse, Xavier, Editor, *People Building Business: Proceedings of the National Workshop on Community College System*, February 2000, MCRDCE Publications, Chennai – September 2000.

Alphonse, Xavier, *English Made Simple: A Text Book for Community Colleges in India*, ICRDCE Publication, Chennai, September 2006.

Alphonse, Xavier, *Exploration, Experience, Empowerment and Employment* – A Collection of selected research articles and features from Journals, Magazines and News papers from 1997 – 2009 on Community Colleges in India, ICRDCE Publication, Chennai, January 2010.

Alphonse, Xavier, Mansingh, David, Nam Vazha Piranthavarkal, *History, Growth and Development*, ICRDCE Publication, Chennai, April 2011.

Alphonse, Xavier, *Marching with the Marginalised: The Contribution of MCRDCE to the Community College Movement in India*, MCRDCE Publication, Chennai, December 2005.

Alphonse, Xavier, *Miracles of Hope – Success Stories of the Community College Students*, MCRDCE Publication, Chennai, March 2005.

Alphonse, Xavier, *Mismatch: Establishing and Developing Community Colleges in India*, MCRDCE Publication, Chennai, June 2002.

Alphonse, Xavier, *Power Within – The Proceedings of the Two Days State Level Convention of Industrial Collaborators and Community Colleges of Tamil Nadu and Karnataka*, ICRDCE Publication, Chennai, April 2008.

Alphonse, Xavier, Prince, *Queenie and Jayakumar, Saradha, Child is the Future –Text Book on Early Childhood Care and Education*, (Volume I and II), ICRDCE Publication, Chennai, January 2011.

Alphonse, Xavier, *Reaching Beyond – Profile of Community Colleges in India* (Volume I and II), ICRDCE Publication, Chennai, June 2007.

Alphonse, Xavier, *Set the World on Fire*, MCRDCE Publication, Chennai, December 2002.

Alphonse, Xavier, *Symphony Goes on... Legacy of Mother Teresa to the Modern World*, MCRDCE Publication, Chennai, October 2003.

Alphonse, Xavier, *The Contribution of MCRDCE to the Community College Movement in India* (1995 - 2001), MCRDCE Publication, Chennai, December 2001.

Alphonse, Xavier, *The Growth and Future of the Community College Movement in India* (1995 - 2003), MCRDCE Publication, Chennai, July 2003.

Alphonse, Xavier, *Walking the Extra Mile: A Textbook on Interpersonal Relationship and Communication Skills*, MCRDCE Publication, Chennai, March 2005.

Alphonse, Xavier, *We Shall Overcome: A Textbook on Life Coping Skills*, MCRDCE Publication, Chennai, March 2004.

Neglected Majority - *The Problem of School Dropouts and Possible Alternatives*, Co-authored by Dr. Peter Xavier, S.J., MCRDCE Publication, Chennai, March 2005.

Ramakrishna, Ganapati, *Community College for India, Madras Institute for Development Education*, Chennai 1980.

Articles:

"A New Breed of College comes to India", *The Community College Times*, July 29, 1997.

"Access and Equity in Higher Education", *Selections from University News* – 15, Association of Indian Universities, New Delhi, 2004. Alphonse, Xavier, "Community College: Meeting Society's Needs", *University News*, Vol. 37 No. 36, September 6, 1999, pp. 131-144.

"Community College Movement", *University News*, New Delhi, Vol. 37:1, January 1999.

"Community College System on Rise", *Madras Universities*, Vol. 27, No. 2, 1st of September 2003.

"Community Colleges in India look to the West", *Community College Times, American Association of Community Colleges*, Vol. 15, No. 21, 28th of October 2003.

"Striving for Recognition – Community College", *University News*, New Delhi, Vol. 37:44, November 1, 1999. (Campus News)

"Ten Years of Community Colleges in India" *The New Leader*, October 16 -31, 2005.

Alphonse, Xavier and Joe Rajan, "Melrosapuram Rural Community College – An Educational Alternative", *University News*, New Delhi, Vol. 36 : 23, June 8, 1998.

Alphonse, Xavier and Pushparaj, "Madurai Community College – An Educational Alternative", *University News*, New Delhi, Vol. 35:41, October 13, 1997.

Alphonse, Xavier and Valeau Edward, "Indian Community College System: Democratic Response to Globalization" Community College Models, *Springer Science + Business Media* B.V. 2009.

Alphonse, Xavier, " Development of Colleges" in the XIth Five Year Plan 2007 – 2012, *New Frontiers in Education*, Vol: 36 No: 3, July – September, 2006

Alphonse, Xavier, "Achievement of Community College" *University News*, New Delhi, Vol. 45 No. 35, August 27 – September 02, 2007.

Alphonse, Xavier, "Best to the Least: Community College Movement in India- An Update" *New Frontiers in Education*, Vol. 32:2 April-June 2002.

Alphonse, Xavier, "Beyond the Frontiers: The Growth and Future of the Community College Movement in India (1995-2004)", *New Frontiers in Education*, Vol. 34:2 April-June 2004.

Alphonse, Xavier, "Community College – The Movement in India", *Digital Learnikng*, Vol. 5:6, June, 2009.

Alphonse, Xavier, "Community College – The Scope and Space for the Disadvantaged for Education and Employment", *University News*, New Delhi, Vol. 47:52, December 28, 2009 – January 03, 2010.

Alphonse, Xavier, "Community College as an Alternative System of Education", *Christian Manager*, Vol.8:6, August - September 2008.

Alphonse, Xavier, "Community College Just the Job for Poor", *Cath News India*, November 24th, 2010.

Alphonse, Xavier, "Community College Movement at a Glance (1995 -2009)", *New Frontiers in Education*, New Delhi, Vol. 42:4, October – December, 2009.

Alphonse, Xavier, "Community College Movement in India – From Adoption to Extension Nationwide", *Changing Colleges*, December 2000.

Alphonse, Xavier, "Community College Movement in India: The Pioneering contribution of Jesuits", *Jivan*, Chennai, April 2006, pp. 4-8.

Alphonse, Xavier, "Community College Movement: An Overview, *University News*, New Delhi, Vol. 38:35, August 28, 2000.

Alphonse, Xavier, "Community College System and its Future in India", *New Frontiers in Education*, Vol:,36 No: 3, July – September, 2006.

Alphonse, Xavier, "Community College System towards Vertical Mobility" *National Qualification Framework*, 25th and 26th of July 2000.

Alphonse, Xavier, "Community College System towards Vertical Mobility" *New Frontiers in Education*, Vol. 30:3 July-September 2000.

Alphonse, Xavier, "Community College System: Empowerment Endorsed", *University News*, New Delhi, Vol. 44 No. 13, March 27-April 02, 2006.

Alphonse, Xavier, "Community College: An alternative to Included the Excluded in Higher Education", *New Frontiers in Education*, New Delhi, Vol. 42:1, January – March, 2009.

Alphonse, Xavier, "Community College: Education for Livelihood" – Empowering the Marginalised, Swami Vivekananda Rural Community College, Souvenir 2007. May 2007.

Alphonse, Xavier, "Community College: Towards National Recognition", *University News*, New Delhi, Vol. 46:51, December 22-28, 2008.

Alphonse, Xavier, "Community College: Towards National Recognition", *New Frontiers in Education*, New Delhi, Vol. 42:3, July – September, 2009.

Alphonse, Xavier, "Community Colleges – Enlightenment and Empowerment," *New Frontiers in Education,* AIACHE, New Delhi, Vol. 35:3, July – September 2005.

Alphonse, Xavier, "Community Colleges: A National Phenomenon", *University News*, June 25 – July 1, 2001.

Alphonse, Xavier, "Community Colleges: A Policy Report", *New Frontiers in Education*, AIACHE, New Delhi, Vol. 24:2, April – June 1999.

Alphonse, Xavier, "Community Colleges: Norms and Guidelines for Recognition and Approval" *New Frontiers in Education*, Vol. 24:4, October – December 1999.

Alphonse, Xavier, "Community Colleges: Opportunity is the key to Success", *New Frontiers in Education*, Vol: 37 No: 1, January – March 2007.

Alphonse, Xavier, "Decennial Celebrations", *University News*, New Delhi, Vol.47:13, March 30 to April 05, 2009.

Alphonse, Xavier, "Education for Empowerment through Community College", in *Higher Education Quality and Management*, Gyan Publishing House, 2010.

Alphonse, Xavier, "Empowering the Disadvantaged", *The Hindu*, May 9, 2000.

Alphonse, Xavier, "Empowerment of Socio-economically Weaker Sections through the Community College System and the Support of the Universities in India", *University News*, New Delhi, Vol. 43 No. 47, November 21-27, 2005.

Alphonse, Xavier, "Learning for Livelihood", *Frontline*, Vol. 23 No. 2, January 28-February 10, 2006.

Alphonse, Xavier, "Madras Community College – An Educational Alternative", *University News*, New Delhi, Vol. 34:36, September 2, 1996.

Alphonse, Xavier, "Marching with the Marginalised: The Community College Movement in Fulfillment of its Mission", *New Frontiers in Education*, AIACHE, New Delhi, Vol. 34:4 October – December 2004.

Alphonse, Xavier, "National Consultation of Community Colleges in India", Campus News, *University News*, New Delhi, Vol. 43:16, April 18-24, 2005.

Alphonse, Xavier, "National Workshop on Quality Management of Community Colleges", Campus News, *University News*, New Delhi. Vol. 49 No. 22 May 30 – June 05, 2011.

Alphonse, Xavier, "National Workshop on the Institutionalization of the Community College System in India", *University News*, New Delhi, Vol. 47: 36, September 07-13, 2009.

Alphonse, Xavier, "Presentation on Community College as an alternative System of Education", *New Frontiers in Education*, New Delhi, Vol. 40:4, October – December 2007.

Alphonse, Xavier, "Role of Community Colleges in the Promotion of Access and Equity" in *Perspectives on Governance of Higher Education* published by Bharati Vidhyapeeth Deemed University. November 2010.

Alphonse, Xavier, "Seminar on Community Colleges", *University News*, New Delhi, Vol. 38:17, April 24, 2000. (Campus News).

Alphonse, Xavier, "Seminar on Indian Community College System", *University News*, Vol. 43:10, March 7-13, 2005.

Alphonse, Xavier, *The Growth and Future of the Community College Movement in India* (1995-2003)", July 2003.

Alphonse, Xavier, "The Growth of the Community College Movement in India", *Christian Manager*, Chennai, Vol. 10 No. 5. June-July 2010.

Alphonse, Xavier, "The Stages and Dynamics of the Community College Movement in India (1995 – 2001), *New Frontiers in Education*, AIACHE, New Delhi, Vol. 31 No. 2 April – June, 2001.

Alphonse, Xavier, "TNOU Community College Model in Collaboration with ICRDCE - Chennai", *New Frontiers in Education*, New Delhi. Vol. 43, No. 3, July- Sep, 2010.

Alphonse, Xavier, "TNOU-ICRDCE Consultation Meeting on Community College", *University News*, New Delhi. Vol. 48 No. 31 August 02-08, 2010.

Alphonse, Xavier, "To Include the Excluded", *New Frontiers in Education*, AIACHE, New Delhi, Vol. 27:4, October – December 1997.

Alphonse, Xavier, "To Include the Excluded", *The Hindu*, Madras, January 20, 1998 and January 27, 1998.

Alphonse, Xavier, "Total Quality Management of Community Colleges", *New Frontiers in Education*. Vol. 44 No. 1 Jan-Mar, 2011.

Alphonse, Xavier, "Total Quality Management of Community Colleges", Communication, *University News*, New Delhi. Vol. 49 No. 26, June 27 – July 03, 2011.

Alphonse, Xavier, Community College: Meeting Society's Needs", *University News*, New Delhi, Vol. 37:36, September 6, 1999.

Alphonse, Xavier, Cover Story of Community Colleges "A People's Movement", *Edu Tech*, Volume 01, Issue 07. May 2010.

Alphonse, Xavier and James C., "Best to the Least : Education for Livelihood – Community Colleges in India", *University News*, Vol. 42 No. 14, April 5-11, 2004.

Bhattacharya, Sandhya, "Community College Initiative", *Education World*, April 2000.

Community Colleges: Experiments and Challenges", *AIACHE Newsletter*, New Delhi, April, 1999.

D'Souza, S. Victor, "Restructuring Higher Education in India – Relevance of the American Community College", *New Frontiers in Education*, AIACHE, New Delhi, Vol. 21:4, 1991.

Document – "Indian Community College System" *New Frontiers in Education*, AIACHE, New Delhi, Vol. 35:3, July – September 2005.

Heimer, Muriel Kay, "The Community College : Opportunity, Accessibility, Excellence, *New Frontiers in Education*, Vol. 27:1, 1997.

ICRDCE Launched in Chennai, *University News*, New Delhi, Vol: 44 No: 42, October 16-22, 2006.

Indian Community Colleges Showing Progress, CCID, May 2006.

Mathew C. Ninan, "Higher Education and Social Responsibility", *New Frontiers in Education,* AIACHE, New Delhi, Vol. 36:1, 2006.

Mehrotra, S.N. "The College and the Community", *New Frontiers in Education*, AIACHE, New Delhi, Vol. 2:2, 1971.

Rao, Sudha K., "Community Colleges in India: Need and Relevance", *New Frontiers in Education*, AIACHE, New Delhi, Vol. 24:3, 1994.

Shah, S.Y., "Indian Scenario of Lifelong Learning" *University News*, New Delhi, Vol. 46 No. 39, October 05, 2008.

Book Reviews

Alphonse, Xavier, "Changing Track" – Community Colleges in India, *The Hindu*, September 9, 1997.

Alphonse, Xavier, "Changing Track": Plea for an Educational Alternative, *University News*, New Delhi, Vol. 35:33, August 18, 1997.

Alphonse, Xavier, "Including the Excluded", *The Hindu*, August 8, 2000.

Alphonse, Xavier, "Including the Excluded", *University News*, New Delhi, Vol. 38:20, May 15, 2000.

Alphonse, Xavier, "Mismatch", *Southern Economist,* Bangalore, October 1, 2003.

Aludiapillai, K., "Marching with the Marginalised – The Contribution of MCRDCE to the Community College Movement in India (1995-2005)", *University News*, New Delhi, Vol. 44 No. 25, June 19-25, 2006.

Mohanty, Ajay Kumar, "A Well Planned Book – Community College – Empowerment Endorsed: The History of Recognition and Accreditation of Community Colleges in India", *University News*, New Delhi, Vol. 44 No. 37, September 11-17, 2006.

Muthukumaran, "Best to the Least: Profile of Community Colleges in India, *University News*, New Delhi, Vol. 43 No. 47, November 21-27, 2005.

News Paper Clippings

"Education has to be responsive to Industry", *The Hindu,* August 19, 1992.

"Needed: Community Colleges", *The Hindu,* 1994.

"UGC to promote Community College", *The Hindu,* April 4, 1995.

"Colleges asked to provide Work-Oriented Skills", *The Hindu,* July 2, 1996.

"Education must be tuned to Societal Needs", *The New Indian Express,* August 5, 1996.

"Community College Set Up", *The Hindu,* August 5, 1996.

"Varsity Plans to start Community College", *The Hindu,* March 18, 1997.

"Need to set up Community Colleges", *The Hindu,* April 16, 1997.

"Community Colleges can Bridge Education, Employment Gap", *The Indian Express,* August 12, 1997.

"Community College catering to the Society"– Pondicherry Panorama: A Feature, *The Hindu,* May 30, 1998.

"Community Colleges meet opens today", *The Hindu,* January 8, 1999.

"Community Concept Hailed", *The Hindu,* January 12, 1999.

"Corporation, Industry come together to generate Employment for school children", *The New Indian Express,* January 25, 1999.

"Job Skills for the Underprivileged" *The Hindu,* February 1, 1999.

"Community Colleges: A Boon to Non-Formal Students" *The Hindu,* May 29, 1999.

"Making their dreams a reality", *The Hindu,* June 28, 1999.

"Need for Alternative System of Education felt", *News Today, February 19, 2000.*

Sankarnarayanan, Harini, "Affordable Higher Education for all – Community Colleges are fast becoming an Attractive Option, Reports" *The Economics Times,* February 27, 2000.

"Community College concept catching up in State", *The Hindu,* March 23, 2000.

Alphonse, Xavier, "Empowering the Disadvantaged" *The Hindu,* May 9, 2000. (Open Page, Education).

"Bridge Gap between Education, Employment", *New Today,* May 21, 2000.

"Meet on Community Colleges", *The Times of India, Mumbai,* September 21, 2000.

"Accent on role of Community Colleges", *The New Indian Express,* October 10, 2000.

"Separate authority for Community Colleges Mooted", *News Today,* October 11, 2000.

"Call to promote Life-Oriented Education", *The Hindu,* October 13, 2000.

"Building Youth for the Future", *Nagaland Page,* October 26, 2000.

"Workshop on Community College", *Nagaland Post,* October 26, 2000.

"Workshop on Community Colleges Inaugurated" *The New Indian Express, Kochi,* 19th January 2001.

"Community Colleges: Centre looking for lead from Tamil Nadu", *News Today,* 19th February 2001.

"Alternative Colleges, an Emerging Concept", *News Today,* 23rd February 2001.

"Community College workshop tan a ni", *Hnethu,* 15th of March 2001.

"Community College seeks inclusion in 10th Plan", *News Today,* 5th of April 2001.

"Recognition of Community Colleges urged", *Trinity Mirror,* 12th April 2001.

"Community Educational System should recognised: MCRDCE", *The Indian*

Express", 13th of April 2001.

"Government assures Community Colleges of all help", *News Today,* 22nd of April 2001.

"Students make a beeline to Agri Community College – The Institution, first in Tamil Nadu to offer Job-Oriented Courses at nominal fees", *The New Indian Express,* 21st of April 2002.

"Fostering Education", *The Hindu,* 29th of July 2002.

"Community College comes up at YWCA", *News Today,* 2nd of August 2002.

"Need to change education system stressed", *News Today,* 21st of August 2002.

"St. Anne's to tie up with Delhi School", *The New Indian Express,* 1st of September 2002.

"Education that ensures gainful employment", *The Hindu,* 5th of October 2002.

"Community College system aiming at uplifting the marginalized", *The New Indian Express,* Kochi, 12th of October 2002.

"Workshop on skill based education today" *The Times of India,* Lucknow, 25th of October 2002.

"Community Colleges start scripting course to success", *The New Indian Express*, 26th of December 2002.

"Community College for poor students", *The Hindu, Eluru,* 26th of January 2003.

"Community Colleges could help tackle dropout", *Herald*, 28th of April 2003.

"Academics advocate Community College for Goa", *Herald*, 28th of April 2003.

"Make me Fit for Life", *The Herald*, May 2-8, 2003.

"Community Colleges ideal for dropouts", *The Hindu,* 31st of March 2004.

"St. Aloysius College holds workshop on Community College", *The Hitavada,* 4th of April 2004.

"Interview on Community Colleges", *Mylapore Times,* May 29 – June 4, 2004.

"Fit for Life", *The New Indian Express, City Express,* 16th of June 2004.

"We Shall Overcome" – Book Review, *The Hindu,* 22nd June 2004.

"NGO to start Community College", *The New Indian Express,* Trichy, 22nd of July 2004.

"Community College launched", *Bhopal Today, Chronicle,* 31st of July 2004.

"Panel formed to prepare comprehence policy Document" *The Hindu*, 10th of October 2004.

"V-C pushes for 'para-formal' education", *The Hindu,* 13th of November 2004.

"Book on Community Colleges released", *Indian Express,* 13th of November 2004.

"VC outlines the key to higher education", *News Today,* 13th of November 2004.

"HRD Ministry seeks report from UGC", *The New Indian Express,* 9th of February 2005.

"Will Community College concept do the trick?" *News Today,* 9th of February 2005.

"Economic Growth linked to Community Colleges", *City Express,* 10th of February 2005.

Integrate Community Colleges into Higher Education Scheme", *The Hindu,* 10th of February 2005.

"Higher Education for all", *The Hindu, Education Plus,* 14th of February 2005.

"Thrust on Community Colleges for Better Education", *Indian Express,* 12th of March 2005.

"Decision on Potential for Excellence Status to Variety" *The Hindu*, 7th of March 2005.

"Community Colleges need Government support", *The Hindu,* 12th of March 2005.

"Community Colleges may be the answer", *News Today,* 13th of March 2005.

"In service of poor", *The Hindu,* 15th of April 2005.

"Empowering the powerless", *The Hindu,* 18th of April 2005.

"Educate and Enlighten", *Deccan Herald,* 7th of July 2005.

"Rural youths need help for empowerment", *The New Indian Express,* 3rd of August 2005.

"Community Colleges play vital role", *The Hindu,* 12th of September 2005.

"College to empower the poor", *The Hindu,* 9th of October 2005.

"Community Colleges a boon to the poor", *The New Indian Express,* 7th of December 2005.

"Empowering the Marginalised", *Education Plus, The Hindu,* 19th of December 2005.

"Technical Courses for the tsunami victims", *The Hindu, Vellore Edition,* 20th of December 2005.

"Education for a Livelihood", *The Hindu,* 21st of December 2005.

"Efforts of Community Colleges earn praise", The *Hindu*, 24th of December 2005.

"The Cultural fest for Community Colleges", *The Hindu*, 24th of April 2006.

"Allow SSLC passed students to take diploma courses" *The New Indian Express,* 12th of August 2006.

"Call for three-tier System in higher education" The *Hindu,* 12th of August 2006.

"Consultation on Community Colleges" *The New Indian Express,* 31st of August 2006.

"Community College System in focus" *The Hindu,* 31st of August 2006.

"Dropping the dropout rate" News *Today,* 2nd of September 2006.

"ICRDCE launched in Chennai" *The Hindu,* 11th of September 2006.

"A College that produces entrepreneurs" *Times of India,* September 2006.

"Another Community College in Kovai" *Cheran Times,* 23rd of December 2006.

"Tamil Nadu Open University Convocation today" *The Hindu,* 11th of January 2007.

"A pioneer Community College" *The Hindu*, *Education Plus*, 28th of May 2007.

"UGC for Expansion – Community Colleges" The Asian Age, 20th of June 2007.

"Community College a boon for Society" News Today, 1st of July 2007.

"Revising Guidelines for Autonomous Colleges" *The Hindu*, 1st of July 2007.

"IID Community College Graduation Day" *The Hindu*, 2nd of July 2007.

"Bhopal Community College Evaluated" Central Chronicle, Bhopal, 15th of July 2007.

"Job Skills for the Less Privileged" *The Hindu*, *Education Plus*, 13th of August 2007.

"Community College a Boon to the Poor" *The Hindu*, District Plus, 25th of August 2007.

"85 Students of Corporation Community College get jobs" *The Hindu*, 17th of November 2007.

"Ensuring equity through Community Colleges" *The Hindu*, *Education Plus*, 3rd December 2007.

"Govt. to launch skill development programme" *The New Indian Express*, 8th of December 2007.

"Community Colleges reaching out to Poor" *News Today*, 23rd of December 2007.

"Community Colleges May Come under Open University System" *The Hindu*, 4th January 2008.

"Students of Community Colleges Shine" *The Hindu*, *Education Plus*, 14th of January 2008.

"Education is Key to Success", News Today, 3rd of February 2008

"50,000 Community Colleges set to Come Up, *Deccan Chronicle*, 1st of May 2008.

New norms for 'dropout' College, *Deccan Chronicle*, 19th of June 2008

"Community Colleges act as a Confidence Booster, Educational Plus, *The Hindu*, 30th June 2008.

Community Colleges now under TN Open University, *The New Indian Express*, 18th of June 2008.

"Community Colleges to help students, *Deccan Chronicle*, 6th of August 2008.

Tamil Nadu Open University Shows the way for School Dropouts, *The Hindu*, 16th of August 2008.

"Community Colleges to assept applications for associate degrees, *The Hindu*, 2nd of February 2009.

"Groom 'ED' TO Work, *The Times of India*, *Education Times*, 23rd of February 2009.

Government to Recognize Community Colleges, *Trinity Mirror*, 8th of May 2009.

Colleges to offer associate Degrees, *The New Indian Express*, 10th of March 2009.

Community Colleges can Transform Students, *The New Indian Express*, 2nd of July 2009.

Associate Degree, Community Colleges get UGC nod, *Deccan Chronicle*, 23rd of June 2009.

Community Colleges should consider developing skill-based Curriculum, says Thiruvasagam, *The Hindu*, 2nd of January 2010.

Focus on More opportunities for Community College Students, *The Hindu, Education Plus*, 18th of January 2010.

Universities to start Community Colleges for unskilled Workers, *The Hindu*, 10th of June 2010.

TN varsities to start Community Colleges to help dropouts, *The Times of India*, 10th of June 2010.

18 New Community Colleges get Open University Approval, *The Hindu*, July 9th 2010.

A Community College for Women, *The Hindu, Education Plus*, 30th of August 2010.

Community Colleges are here, *The Hindu, Education Plus*, 22nd of November 2010.

Giving Community Colleges their due, *The Hindu, Education Plus*, 6th of February 2011.

Community Connect, *The Times of India*, 14th of March 2011.

Index

U